PHOTOGRAPHY AND SEPTEMBER 11TH

PHOTOGRAPHY AND SEPTEMBER 11TH

Spectacle, Memory, Trauma

Jennifer Good

B L O O M S B U R Y
LONDON • NEW DELHI • NEW YORK • SYDNEY

Bloomsbury Academic
An imprint of Bloomsbury Publishing Plc

50 Bedford Square
London
WC1B 3DP
UK

1385 Broadway
New York
NY 10018
USA

www.bloomsbury.com

Bloomsbury is a registered trade mark of Bloomsbury Publishing Plc

First published 2015

British Library Cataloguing-in-Publication Data
A catalogue record for this book is available from the British Library.

ISBN: HB: 978-1-4725-3331-9
ePDF: 978-1-4725-2897-1
ePub: 978-1-4725-2779-0

Library of Congress Cataloging-in-Publication Data
A catalog record for this book is available from the Library of Congress.

Typeset by Integra Software Services Pvt. Ltd.
Printed and bound in Great Britain

For Nora

CONTENTS

LIST OF ILLUSTRATIONS

ACKNOWLEDGEMENTS

My thanks to Davida Forbes at Bloomsbury for her guidance, insight and patience, to the University of the Arts London for research sabbatical funding without which the manuscript for this book could not have been completed and to my colleagues at London College of Communication, particularly Paul Lowe, for their support and advice. Thanks also to the students and staff of the Art History department at the University of Nottingham for the various roles they played in the earliest stages of the research, particularly Simon Baker, and also Mark Rawlinson and Marquard Smith, for their detailed and formative comments. As well as years of friendship and moral support, Suzy Freake provided specialist feedback on Chapter 3 for which I am most grateful. Special thanks to Professor John Tulloch for his generosity and guidance over several years in refining the vision of the book and preparing it for publication, and to the anonymous peer reviewers whose feedback at the proposal and manuscript stages was invaluable. Finally, biggest thanks to my parents, Ken and Mary Good, for their constant encouragement in every chapter and for making it possible in the most practical of ways to get the job done.

PREFACE: *I WAS THERE*

Photographs that everyone recognises are now a constituent part of what a society chooses to think about, or declares that it has chosen to think about. It calls these ideas 'memories', and that is, over the long run, a fiction. Strictly speaking, there is no such thing as collective memory – part of the same family of spurious notions as collective guilt. But there is collective instruction.

SUSAN SONTAG[1]

My first encounter with the news of a plane hitting the World Trade Center towers came not via broadcast media but by phone. I had just landed back in London after the university summer break and received the call from my boyfriend as I waited at baggage claim. A passenger jet had crashed into one of the twin towers, and people were jumping. Throughout my long bus journey back to campus, he checked in with updates as the story unfolded, and I tried to put together mental images of the improbable scenes he was describing as he sat in front of his television screen. A second plane … fire, dust and smoke … collapse. Hundreds dead. Thousands. I eventually arrived at my empty house, turned on the TV and sat transfixed until long after midnight with my coat on and my unopened suitcase by my side. I watched the planes hit and the towers fall again and again and again.

I was not in Lower Manhattan, but I was *there*. Is it wrong to say this? Is it not disrespectful – outrageous even? – to compare my experience to that of those who inhaled the dust, ran for their lives or lost family members? Of course it is. But, in another sense, as specific as my own Euro-American perspective was, I was as 'there' as the majority of people who experienced the event around the world, were moved, impacted and changed by it. That afternoon, once I had landed on my couch and turned on the television at a remove of a few hours and thousands of miles, time and space somehow took on a new character. I watched the images on repeat as breaking, rolling 'tele-presence' took over scheduled programming on every terrestrial channel. News anchors abandoned by their usual air of reassuring authority tried to make sense of what they were seeing based on no more information than I myself could see before my eyes. They did their best to guide me as the early images of the first impact's aftermath were supplemented and mixed with later developments and live footage from the scene as it unfolded. Neither of us, it seemed, could be sure what was 'real time' and what was not (was that the first plane or the second? Oh my god, is it happening again?). I would not articulate this clearly until several years later, but somehow, on that day, being in a particular place at a particular time was crucial, and yet did not mean what it might have meant before in quite the same way.

Everywhere I went over the several years of researching this work, people told me stories. This is an unusual response to hearing about someone's academic research, which can sometimes be a conversation-killer. When I answered the question, 'what are you working on?', invariably in response came a personal story of where this person was at the time they had heard or seen the news. These ranged from experiences of watching from bedroom windows in downtown New York as the towers fell, to those who remember sitting in front of TV screens on the other side of the world, as I had done, and searching for the words to explain to their kids what they were seeing. I learned that personal testimony, even for those whose experience had been no more first-hand than mine, was important. I learned that the ownership and narrative retelling of these stories was also important. But, even more than that, I learned the importance of pictures. Often, a person's way of telling me that they were 'there' was to talk about the photograph that had moved them the most. The specific picture varied from person to person and might have been encountered hours or weeks afterwards, but as I heard these stories, it became clear to me that this was a kind of personal witnessing that had its own special importance. And, just as the distanced, mediated nature of the experience could be said to involve a kind of shift in the meaning of time and place, so the respective roles of words and pictures had somehow been altered too. Whereas in the usual order of things we would hear a breaking news story and then see the photographic evidence that made it real, this time the pictures came before the explanation. Finding words was a new sort of challenge (my friends had to try to explain unspeakable things to their children before – war, violence, loss – but never as it was happening live in front of their eyes in a repeated televised loop), and words took on a new relationship to images. Like the TV newsreaders who struggled to believe their autocues and their eyes, my experience of seeing the captionless images and being lost for words was typical of millions. I might have been able to utter, 'the twin towers have fallen down', but because everyone was seeing it all at once, as soon as the words became sayable, they were already redundant. In actuality, what happened was that I called my family to say that I did not know what to say. We sat on our respective couches, eyes fixed on our screens and shared our silence down the telephone line.

As the days went by, the images sank in, the words gradually took shape and the pieces of the story fell into order, what was forming as we watched came to be called 'collective memory'. But, although we were no doubt sharing something, 'memory' was not the right word for it. We were participating in a new kind of witnessing, which might have been said to have augured in a whole new age of mediated atrocity, if anything comparable had ever happened since. We were seeing sights that were in both the past and the present at the same time. They were being endlessly recalled to our minds not by our own bidding but by screens and pages everywhere. They were visible before they were nameable. And, in the instant that they became nameable, they were called 'war'.

INTRODUCTION

This book is about the role that photographs played following the events of September 11th 2001: about what was seen photographically and how. It is concerned not only with the images that international media audiences saw on that day and continued to see, but the processes of seeing, understanding, remembering and bearing witness through photographs. Hiro Oshima is a New Yorker who took a series of photographs as he made his way uptown following evacuation from his Lower Manhattan apartment building, some of which went on to be distributed by Getty Images and acquired by the National September 11 Memorial Museum. One of his pictures (Figure I.1) shows a crowd of people gathered at an intersection. Most look upwards, mesmerized by the same view, and tense confusion pervades the scene. The man in the central foreground is the one who seems to have the clearest grasp of what he is seeing, his face and body language conveying utter desperation. He looks as if he is on the point of turning and running, but he cannot take his eyes away. He is caught between two forces. The subject of this picture, like many taken in downtown New York City on that day, is not the stricken twin towers themselves, but the reactions of the watching people. This is a type of news photograph that has a particular history, being reserved for the greatest catastrophes and the most shocking violence. At such moments, it seems photographers recognize that the impact on witnesses is as much a part of the story as the view before their eyes. Barbie Zelizer, professor of communication and former journalist who has discussed the media responses to both September 11th and the Holocaust, suggests that pictures of this type are important to the viewing public because seeing others bear witness to exceptional events helps us to find our own reaction – to see for ourselves, as it were, placing and integrating our feelings within a set of others and inviting us into a group identity as a seeing public.[1] This in turn helps us to feel more stable and situated in unstable, fragmented and chaotic times.

The photograph shows something of a cross-section of New York society. People of different ethnicities, backgrounds and occupations stand together as common witnesses to the same horror. Without knowing the context of this

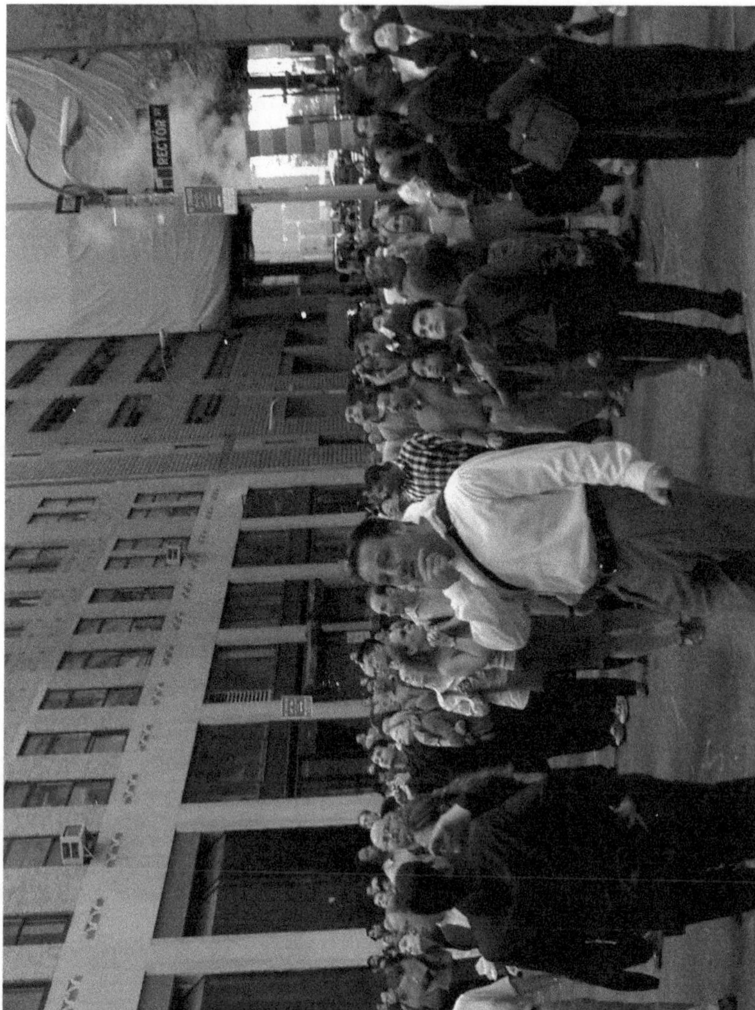

Figure I.1 New Yorkers watch as the World Trade Center burns following terrorist attack. Photo by Hiro Oshima, WireImage/Getty Images.

picture, we might think it was a still from a Hollywood disaster movie. Maybe these people are watching as King Kong terrorizes their city, or as hostile aliens open fire from the sky. A great many people testified to the feeling that September 11th was 'like a movie', and some (most notably Slavoj Žižek[2]) have written in depth about what this comparison means. One fairly obvious suggestion is that describing the experience in this way makes it easier to confront because it is a familiar category, and because there was simply nothing from real life to compare it to. Most fundamentally though, photographs of this kind demonstrate what an important part looking, watching, witnessing and spectacle played in the story of September 11th. Though it was for a long time deemed unacceptable to say so, this was a spectacular event: a terrorist attack designed to operate on both literal and symbolic levels, but which surely achieved the latter with a degree of success beyond the perpetrators' wildest dreams. The photographs it left behind are deeply affecting in some cases because they capture directly the magnitude of the spectacle – pictures like Spencer Platt's (Figure 1.1) being one of the most widely reproduced examples. In others though, it is because they draw our imagination to fill the gap between what is pictured and what we know took place but never really saw: the deaths of thousands of people. The overwhelmed faces of these New Yorkers show that there was, on one level, too much to see on that day. But, this photograph, for which Hiro Oshima turned his camera away from the scene of death, and in which witnesses are the story, also points towards another truth: that there was not enough. Bound up in the media coverage of the event are these dual problems of invisibility and overvisibility: on the one hand, the marginalizing of particular kinds of image, but perhaps more crucially on the other, the repetitive overvisibility of others. There were sights from that day that the world did not see and perhaps should have, but as the Western media landscape was flooded as never before with photographs of a single subject, and appetite for them seemed, in turn, to be insatiable, the overwhelming issue was not one of censorship, but a dazzling, disabling, visual overload.

Whose job is it to talk about photographs of September 11th? Within whose disciplinary remit do they fall: Journalists; Art historians; Psychologists; Scholars of media studies, political science, cyber-culture or history? Each of these can account for an element of the photographs' collective impact. But, the network that takes shape between and around these images touches on so many different types of question, crossing so many lines, that a new problem emerges. What is the framework that can address in enough depth the social and political implications of this exceptional image-event?[3] The American state, the culture industry and the public imagination were each, in their way, stretched by it, and there has been no going back. Some of the specific areas in which this stretching has occurred (the journalism industry, the field of trauma studies, foreign policy discourse and others) have recognized the enormity of what September 11th means for them and have discussed at length, if not resolved, their new parameters. But, in all of this talking, all the analysis and debate that has ensued in the past decade, the photographs somehow remain unaccounted for. Even those who have written about them in the most powerful ways have rarely gone further than a kind of fragmentary, subjective confession; acknowledging that they raise questions that are deep, consequential – urgent, even – but surely not answerable. Scholarly minds have pointed to these questions, listed them and sometimes attempted to address them in microcosm through the study of isolated examples. But, in the face of the photographs' collective power, they have retreated.

In her essay, 'I Took Pictures: September 2001 and Beyond', Marianne Hirsch offers a series of suggestive meditations based on her own experience of photographing the 9/11 site.[4] She asks questions about the relationships between photography, trauma, witnessing, memory, testimony and grief, and specifically about the meanings of these images for those who were not there, but she does not set out to answer them. Similarly, E. Ann Kaplan, in 'A Camera and a Catastrophe', offers very personal reflections on photography and her own experience of trauma, going on to discuss the notion that Americans have indulged in a kind of 'over-psychologising' in the post–9/11 period.[5] She argues for a politically critical response to the events that also make room for empathy and emotion, but again, as probing as her essay is, its short form limits the theoretical rigour that would follow these arguments through. In other cases, scholars have dealt with individual images in great analytical depth, but at the expense of accounting for their implications within wider networks of political affect. Notable examples are discussions of Richard Drew's 'Falling Man' photograph by Andrea Fitzpatrick and Rob Kroes.[6] These essays situate this particular photograph within discussions about, respectively, photography theory and the contested realm of the 'iconic', but they cannot within their remits relate it fully to an extended political critique of the dominant readings or ideological mobilizations of September 11th photography as a body. *En masse*, the photographs remain unspeakable.

Conversely, as there have been important critical essays focussing on photographic subjects but in limited form, there have also been full-length scholarly texts that explore the subject of September 11th but do not primarily address photography. Some are political critiques (the Retort group's *Afflicted Powers*, Daniel Sherman and Terry Nardin's *Terror, Culture, Politics*), some discuss the impact of the attacks on journalism (Barbie Zelizer and Stuart Allan's *Journalism After September 11th*) or popular culture (Normal Denzin and Yvonna Lincoln's *9/11 in American Culture*, and Jeff Birkenstein, Anna Froula and Karen Randell's *Reframing 9/11*), and crucially in relation to this book, there are those that discuss the intersection of psychology and culture in terms of trauma and commemoration (David Simpson's *9/11* and Judith Greenberg's *Trauma at Home*). A final category is that of work that addresses the visual character of the September 11th attacks and the subsequent 'War on Terror' in ways that directly impact discussions of photography, but without using photography as their core material (the most important of these to date are W.J.T. Mitchell's *Cloning Terror* and Karen Engle's *Seeing Ghosts*, in both of which photography is addressed not as a unique medium with its own specific characteristics and implications, but merely as part of a wider cultural landscape of signs). One of my aims here is to provide fully worked answers to some of the questions that have been raised about photography within these various works, to elaborate and to 'join the dots' between shorter and/or less specific analyses that have gone before. Partly because of these others – in particular the essays (more numerous than those highlighted above) that have treated individual photographs in depth, I have resisted spending time on sustained analysis of the best-known September 11th photographs here. In their book about the most famous photojournalistic images of the last century, Robert Hariman and John Louis Lucaites warn against 'produc[ing] social theory at the expense of what the images are actually doing'.[7] This is an inherent risk for a project that seeks to go beyond the close reading of pictures towards an account of their collective influence, but I take that risk in the knowledge that it is impossible to understand what these images are doing without looking at what they are doing together, as a cumulative, spectacular force, and also by acknowledging that this book is part of a bigger picture too, in which I build on the work of others and write together with them.

It is a sensitive thing to make a critical analysis of objects connected with such grief and distress. There is much in the photographic record of September 11th that would seem to stand outside the purview of academic interrogation, and to suggest that critique would be improper or at least excessive. But, these are public images, part of a public discourse concerning the meanings of and appropriate responses to a national atrocity and an event of global consequence. Writing in 2006, David Simpson warned that in the case of September 11th, 'the repression of theory itself in its conventional appearance of foreignness and hostile rhetorical difficulty is one mark of the willed ignorance maintained by the major media inside the United States, and by many among its intelligentsia, about what the rest of the world thinks of us'.[8] The suggestion that, even after the passage of five years, there has been an enduring repression of theory by those in power in the United States, and of the self-critical attitude that it might entail, is a serious one. In the face of images that are declared to be beyond critique, there is perhaps a similar and equally serious kind of 'willed ignorance'. As I will argue, while in some quarters there has been genuine and sustained critical enquiry into the meanings of this event, the study of its images, and photography in particular, has failed to happen in quite the same way.[9] Since the 1970s, those of us working in the field of photography, whatever disciplinary titles we give ourselves, have shared in the renewed energy that critical theory has brought to bear on the study of cultural production across the humanities. But, theory, the argument goes, is in opposition to reality and so can have little to do with violence and death, which are completely real; nor can it comment on emotion, as it is essentially impersonal and abstract. The use of theory has at times been seen as a reductive attempt to demystify grief and trauma or to deconstruct them in ways that are threatening, invasive and disrespectful. These misunderstandings, as Simpson points out, are exacerbated by a defensive anti-intellectual stance within certain sections of Conservative US society, where intellectualism is associated with radicalism, or liberalism, or both, and is therefore held in disdain. And so, by the same gesture that distances powerful photographs from critique and even language itself, theory is often, at best, held at arm's length.

In a sense, this is where it should be. 'Critical distance' is what accounts both for theory's great value and its popular dismissal. Within his own field of 'cultural memory-work', Dominick LaCapra defines theory as 'sustained critical and self-critical reflection addressed to practices, texts, or sets of facts'. For him, this involves a careful accounting for the subjective and the personal, holding them in a tension that does not threaten but invigorates analysis and allows for more profound levels of rigour: 'ideally, such reflection increases self-understanding and provides a measure of critical distance on problems without implying a denial of one's implication in them'.[10] Theory allows us to take a step back from the texts and images that preoccupy us and simultaneously to acknowledge their great power. A synonym for the other or the foreign, theory offers understanding outside of the consensus, and it is this outside-ness that can make it seem inappropriate to the task of commenting on human atrocities or emotional issues. But, when the stakes are so high, a position outside of the consensus is exactly what we must seek to adopt, not least because, in this case, it represents an alternative to the national self-regard that dominates world politics. Further, as David Simpson has also argued, the most important contribution of theory is the access it can give to an improved understanding of the human 'other'. This is especially urgent when America's other is the Iraqi or the Muslim, and the difference has been formulated using terms like 'the fallen heroes of 9/11' versus 'the axis of evil'.

In New York, in late 2001, Giovanna Borradori conducted extended interviews with Jaques Derrida and Jürgen Habermas, questioning them as to how the discourses of philosophy and critical theory should respond to what had just happened. The result was an extraordinary example of theory's application to the cultural and social conditions of the moment, as both of these intellectual giants were called upon to bring their entire bodies of thought to bear on one – at the time, very recent – historical event. For Habermas, critical theory means philosophy aimed at carefully diagnosing and remedying the ills of modern society and carrying a burden of political responsibility in the public sphere.[11] For him, theory and practice are essentially interdependent. In the tradition of Kant and the Enlightenment thinkers, the effective work of critical theory relies on universally valid principles that hold across historical and cultural specificities. For Derrida, on the other hand, the most significant precondition for Enlightenment (defined as justice and freedom for all) is the careful deconstruction of apparently universal principles. As Borradori puts it in her summing up of his position, 'social critique and ethical responsibility require the deconstruction of falsely neutral and potentially hegemonic ideals. Far from curtailing the demand for universal justice and freedom, deconstruction renews it infinitely'.[12] In the light of this particular twenty-first-century event, both Habermas and Derrida return to radical principles that first had their widespread expression in the 1970s and 1980s. However, while Habermas (whose work, influenced by Marx and the Frankfurt School, is perhaps more easily applied to the discussion of politics and the public sphere) emphasizes the application of critical theory to the crises at hand, Derrida's primary contribution within this process is to provide the means to deconstruct the received concepts, ideas and ideals implicated within these crises (primarily, in the case of September 11th, the notion of terrorism itself). In light of this example of a meeting between theory and politics at the knife-edge of history, I would add that a due regard for theory must bring with it an attitude of humility, because its very difficulty can remind us of how little we really understand. It is via the remove of a theoretical stance that we realize, as Derrida himself commented, that 'we do not yet know what we are talking about'.[13]

Within popular American public discourse, two predominant types of conversation have addressed photography's role in the aftermath of the September 11th attacks: one that sees their power as being purely personal and emotive, claiming the untouchable, even mystical authority of the first-person narrative, and a second that mobilizes this untouchable authority in the name of military, or at least ideological, retaliation. Both of these were set out neatly by Colin Powell in a speech in 2004, at the official launch of a world-travelling exhibition of work by photographer Joel Meyerowitz staged by the US Department of State: 'September eleventh was a very personal experience for each of us … These images remind me that our country, our people and our families are very precious and that we must do all we can to protect them from the scourge of terrorism [… The photographs] gave us the opportunity to lead a worldwide coalition to go after not only the perpetrators of these attacks, but to go after terrorists around the world.'[14] The danger of this leap from the emotive to the militant, made uniquely possible by photography (the word 'opportunity' is surely the most troubling in Powell's whole speech), will be discussed later. But, in the meantime, there is a warning here about the way in which photography's apparent self-evidence – the transparent authority that it claims, and its easy isolation from the flows of political power – is at the outset in danger of shutting off the kinds of conversation that need to be had about it. In the words of Victor Burgin,

> the very 'natural' casualness of the scene presented to us disarms … analysis, which it characterises as an excessive response. But excess production

is generally on the side of ideology, and it is precisely in its apparent ingenuousness that the ideological power of photography is rooted – our conviction that we are free to choose what we make of a photograph hides the complicity to which we are recruited in the very act of looking.[15]

To address this situation and to free ourselves from the complicity into which the photography of September 11th draws us, it must be removed from its untouchable, reified position beyond the boundaries of critique. We must try to unravel its chains and networks, differentiate the levels on which it operates and identify their connections and the kinds of intentionality involved. And, simultaneously with all of this, we must somehow maintain a recognition of what we are looking at: the deaths of thousands of real people and the psychological destabilizing of many more thousands of others.

In the usual course of academic commentary on world events, there is time for critical thinking, assessment and rational exchange before conclusions are drawn. This distance, both temporal and conceptual, is what lends academia its authority in such situations. The events of September 11th seemed to disrupt this luxury. The uniqueness of this situation was highlighted by Habermas and Derrida: their comments just weeks after the attacks, while full of insight and prescient commentary on the moment at hand, were essentially reserved, mindful of the fact that, as Habermas put it, 'only in retrospect will we be able to understand … for now we do not know'.[16] He also recognized, however, that in a culture mediated by spin, PR and high-speed information exchange, the receiver (or ordinary citizen of the United States) was at a disadvantage, as consensus and understanding could be so easily engineered by those given the authority to distribute information. Arguably, it makes sense to leave the analysis of these images and their uses until enough time has passed for some critical distance and perspective. No doubt, in the years to come, valuable knowledge will be produced which could not have been produced any earlier. Again, however, it is the belief that such work might have present consequence, and that there is moral responsibility involved, that should motivate us to ask sensitive and dangerous questions at what is still, over a decade later, a sensitive and dangerous time. Historicizing the present, or at least the very recent, is a difficult project for those of us studying culture, as opposed to, say, political theory, social science or legal procedure. Conversely though, there is also danger in waiting too long, as David Simpson argues:

> Taking time for the effort at an inquiry … in the light of theory raises the question of whether there is still time, whether it is too late … The breakneck speed with which the tragic events of September 11th have been cashed in for the pursuit of long-mediated military adventurisms and global realignments (intended or not) must make us wonder whether taking the time for sustained reflection is still worth doing. Scholarly time looks its best when there are no

critical events going on around it: then it can reflect and project and even hope to appear prescient. When things speed up, we scholars run the risk of being left behind, assimilating yesterday's news.[17]

What does it mean to write about these images as I do here and now, in 2014 rather than 2001, and from Britain as opposed to the United States or anywhere else? This work is, in part, about how the roles and meanings of photographs change as they move between contexts, but also as they cross these spatial and temporal distances. In his book, *Open Sky*, Paul Virilio uses the terms 'underexposure' and 'overexposure' to set out a radical new understanding of time in the age of 'real-time' continuous tele-presence and virtuality. Rather than unfolding in the form of conventional narrative succession (before, during, after), media audiences are increasingly accustomed, he says, to perceiving time in terms of abrupt and discontinuous irruptions of varying intensities. These irruptions of what he calls 'chronoscopic time' are characterized as underexposure, exposure and overexposure. Chronoscopic time is essentially a violent process of intense compression by which narrative time implodes, and all that is left is an obsessive fixation with the real-time instant: the exposure. By this definition of exposure, Virlio's concern is not the exposure of viewing subjects, as one might describe exposure to UV rays for example, but the exposure of *things to audiences*: how the visible and represented world – including time itself – is presented to our vision and experience. This is not a psychological or a psychoanalytic model, but I would like to employ it in the service of one.

Virilio's discussion of space and time begins in the mysterious, almost transcendental territory of astrophysics, from which he gleans that time is 'no longer exclusively the time of classic chronological succession, but now a time of (chronoscopic) exposure of the duration of events at the speed of light'.[18] Developing the theme of light as understood within the realms of astrophysics and quantum theory, he then links the 'exposure' of chronoscopic time to the mechanics of the photographic process. Recognizing the capacity of the camera to interfere with conventional time by freezing and isolating instants from the flow of temporal experience, he notes that in the making of a photograph, time is 'no longer the same as time passing, but essentially a kind of time that gets exposed, that "breaks the surface" – surfaces; and this exposure time then succeeds the classic time of succession. The time of the sudden *take* is accordingly, from the beginning, time-light'.[19] He goes on, 'this is confirmed by the various technological experiments with "exposure time", from Niepce and Daguerre's dark room through Marey's chronophotography to the present-day elementary particle accelerators which are veritable telescopes of the infinitely small.'[20] He seems to mean all of this as an elaborate metaphor – a useful way of illustrating an abstract point – but surely it is more than that. The photographic process is not just a useful metaphoric device, it is the very location and instance of what he is talking about, especially in psychological terms. Time erupts: time, light, the object and the image are all, simultaneously in the photographic instant, exposed, and this must translate in the experience of looking at the resulting photograph, whether minutes or years later, as another layer of exposure: what he himself calls the 'relativistic eternal present … when the successive moments of time are equally present in a single perception that makes them a landscape of events'.[21]

The application of these ideas to the mediated representation of September 11th is irresistible. The crowd of New Yorkers in Oshima's photograph is suspended in an eternal present. The central protagonist is held for all time in the tension between looking and running away. Photographs like this are sometimes said to 'sum up' the magnitude of a whole event. When people say this, they mean that by the skill or luck of the photographer, or the chance arrangement of details in front of the camera, the many moments of that long day are somehow equally and simultaneously present within the frame, creating a symbol that is more evocative than the sum of its elements. Here is a single, collapsed present in which the succession of moments takes spatial form as 'a landscape of events'. Writing shortly after the attacks in *Rolling Stone* magazine, David Foster Wallace recalled, 'from the door to the kitchen I remember seeing the second tower fall and being confused about whether it was a replay of the first tower falling'.[22] Similarly, there are stories of small children confused by the endless repetition of collapsing buildings on TV, thinking that all the towers in all the world were falling down. For these children, for Foster Wallace, and so many millions of viewers around the world, the succession of events was violently collapsed into a single shattering irruption. It was overexposed, and so were we. This character of simultaneity is by definition present in the photographs over a decade later just as it was in 2001. And, so talking about them now involves a recognition of this eternal present, as well as of the changes that have taken place outside the frame over time. One of the biggest of these is a broadening in the kind of language that we can now use to tackle what we see. There may never be an ideal time or a safe distance, but where words like 'spectacular', 'manipulation' or even 'beauty' were once unacceptable, they can now be part of the conversation about September 11th's visual character. There is still risk involved in navigating the 'too soon' and the 'too late', but in the meantime, writes W.J.T. Mitchell, we have a responsibility to commit to 'untimely utterances and awkward silences … examining what cannot or should not be said', and 'reflecting on the conditions of sayability and the unspeakable'.[23]

Another change is in the realm of images that can now safely be talked about. It took some time for photographs of the so-called 'jumpers' to easily be looked at, let alone discussed in all but the most hushed tones. But, this shifting of the parameters of taboo over time is exemplified best of all by the case of '9/11's most controversial photo', taken by Magnum photographer Thomas

Hoepker. This picture, of five young people watching idly from the Williamsburg waterfront as the towers burn, appeared five years late, the photographer judging it too 'confusing' to be included in the public account of the tragedy any sooner. When it was finally published in 2006, Fred Rich of *The New York Times* condemned the picture's subjects (or victims) for moving on too fast, daring to enjoy the Autumn sunshine while the day of death was still unfolding. 'The young people in Mr. Hoepker's photo aren't necessarily callous', he wrote, 'they're just American. In the five years since the attacks, the ability of Americans to dust themselves off and keep going explains both what's gone right and what's gone wrong on our path to the divided and dispirited state the nation finds itself in today.'[24] The consensus seemed to be that the picture was ahead of its time. It showed something that was happening then and there, but too soon to be accepted by the rest of us. In the photographer's words, it 'didn't "feel right" at this moment and I put it in the "B" box of rejected images.'[25] Later, as the attack's ten-year anniversary came and went, this same picture was being called 'iconic', precisely because it holds, compressed in its eternal present, all the attendant ambiguities of moving on.[26]

Despite the tempting etymological connections, Paul Virilio's particular use of 'underexposure' and 'overexposure' remains fundamentally different from the more literal 'invisibility' or 'overvisibility' of specific photographs. But, taken together, these two pairs of terms prepare the ground for an understanding of the roles that photography has played in and around September 11th, in accounting first for what there was to see, and subsequently for how it was experienced and re-experienced from the very first moments right through to the present. As I have already begun to argue, the media spectacle of '9/11' was so overwhelming that it created new problems for seeing and processing visual information. The global, instantaneous, simultaneous and seemingly endless exposure of spectacular terror happened before it could be explained in words. While the first imagery that many people saw of 9/11 was on television, the particular widespread attachment to still photographs in attempts at memorializing and recovery was, I argue, very special. And so, the focus throughout this book is on still photography. It begins in the first chapter by examining the dazzling and emotive ways in which photography was used to construct so-called 'public' or 'collective memory' of the event. This involves the analysis of two sources: first, the uses of photography and framing text in major regional US newspapers in the days following the attacks, and second, a number of high-profile commemorative photography books. In both of these settings, an array of hugely powerful photographs was harnessed to push forward particular interpretations of the event, very often with reference to the prevailing idea of public memory. As well as Guy Debord's concept of the Spectacle, Theodor Adorno's work on the culture industry is used, paying special attention to his suggestion that a whole society can be 'infantilised'; its desires shaped by means not of censorship, but of distraction, and via what might be called a regime of 'regressive seeing'.

The next chapter begins to deal with the contested but ubiquitous notion of 'trauma'. I argue that the experiences of many millions of indirect witnesses of the September 2001 attacks via broadcast media and photography involved a particular kind of trauma – one that presents problems for the existing field of trauma theory because normal processes of seeing and understanding were disrupted in completely new ways. As language struggled to keep up, many testified that words seemed inadequate, while images somehow came closer. In this chapter, the work of both Sigmund Freud and Jacques Lacan is used to consider the structural nature of psychological trauma and specifically the ways in which the perceived dichotomy between words and images affects the discussion of this event's overwhelmingly visual media presentation. In combination with more recent thinking on photography and trauma, these two very different foundational figures of psychoanalysis provide the basis to argue that the event's mediation was in itself traumatizing, specifically because of a radical disruption within the two binaries of time and space, language and image.

Some of the most powerful September 11th images are of buildings, both shattered and whole, which, in a long-established photojournalistic convention, stand in for human bodies. Chapter 3 considers two alternative ways of understanding these pictures of buildings. Holy and sacred on the one hand, as they take on flesh in the redemptive Christian narrative of the sanctified suffering body; dark and alienating on the other, as the original expression of Freud's 'uncanny', the domestic space made strange; or worse, Lacan's elusive 'real'. The bewildering uncanniness of the attacks as a technologically mediated event experienced by so many so immediately yet from a distance as if by proxy accounts for the rush by both government and media to make sense of it in terms that served their own interests, perhaps most significantly the terms of religion.

Very soon after the 'collective memory' of September 2001 was established, individuals and groups began using photography in various ways to process their own feelings and offer tributes to the dead. The next chapter looks at some of the ways in which photographs were appropriated and assimilated, most significantly within 'communities' of blog-style vernacular photographic memorial websites, and also in large-scale exhibition projects like *Here is New York* and *The September 11 Photo Project*, both of which emphasized their independence from the mainstream media and their privileging of vernacular or 'democratic' views. But, perhaps these projects were not as independent as they might have hoped or seemed to be. The ideas of both Michel Foucault and Theodor Adorno are used here to think about the troubling ways in which particular readings of photographs worked their way from the mainstream press into individual expressions of grief.

For some people, collecting and looking at endless streams of photographs, whether in group exhibits or personal web pages, felt like a cathartic experience that helped in coming to terms with the event. But, with the passing of time, the repeated seeing of such violent images might also have served paradoxically to re-enact or reinforce the trauma again and again. If photographic representation played a role in compounding or even creating the initial trauma, Chapter 5 asks what we might then say about its use in so many people's varied attempts at recovery. Clinical psychologists have suggested that while it is natural to make recourse to pictures of whatever kind in approaching 'unspeakable' experiences, for true recovery to happen these visual fragments must be assimilated and made subject to a narrative. But, because of the media's handling of these events, this transition into critical narrative-formation was made almost impossible. Instead, the dazzling, synchronous visual spectacle, and the ideological determinism that were built into it from the outset, prevailed.

The complexity and impact of the photographic representation of these events, both within the United States and internationally, call for a kind of critical conversation that reaches outside the academic disciplines in which photography is conventionally studied. A need for 'interdisciplinarity' is reflected by the range of theoretical frames used throughout the book, which vary according to the different stages of the story and the different media being examined but move between two broad categories: on the one hand, a concern with political and cultural factors that is informed primarily by the thinking of the Frankfurt School, Debord and Foucault, and on the other, the psychoanalysis of Freud and Lacan. Framing all of this and implicit throughout is the recurring question of time, which, having been articulated by way of Paul Virilio, is addressed both to the photographic seeing of the September 11th attacks and the complexities of writing about them in the present. Moving at such a pace between the work of figures from Freud to Adorno and those on the more contemporary edge of fields like trauma studies and cyber culture, there is a risk of disjointedness. The reason for this diversity, though, is that the visual phenomena that make up the representation of September 11th constitute a deeply interdependent network that transgresses the disciplinary boundaries of photography, media, cyber-culture, psychology, critical theory and politics, and studying them in isolation has only taken us so far. Photography, trauma, global media and terrorism have each been theorized extensively in their own various contexts, but the extraordinary things that happened when these elements came together in this event and its aftermath – the unprecedented level of photographic coverage of an attack designed to operate overwhelmingly on the level of visual symbolism, the spectacle of its media coverage, the outpouring of public emotional expression by means of this very same photography and the unique convergence of visual and verbal rhetoric in support of war – have not.

1 SPECTACLE AND COLLECTIVE MEMORY

A journalist asked me, isn't this propaganda? I told him, propaganda for what?[1]

It is now no longer the taboo it once was to describe the September 11th attacks as spectacular. They were designed to do as much damage to America on a symbolic level as on the level of material destruction and death. It is also now widely accepted that as an act of spectacular terrorism, this was destined, if not deliberately planned, to be the first move in an enduring war of images. In this sense, it was, according to one especially daring *Washington Post* reporter, 'a masterpiece'.[2] My subject here is not this symbolic manoeuvre itself, but the victims' backlash. What agendas, constraints, tropes and modes of address characterized the visual representation of the attacks in the American media, and why? Has the United States' position within the image war been strengthened or compromised by its response? What journalistic conventions were broken or adhered to in this process, and what were the implications? Lower Manhattan was filled with cameras on that day. Professional and amateur photographers in their thousands created a record more comprehensive than that of any other public event in history. And, this supply was equally met by demand. The following day's newspapers were taken over by photography, with text largely relegated to margins and captions. Photo editors faced an unusual problem – instead of struggling to find the right pictures, they struggled to fit all the pictures in, in many cases responding by creating special editions and photographic supplements in which words could be dispensed with almost completely. Barbie Zelizer has argued that the American media's photographic presentation of the attacks was 'dazzling', and that the sidelining of words that was associated with this had political consequences. Critical questions about what had led to the attacks, their possible prevention and the nature of the Bush administration's immediate response and subsequent military action were deflected by means of a spectacular image overload.[3] While the deliberate hiding of particular images from public view may indeed have been an issue, a more fundamental problem was the disabling of public critical engagement by an abundance of images that did not reveal the whole truth but seemed to satisfy by their sheer volume and impact. This dazzling effect operated on two levels. The first was the immediate photographic news coverage that took place in the days following the attacks: the high-pressure editorial decisions regarding what, and how much, to publish of the first visual details at the World Trade Center and Pentagon sites. This early stage could be called, in the pseudo-military terminology of an image war, defensive. Then, as well as documentation of the slower processes of recovery and response, later stages involved more calculated uses of photographic imagery for propaganda purposes: carefully orchestrated PR appearances by political figures at the site, for example, and perhaps most striking of all, the US Department of State's touring photographic exhibition, *After September 11: Images from Ground Zero*.

Though television was the medium that first broke the news of the September 11th attacks to American and international audiences, our subject here is the printed press.[4] One reason for this focus is that, due to the dangers of close-range filming and the difficulties of transmission, most of the video coverage of Lower Manhattan that day was gathered by news teams positioned at high vantage points on buildings that were a safe distance away from the World Trade Center. This, and the unprecedented decision quickly made by news networks to share footage, means that most of the early moving images seen around the world were essentially the same wide-angle, long-range views, repeated over and over again. Still photography, on the other hand, provided much greater diversity and detail. The pictures that made it into the following day's newspapers via the Associated Press, Reuters and other agencies not only framed the burning towers from a frontal, bird's eye perspective but also from myriad positions on the streets below. Photographers were able to capture the unfolding human drama as well as the big picture, in some cases having to negotiate risks to their own safety and inhaling the same dust and smoke as their subjects. Further, in keeping with, but also somewhat crippled by, television's special role as the medium best equipped to relay breaking news in real time, TV news networks were able to present only what their live cameras were taking in minute by minute, in many cases struggling to comprehend what they were seeing even as they were broadcasting it. The printed press, on the other hand, had at least a little time to make decisions about its picturing of the events.[5]

The appetite for printed news in America in the aftermath of September 11th was so huge that before long, as well as reporting the unfolding story, newspaper editors realized that they themselves were becoming part of the story. This event called for unprecedented decisions to be made regarding editorial content, distribution and print volume. As the *Los Angeles Times* reported on 13 September, at least 100 newspapers published 'extra editions' on the Tuesday afternoon, with front page headlines declaring, 'TERROR', 'OUTRAGE', 'DAY

OF EVIL' and 'BASTARDS!' in much larger-than-usual type.[6] The same article reports that on Wednesday morning, the *Los Angeles Times* itself had printed 180,000 more copies than usual, and 50,000 more by noon. The *New York Times* printed 450,000 extra on Wednesday, approximately doubling its usual print run, and spokesmen said there would be an expected 900,000 further copies on Thursday. *TIME*, America's largest weekly news magazine, posted stories and pictures from a special 40-page 'memorial' edition on its website on Wednesday evening, expecting to publish seven million copies by the end of Thursday, and *Newsweek* also quickly produced two million copies of a 64-page special edition that contained no advertising.[7] On its now famous 'US attacked' cover, the *New York Times* featured an extra-large typeface used only twice previously by the paper, for the first manned moon landing and the resignation of Richard Nixon. The *Chicago Tribune* (which initially increased its press run by 15 per cent and by Thursday had printed another 900,000 extra copies) remarked that the nation's newspapers presented widely varying tones, or 'more personality' when compared to the relatively homogenous coverage provided by television news. This was, it said, 'a reflection of papers' traditional role as records not only of the moment, but historical markers destined to be keepsakes'.[8]

Despite this perceived diversity, however, a close look at how newspapers used photographs during these first few days reveals that the range of views represented is in fact very narrow. In her own survey of the attacks' printed press coverage, Zelizer has identified four prevailing categories of photograph.[9] Three of these are photographs showing the towers' ruins being observed by witnesses (usually uniformed rescue workers or other figures of authority), those showing witnesses watching as the attacks unfold, but not showing the scene itself (as in Figure I.1) and images of people looking at photographs or taking photographs. The first and most prominent category, however, consists of images of the World Trade Center towers themselves during or just after the impact of the second plane. Included in this category is Spencer Platt's view shown in Figure 1.1, and the photograph taken by Steve Ludlum that appeared on the front page of the *New York Times* the following day. Ludlum's picture provides a wide-angle view showing the intact Brooklyn Bridge in the foreground and the exploding twin towers surrounded by the other (as yet) undamaged buildings of the financial district. John Loengard, former director of photography at *LIFE* magazine, offers his opinion of why this image was chosen for the *Times* front page, saying that it 'put the event in a context – human habitation, the size of the city – whereas many of the others were focussed directly on the towers'.[10] It is perhaps significant that the paper chose to lead with a photograph in which the scale of the catastrophe is clear but is set within a larger context of relative normality. This is in contrast to *TIME* magazine's commemorative cover, featuring a photograph by Lyle Oweko that shows the exploding towers in dramatic foreshortened isolation, evoking not steadfastness, but epic, almost

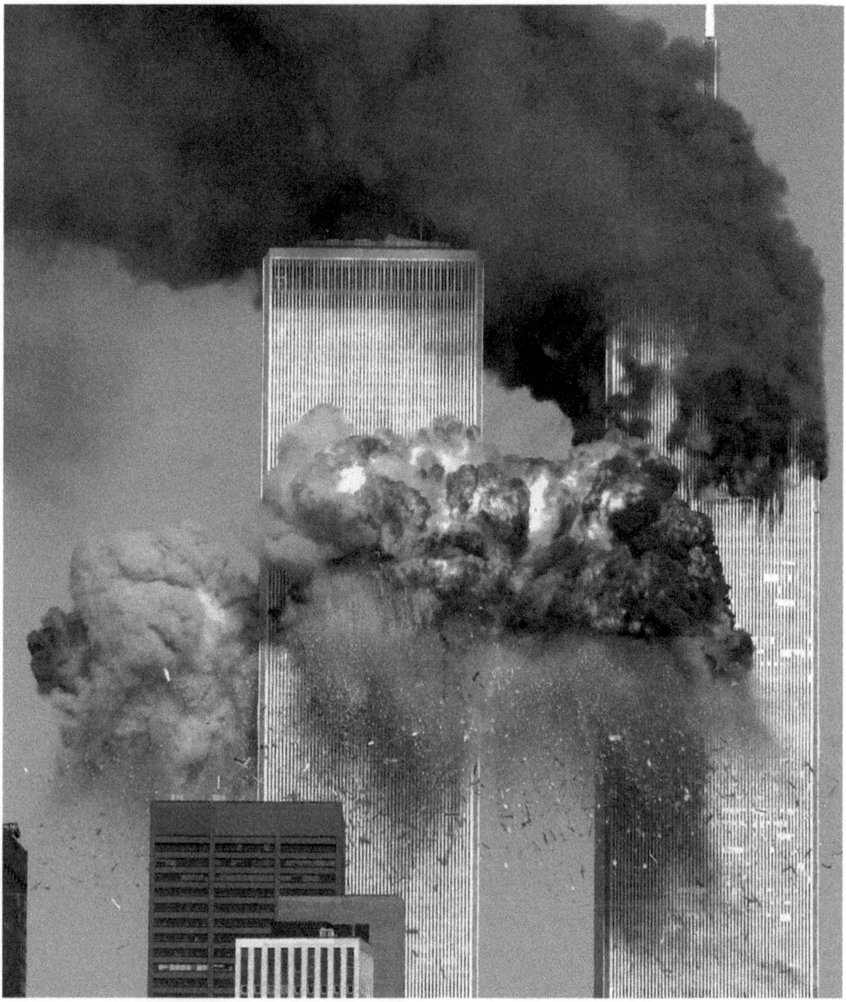

Figure 1.1 Hijacked United Airlines Flight 175 crashes into the South Tower of the World Trade Center 9.03 a.m. September 11th 2001. Photo by Spencer Platt, Getty Images.

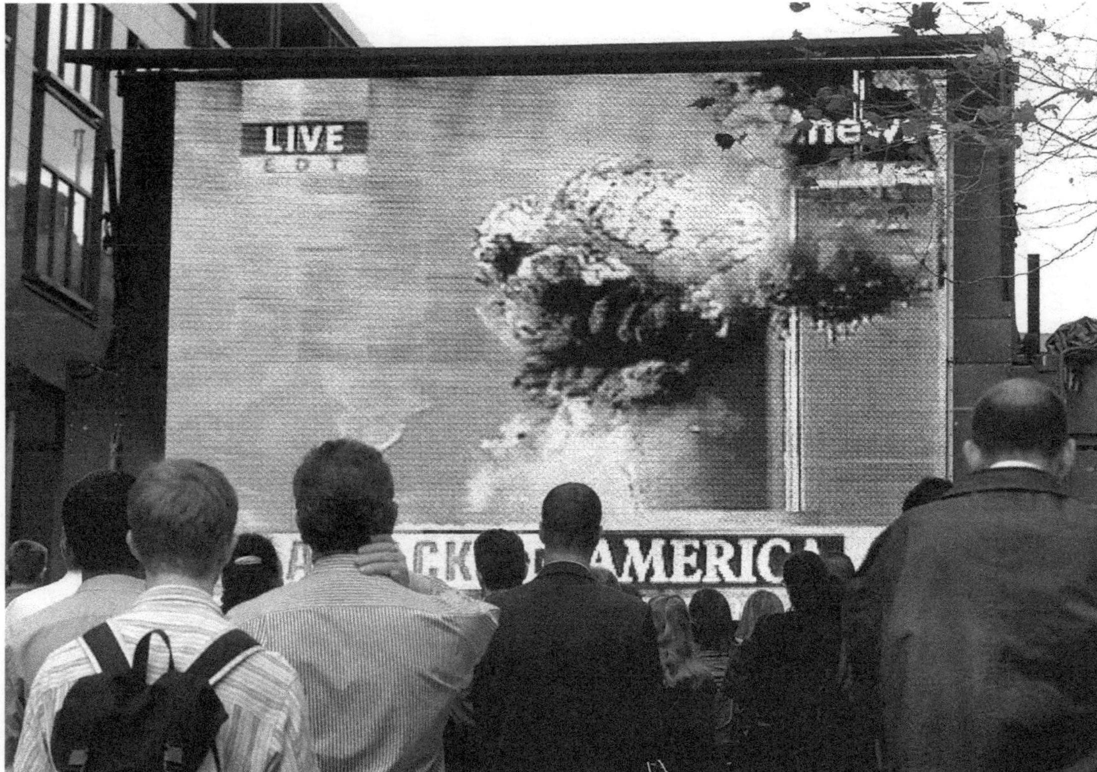

Figure 1.2 Workers watch a giant screen in Martin Place, Sydney, 12 September 2001, showing images of the twin towers of the World Trade Center after they were hit by two hijacked passenger jets. Photo by Greg Wood, AFP/Getty Images.

cinematic destruction. These and other views of the towers were by far the most common choice for the front pages of papers around the country, and they continued to appear long after the rubble was cleared. The *New York Times*, whose front page featured not one, but five photographs of varying sizes, has become invested with historical meaning as a commemorative object in itself, as the *Chicago Tribune* predicted many papers would. The context of the action shown in Ludlum's dominant image is illustrated by four supplementary views: United Airlines Flight 175 before impact with the south tower (forming a kind of inverted 'before and after'), firefighters in the towers' wreckage, the scene of the Pentagon attack and a wounded female victim receiving first aid near the World Trade Center site – a relatively graphic illustration of actual bodily injury that proved very rare in the American press from this point onwards.

Another unconventional photojournalistic trope, and one that is associated with Zelizer's category of pictures that show people looking at pictures, is pictures of people looking at screens.[11] Appearing frequently in newspapers far beyond New York and Washington are a notable number of photographs of people looking at footage of the attacks on screens, often in public places and in groups (Figure 1.2). Further illustrating the nationwide and international impact of the event, it is again not the attack itself that is the 'news' signified by these images, but the act of watching, particularly when this watching is a collective activity and one that marks an exception to people's usual habits of news consumption. Photographs of photographs and photographs of screens all involve a layering of refracted gazes, each layer redoubling the burden of spectacle. So heavy was this burden – the imperative not only to bear witness to the devastation of the buildings but to the devastation of other witnesses – that it seemed to create the need for a further category, in which figures of authority appear in the frame looking along with us and on our behalf. From around 15 September, photographs and footage began to appear of political leaders arriving to observe for themselves the scene in Lower Manhattan. The *New York Times* ran a large picture of President Bush and other officials at Ground Zero with the caption, 'President Bush surveyed what looked like a war zone yesterday at the World Trade Center site. Representative Jerold Nadler, Governor Pataki and Mayor Giuliani accompanied him.'[12] The authority of these witnesses can be seen, Zelizer says, as a symbolic invitation, providing a prompt for viewers in their own reactions. These pictures are used, again, not only because of their inherent newsworthiness, but as representative signals of appropriate response. She identifies this particular convention as beginning with the photographic coverage of the liberation of Nazi death camps in 1945, when General Eisenhower and other Allied leaders were brought to the camps to be photographed looking, along with the rest of the world, at the horrors that had been uncovered there.[13] This, she argues, was for international audiences a historical moment of such disorientating atrocity that it essentially called for a demonstration of how to

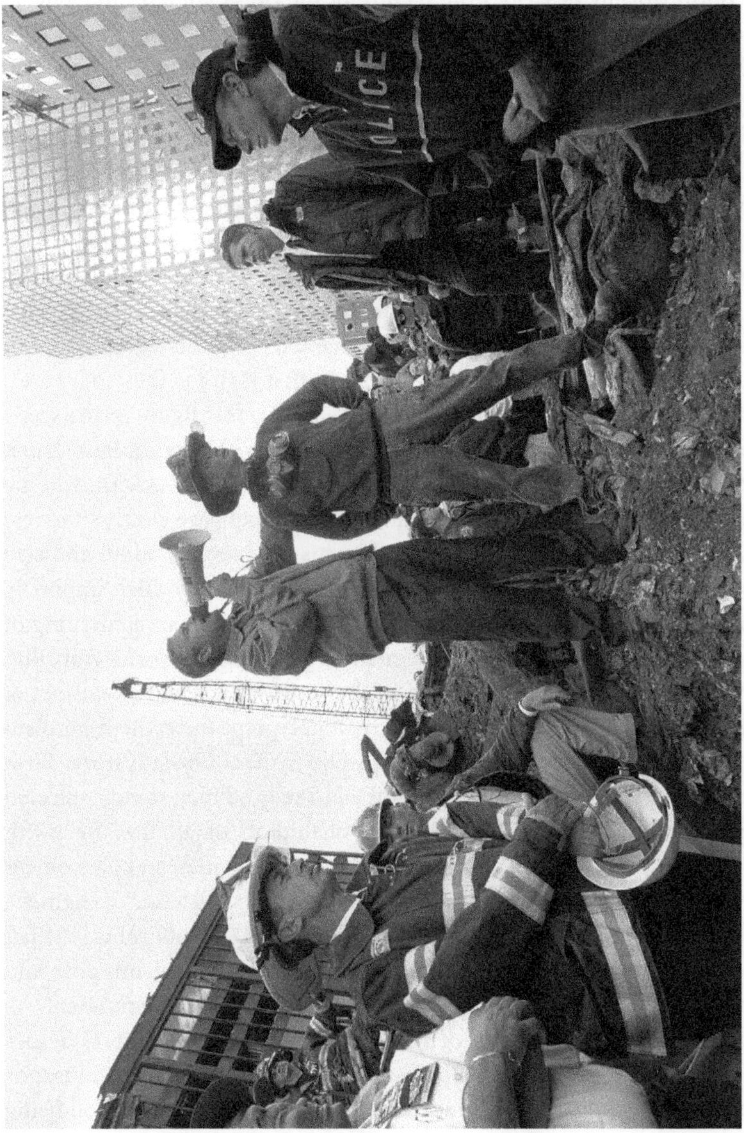

Figure 1.3 U.S. President George W. Bush speaks to rescue workers, firefighters and police officers from the rubble of Ground Zero, 14 September 2001. Standing with Bush is retired firefighter Bob Beckwith and New York Governor George Pataki. Photo by Eric Draper, White House/Getty Images.

see. In this moment, looking was so serious an undertaking that it had to be modelled and led by society's chief witnesses. Of all the post–September 11th photographs consistent with this function, the one shown in Figure 1.3 was the most widely circulated. Mark McKinnon, George W. Bush's media advisor, somewhat optimistically describes the picture of the president atop the 'pile' at Ground Zero with retired firefighter Bob Beckwith as 'the most lasting and iconic image of [his] presidency. It is much like President Reagan's call in Berlin to "tear down this wall," except this moment was unscripted and an antecedent to war, which makes it even more powerful.'[14] Other political and media figures disagree on the point of the image's spontaneity, but not on its value to the president's P.R. The photo opportunity was not only perfectly realized, but essential, says Luc Sante, cultural critic and historian of photography: 'People wanted to see him climbing on top of something [down there] … Even if the calculation was done five minutes ahead of time, it was calculated. I'm positive of it. [It was] part of an image-management strategy that's characterised this administration from the beginning.'[15] And, there can be no doubt that it is, for these purposes, a perfect photograph. The president stands as the uppermost figure in the scene and is the sole focus of the crowd, whom he addresses through a loud haler. But, his body language self-consciously shifts attention on to Beckwith, who by contrast stands, feet planted wide apart, hands on hips and gaze aloft, as the real hero of the moment. This status is reinforced by his age (seventy-nine) and also by the gas-mask-like apparatus worn around his neck, both of which implicitly identify him with the 'greatest generation' and lend this moment something of the glory attributed to America's involvement in the Second World War. But, instead of a uniform, Beckwith is dressed in the scruffy jeans and sweatshirt of the American everyman, and so he is also an archetype of the civilian heroism that has already come to characterize this episode in New York's history. Bush picks out this American hero, elevates him for all to see and then stands reflected in his eminence, identifying himself as the champion of all that Beckwith represents. But, in case the symbol of a hero who is part civilian and part officer is too ambiguous (Beckwith is not just a firefighter, he is a 'veteran' firefighter), the group is flanked in the foreground by a uniformed FDNY official on the left and a police officer on the right, both mirroring one another's solemn pose and facial expression and adding further emphasis to the gravitas of the moment.

Alongside the repetitive scenes of rubble, smoke, rescue workers, heroes and watchers, though, there was an overwhelming absence. In the thousands of photographs that circulated within the public sphere in the week following the attacks, death was everywhere implied, but invisible. The closest that most newspaper editors came to showing dead bodies was in the 'jumper' photographs. Images of falling victims – a sight that for many eyewitnesses was the defining horror of the day – appeared in a handful of papers around the country within twenty-four hours of the attacks but then quickly disappeared from view. Their place was taken by symbols: architectural destruction without any visible trace of the people inside; the streets of Lower Manhattan covered with ad-hoc memorial paraphernalia, crosses and photographs of missing victims; tokens of the invisible dead. A very rare exception, appearing in the *Los Angeles Times* on 14 September, was a large photograph of rescue workers holding a body bag on a stretcher above their heads. The caption reads: 'A victim of the WTC disaster is carried out of the rubble in a body bag, one of 30,000 ordered by city officials as the grim collection of corpses continues.' But the body itself is not visible.[16]

A *New York Times* article on 13 September discussed the dilemma faced by pictures' desks in those chaotic days, regarding what to publish and what to shield from public view. It observed that 'not since the Oklahoma bombing or the crash of a helicopter in Mogadishu, Somalia, have newspaper editors and television producers had so many images available that show the graphic deaths and dismemberments of Americans'.[17] But, several factors were at play in the editorial decisions that had to be made about these pictures. Some, like Erik Sorenson, president and general manager of MSNBC, asked the question, 'when does realistic coverage of a tragedy cross the line into exploitation?' arguing that 'there were plenty of images that told the story without all of the gore'.[18] In the same article, David Westin, president of ABC News, put it a different way: 'the question is, are we informing or titillating and causing unnecessary grief? Our responsibility is to inform the American public of what's going on and, in going the next step, is it necessary to show people plunging to their death?'[19] Conversely, Ed Kosner, editor in chief of *New York Daily News*, who had caused controversy in the first few days with his decision to print a photo of a severed hand, argued, 'you can't do the story without doing the story. It's no time to be squeamish'.[20]

Commonly accepted standards of taste are the most obvious explanation for the invisibility of human destruction in this instance. There would arguably have been little point in causing further distress at such a delicate time, particularly given the very real risk of family members recognizing the remains of loved ones, perhaps even before being notified of their deaths. The convention of picturing architectural wreckage or other signifiers such as lighted candles, blood splatters, strewn items of clothing and personal effects rather than human remains ensures impact without distaste. In the British and American press, unlike that of other parts of the world, it is usual practice to picture a scene of death only after the bodies are out of sight. Most of the horror of these images lies in imagining either what has gone before or what is outside the frame. These images can be metaphorical or even beautiful, suiting a sombre mood rather than illustrating the full impact of 'reality'. This practice could be called euphemistic, implying manipulation or dishonesty, and yet it is sometimes difficult to discern between the dishonest and the considerate. It is also difficult to discern between common decency in the face of grief and manipulation for questionable political ends. That is what makes any detached critical study of this subject both very important and very sensitive. This fine line was negotiated by newsrooms and press offices all over the world in the aftermath of September 11th. In an article titled 'Brokering the Power of the Image', James Kelly, managing editor of *TIME* magazine, reflects on his publication's history in recording the horrors of war, claiming that 'times have changed' since the days when official censorship was what made war fatalities invisible. He discusses the ethical wrestling involved in deciding what to show and what to hold back, and his comments reveal his adherence to the American mainstream press convention of occasionally printing photographs of dead foreigners, but almost never Americans, and certainly never white Americans:

> It is also undeniable that the task of deciding what photos to run in *TIME* has grown much more difficult in the wake of September 11th. In putting together our special issue on the World Trade Center attacks, I considered whether we should use photographs of the many victims who jumped out of windows rather than stay behind and be burned to death … I'm not saying that one decision is right and the other wrong but only that my sensibility led me to pick one over the other.[21]

Kelly's comments highlight two points. First, that September 11th changed photojournalism, and second, the issue of exactly what it is that prompts the decision to print or hide a dead body. For Kelly, it was 'sensibility'. For others, the criteria may have been different.

Zelizer identifies an uncritical acceptance of invisibility in the aftermath of September 11th, suggesting that American society has been complacent about 'seeing less when we should see more'.[22] The main reason for this, she says, is that so little information was made to look like so much, and that the images shown were generally not complex or multi-layered, but easily readable and easily slotted into the pervading interpretive schema. The ubiquity of such images, which Zelizer calls 'pure surfaces', created the illusion of masses of information and infinite visibility, when in fact these huge numbers of photographs were all variations on the same narrow set of themes. Which images were being pushed aside in this deluge? Is it simply the invisibility of bodies and gore that is at issue here? How dangerous or destructive could this invisibility really be? John Taylor, in his book *Body Horror*, equates the absence of horror in the representation of real events, however sensitive, with a 'dangerous poverty of knowledge'.[23] He concludes that if the press has a responsibility to show horror more graphically than it does, this is because of the importance of bearing witness; a debt owed to the dead or suffering to ensure that society learns something and that such a thing cannot happen again. Bearing witness, he argues, is an act of cultivating historical memory: an appropriate sense of things as they happened. The responsibility of the media is to mark out and present events with honesty, and the decision not to show unpleasant details robs the public of the opportunity to bear witness.[24] Taylor seems to be suggesting that the press should be responsible for the deliberate shaping of public memory and for creating a space within which people can appropriately witness, as well as for deciding what is appropriate. The potential for ideological influence seems to lie, for him, in the decision to hide particular pictures. For Susan Sontag, on the other hand, any kind of deliberately cultivated 'public' or 'collective memory' at all, whether or not it is graphic in its presentation of horror, constitutes a dangerous ideology, and this is an inevitable outcome whenever institutions assume control of sets of images:

> All memory is individual, unreproducible – it dies with each person. What is called collective memory is not a remembering but a stipulating: that this is important, and this is the story about how it happened, with the pictures that lock the story in our minds. Ideologies create substantiating archives of images, representative images, which encapsulate common ideas of significance and trigger predictable thoughts [and] feelings.[25]

It is tempting to make generalizations about the political and social factors at play in the control of the visual representation of September 11th. Why, from the state's point of view, was it not in the national interest to see the bodies of victims of September 11th? Wouldn't the heightened outrage have cemented support for retaliation? The ideological motivations and power of the Bush administration were surely implicated, as was the media's compulsion to cooperate with them, particularly as the days and weeks went by and the transition was made from initial knee-jerk reportage to a period of 'making sense', followed by commemoration. It would also be easy to overstate the passivity of the audience at whom this representation was aimed, within and outside the United States. It is on this point that Theodor Adorno's critique of 'the culture industry' presents a useful model. For Adorno and Horkheimer, the culture industry is constituted by the complex and often fluid relationship between ruling ideology, mass media and society and is characterized by the direct control of populations through the manipulation of their desires. This seems to be an ideal framework for the analysis of American culture at this time, when the political administration had such a vested interest in the emotional state of the nation, and the threatened population in turn looked to both government and media for reassurance with an urgency rarely seen before or since. There is a proviso, however, that in his writing on this subject, Adorno can be accused of a certain amount of generalization when it comes to the definitions of the 'ruling ideology'. Those referred to in his work 'The Culture Industry: Enlightenment as Mass Deception' as 'the people at the top', who possess a 'violent monopoly over cultural life', are never identified in very specific detail.[26] In common with his contemporaries within the Frankfurt School, an underlying motivation for much of Adorno's work was to understand the roots of fascism: what the workings of the culture industry might reveal about this extreme ideology, and how such an ideology could possibly have taken hold of a civilized society in the way that it did in 1930s' Europe.[27] While by no means analogous, early twenty-first-century America was also a society gripped by uncertainty, suspicion and conflict, in which what might be called the 'visual culture industry' had a relationship to dominant socio-political forces that warrants a similar kind of attention. Another proviso, however, is that along with the wider Frankfurt School at the point of their writing, Adorno and Horkheimer's concern with culture and subjectivity in *The Dialectic of Enlightenment* (in which Adorno's 'Culture Industry' essay appears) is somewhat detached from the concrete politics of the day, and in particular from the very pragmatic Marxist base/superstructure model which lay at the original foundation of much of their work. One consequence of this is a degree of fatalism. Unlike Marx's, Adorno's critique is not connected to any constructive means of redressing the manipulation or deception in which the masses are caught.

A central argument of 'The Culture Industry' concerns the use of popular media to disable individuals' capacity for critical reflection through what might be summed up as a kind of mass-produced distraction,[28] which Adorno goes as far as to describe as 'psychoanalysis in reverse'.[29] In his words, 'the need which might resist central control has already been suppressed by the control of the individual consciousness.'[30] The key point here is that the culture industry has power over individual consciousness not by overcoming diversity of thought through aggressive ideological control or forceful domination, but by managing in the first place to create a situation in which each 'individual' – reproduced as a subject of mass consumption – is essentially alike. This homogenization of individual consciousness also creates in each subject an appetite for more of the same control: 'freedom to choose an ideology – since ideology always reflects economic coercion – everywhere proves to be freedom to choose what is always the same'.[31] All possible modes of thought and consumption are freely permitted in what is ostensibly a liberal society, but the desires of the population are, Adorno argues, subtly, actively and pre-emptively shaped so that the culture industry is then in turn only 'giving the people what they want'.

This is perhaps the kind of dynamic that is at play when James Kelly of *TIME* magazine says that in the question of how to represent the aftermath of the September 11th attacks, he was not influenced by official censorship but was instead left to the freedom of his own liberal 'sensibility', which led him, as it did countless other editors, to conform to a pattern that aligned with prevailing political convention and intent. In a liberal media environment such as this, as well as communicating visual information, photojournalism also functions precisely to serve the expectations of its audience. It tends to confirm existing ideas rather than introducing new ones and, in a manner that fits precisely with the Adornian model of manipulating individual subjects by 'giving them what they want' within a totalizing framework, reinforces rather than challenges existing beliefs. In other words, news is always presented in relation to things already known. This goes some way towards explaining why the range of photographs was in this instance so narrow, with so little deviation.

There are numerous examples of this kind of reductive logic being played out photographically. One of the most prominent, which lent itself more readily to verbal than visual rhetoric, but was also represented in photographs, was the basic narrative trope of a battle between good and evil. The righteous and morally superior position of the United States was reinforced in images of political leaders, who by means of various gestures and photo opportunities could be seen to step up and offer assurance of retribution. Headlines such as 'President promises to avenge lost lives' and 'Bush vows to respond and calls for calm' were combined with photographs like the one featured in the *Los Angeles Times* on 12 September, of President Bush on the telephone to Vice President Dick Cheney aboard Air Force One, looking capable and determined (Figure 1.4).[32] Other images in support of this same rhetorical message also featured in the *Los Angeles Times* on this date, including one of Bush later in the day, disembarking Air Force One at St. Andrews Air Force Base and addressing the nation from the Oval Office. A photograph of an F-16 fighter en route to Washington, DC, also served to convey the image of a president in control.[33] In his wide-ranging chronicle of the stories behind many of the most well-known September 11th photographs, David Friend suggests that the Air Force One picture was deliberately distributed by the administration to counteract the effect of the earlier photographs and footage of the president at the Florida school where he first learned of the attacks, in which he appears confused, passive and awkward.[34] Ari Fleischer, Bush's then press secretary, explains the effects of the later image:

> On September 11 and the immediate aftermath, the nation did see – whether it was live on TV for extended periods of time or in the snapshot of a photo – a very determined, strong president. That picture caught it. That's one of the reasons that picture resounded so well with the public.[35]

As well as boosting the president's public image, another function of this photograph (also served by the pictures of fighter planes) was to associate the September 11th attacks immediately with war. Bush's declarations to this effect were repeated in many headlines, and the connection extended in some reports to

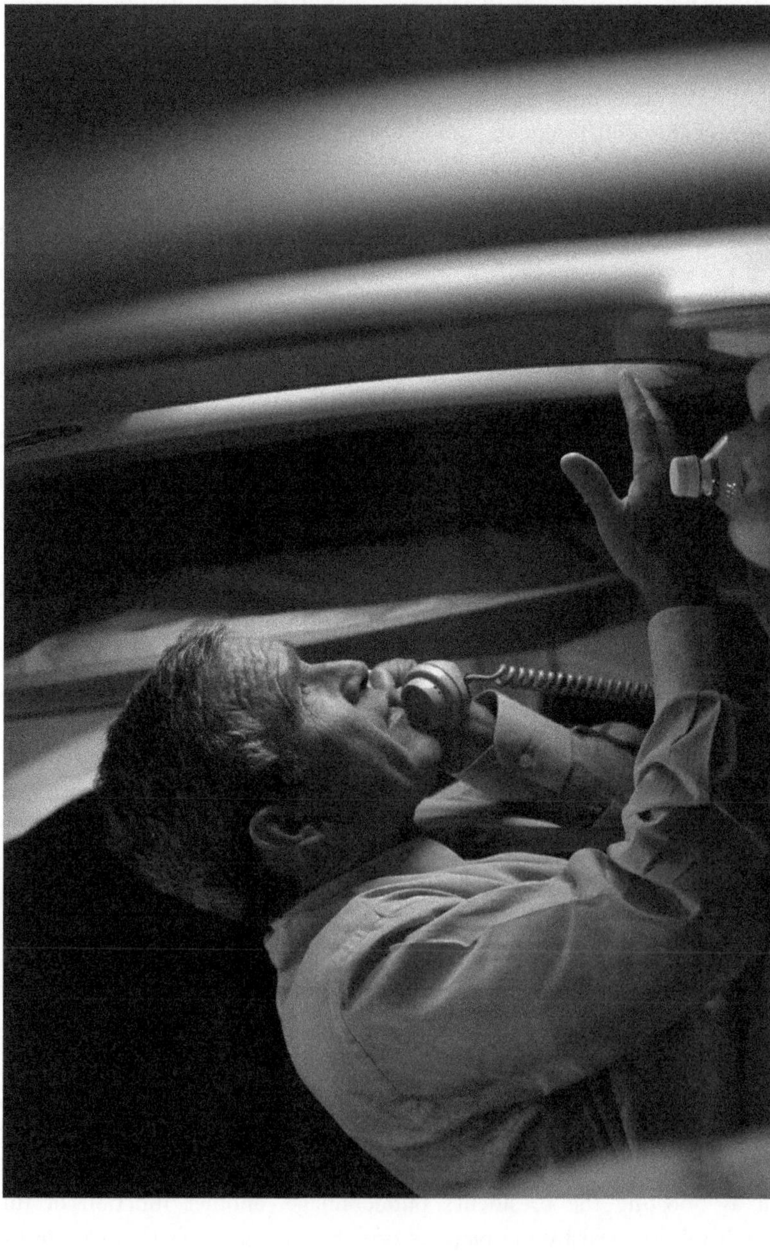

Figure 1.4 U.S. President George W. Bush speaks to Vice President Dick Cheney by phone aboard Air Force One on 11 September 2001 after departing from Offutt Air Force Base in Nebraska. Photo by Eric Draper, The White House/Getty Images.

include the inference that rescue workers at Ground Zero were fulfilling a kind of military duty. At least one article described the firefighters as serving on a 'front line' and went on to say that, on the occasion of Bush's visit captured by Eric Draper in Figure 1.3, they were 'happy to see the Commander in Chief'.[36] The framing of the attacks as an act of war, however, and of the president as a resolute commander preparing to retaliate, was complicated by a simultaneous imperative to convey the opposite image, of emotional sensitivity. This paradox was illustrated by a pair of photographs printed in the *New York Times* on 12 September. One showed a large close-up of Bush in front of the US flag, hands clasped, his expression concerned and reflective, appearing to respond to the situation primarily on the level of its emotional impact. Directly beside this was a smaller photograph of Donald Rumsfeld speaking at the Pentagon. His fist is clenched and raised in a direct, aggressive attitude that contrasts sharply with that of Bush, and the appearance of these images side by side seems to represent a careful balancing act, the two leaders adopting opposite roles that could never have been enacted simultaneously by just one figure.[37]

The open emotion of Bush's demeanour in the days following the attacks was also captured in a famous photograph taken at the Oval Office immediately after his announcement on the telephone to Rudy Giuliani and George Pataki that he had decided to go to New York and visit Ground Zero for himself. The picture, taken by Kevin Lamarque, is a very tightly cropped close-up of the president's face, his mouth strained and eyes glistening with tears. Fleischer, again, expresses satisfaction at this photo opportunity well taken: 'he started to cry at the end of the call. In the classic way that Bush men do, he started to tear up. And there are some wonderful photographs that captured that tear. The press was in the Oval Office for it.'[38] Not everyone saw it as wonderful though. When the picture appeared on the front page of the British *Times*, its caption emphasized further the inner conflict that is visible in the president's face: 'tears well in the eyes of President Bush as he speaks of families and victims during an Oval Office press conference. He said: "I'm a loving guy, and I'm also someone, however, who has a job to do and I intend to do it."'[39] *Los Angeles Times* television critic Howard Rosenberg compared Bush's screen presence during his much-criticized first televised speech to the nation with that of previous presidents Reagan and Clinton: 'throughout this terrible week in US history, Bush has lacked size in front of the camera when he should have been commanding and filling the screen.' Rosenberg picked up in particular on the president's body language ('slinking guiltily'), noting that he appeared like 'a little boy'; genuinely moved, but not strong. 'These are times when America needs a president they can look up to', he concluded, 'not just one who will share in their mourning.'[40] In the *Chicago Tribune*, another reporter described the national White House address as 'thuddingly rote' and complained, 'he had the sentiments right, but this president seems unable to rub sticks together to light a rhetorical fire'.[41] In moments like these, George W. Bush did not make his press officers' job any easier. But nonetheless, the *New York Times* recorded a significant increase in support for the president during this period. 'Few challenged the national leadership at the time', it reported, 'and one late-night television talk show host who questioned the notion that the airplane hijackers were "cowards" was shunned by sponsors, and rebuked by the White House spokesman.'[42]

While images of the president and other political leaders served to enact the simple narrative themes of war and of goodness in the face of evil, pictures of ordinary citizens present at the scene of the attacks upheld and developed these. The principal figure in this process, depicted in countless photographs and in the texts around them, was the hero. Most strongly associated with firefighters, this title was also extended to rescue workers and other uniformed men, but it continued to proliferate as a rhetorical device that eventually came to encompass victims and survivors. Within the mainstream photographic record, images denoting rescue, help and kindness dominated. Crying or injured people were rarely shown alone, and signs of panic were typically counterbalanced by some positive gesture such as an embrace or an act of practical assistance.[43] Particularly prevalent were photographs of uniformed men coming to the aid of civilian women (Figure 1.5), and strong, physically able people bodily propping up those weakened by shock or injury. It is unsurprising that there should have been so many photographs of this kind: many remarkable rescues and small acts of kindness took place that day in view of the many hundreds of cameras present, and a large number of people could no doubt rightly be commended for extraordinary courage and selflessness. But, the extensive use of the word 'hero', the proliferation of photographs like Jennifer Altman's and the almost total absence of any image of untempered distress or untended suffering created in the media an impression of ubiquitous, self-evident, almost transcendental heroism.[44] In his introduction to *LIFE* magazine's anthology of their coverage of the event, former New York City mayor Rudy Giuliani takes the final rhetorical step of ascribing it to all of the victims:

> Even more devastating is the loss of thousands of individuals who were killed in the attack. All were innocent. All were heroes. Those who went to work in the World Trade Center on September 11 were engaged in the quiet heroism of supporting their families, pursuing their dreams, and playing their own meaningful part in a diverse, dynamic and free society.[45]

Among those prepared to question this widespread heroizing was Jürgen Habermas. 'Perhaps the word has different connotations in American English than it does in German', he mused a few weeks after the attacks. 'It seems to me that whenever "heroes" are honoured the question arises as to who needs them and why. Even in this looser sense of the term one can understand Bertolt Brecht's warning: "Pity the land that needs heroes."'[46] Habermas suggests that

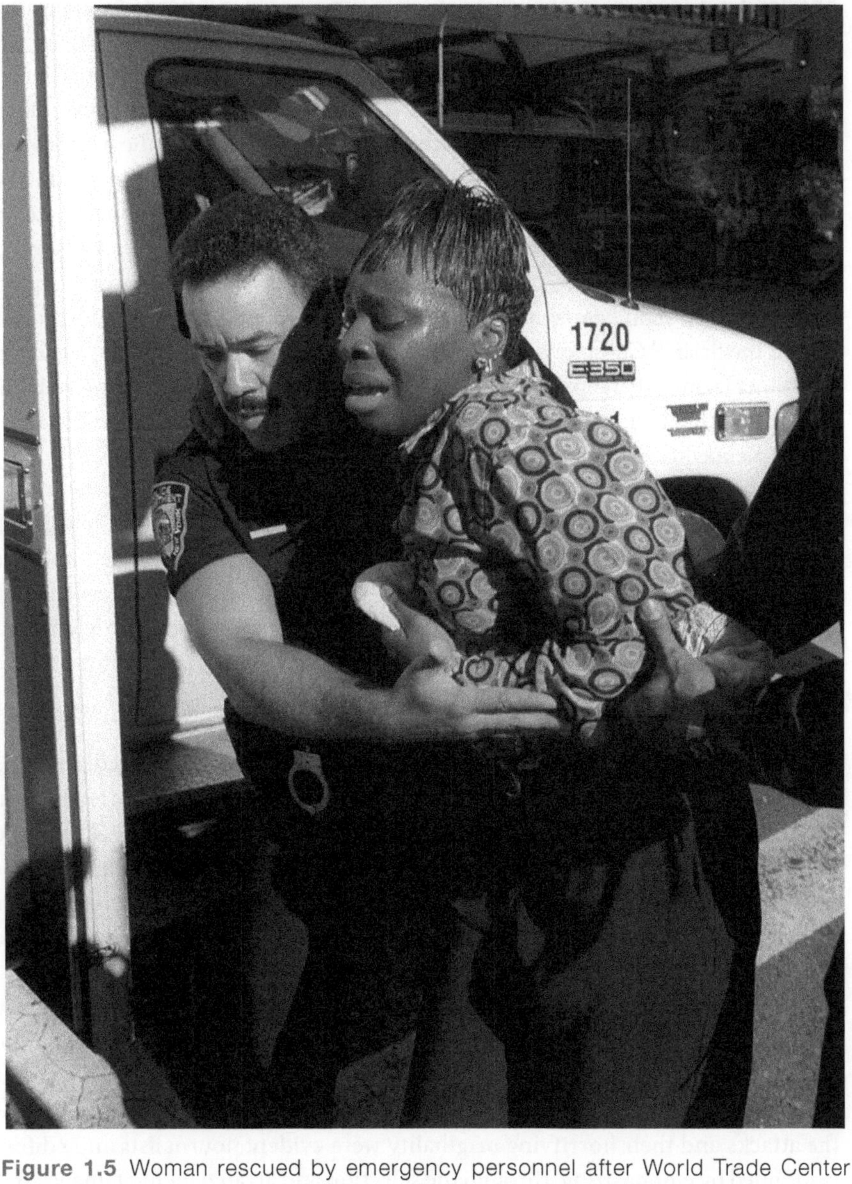

Figure 1.5 Woman rescued by emergency personnel after World Trade Center terrorist attack. Photo by Jennifer S. Altman, WireImage/Getty Images.

when the term is used, as it is by Giuliani, to refer to the normal pursuits of work and family life, it is not because such acts are actually heroic, but because the need to delineate the binary of good and evil, of villain and hero, is so great. The 'land needed heroes' at such a senseless time, because it needed a story that made sense.

In some cases, this impulse became explicitly attached to particular photographs, like that of firefighter Mike Kehoe. The famous photograph, taken by John Labriola, of Kehoe looking fleetingly into the camera as he ascends the stairwell of the North Tower while most of its occupants are escaping in the other direction cast him not only as a hero, but a celebrity. 'Everyone wanted a piece of him', wrote Jodie Morse of *TIME* magazine. 'There were 40 messages a day from reporters... One particularly aggressive fan... wrote almost daily on stationary with pink hearts and drove all the way to New York City... just to see him in the flesh.'[47] Going on to receive a 'Pride of Britain' award and appearing in *TIME* magazine's 'Person of the Year' issue, Kehoe was reportedly bemused and distressed at being honoured in this way when so many of his colleagues had been killed. 'Kehoe had not perished', writes David Friend,

> nor had he saved a single life on September 11. But this slight-of-build son and brother of a fire fighter seemed to personify his profession. Unlike hundreds of firemen who were not caught on film that morning... Kehoe was the one who had walked into the lens as if he were minutes from staring death itself in the face. As such, Kehoe became an inadvertent icon, The Fireman in the Stairwell.[48]

The almost hysterical reaction of admirers, politicians and the media to this 'inadvertent' symbol illustrates the need, pointed out by Habermas, for heroes, their stories, their images and ideally their happy endings. It also illustrates the unpredictable power of the camera to shape people's destinies. Kehoe, by his own admission, was cast as the hero not because he did anything remarkable, or even because he survived, but because he happened to be the one caught by the camera.

The distinct but interrelated tropes of good and evil, hero and villain, military honour and leaders who could both empathize and avenge were slotted by the media into pre-existing narrative templates that readers could easily grasp because they were reassuringly familiar. While the unprecedented nature of the attacks and their horrifying originality were evident, journalists and editors responded by emphasizing, through the selection and arrangement of images and the choice of words, how they could be related to reference points from history – like the attack on Pearl Harbor – or to the fictional plotlines of action movies.[49] This formula, in which events are presented as conforming to what viewers and readers apparently already know, thus confirming their existing matrix of beliefs about the world, often follows catastrophic news events. In John Taylor's words, it necessarily 'arise[s] from the sudden collapse of generally reliable systems', when the known has been undermined.[50] The first question asked in the aftermath of such an event is 'why?', and so, attempts are made early on to impose meaning upon the senselessness. In this case, the restoration of order was enacted in various ways, from the reassuring rhetoric of justice triumphing over evil, to a highlighting of the ways in which particular photographs revealed formal and ideological echoes of images from the past (most famously Thomas Franklin's picture of firefighters raising the flag at Ground Zero with Joe Rosenthal's World War Two Iwo Jima icon). Another means of reconstructing 'reliable systems' was in the use of computer-generated schematic diagrams, or info-graphics. Every major American newspaper featured at least one image of this kind within the first week or so: a clean-lined, sanitized graphic account of the towers' structural damage and collapse, often incorporating a timeline of some kind and giving the impression of a sequence of events that is ordered and clearly apprehensible, with a beginning, a middle and an end.[51]

Having been established, these codes of visual and verbal rhetoric were repeated again and again. Such repetition in the news media of footage and photographs of disasters after their immediate occurrence is not usual. Rather than moving on from 'yesterday's news', papers and magazines were dominated by spectacular photographs of the towers' destruction for weeks, just as the television news sequences had shown the same footage (most commonly the impact of the second plane), on a loop for days. In the next chapter, I will explore the possibility that this repetition caused harm, but Daniel Sherman and Terry Nardin have suggested that it was also implicated in the projection of safety and the restoration of order. The repetition of these images, they argue, reinstated the kind of 'safe spectatorship' that typically characterizes Americans' viewing position in relation to images of atrocity.[52] In short, the images are repeated so many times that they become familiar and are simultaneously consigned to a position of more comfortable distance. Similar to the effect of orderly, tidy and clear schematic diagrams, Sherman and Nardin seem to argue that the device of repetition was used deliberately to lull viewers into a reassuring but false sense of knowledge and control.

As I will later argue, this is questionable. A much clearer consequence of the images' repetition was simply to compound the image overload that broadly characterized the attacks' aftermath. In a formula that corresponds to the culture industry model set out and condemned by Adorno, this overload was not only spectacular, but simplistically homogenized, and it not only suppressed critical reflection and debate, particularly regarding the war in Iraq, but also perpetuated desire for further manipulation by further dazzling, homogenized means. Like (or as) the products of the culture industry, this image spectacle 'impede[d] the development of autonomous, independent individuals who judge and decide consciously for themselves'.[53] In 'The Fetish Character in Music and the Regression of Listening', Adorno uses the example of popular music to explain the process of 'regression' imposed upon audiences by the culture industry. Subjects are, he says, 'arrested at the infantile stage' by the homogenization, standardization and fetishization of music. This is not just a dismissive insult to listeners of popular music (whom Adorno believes to be idiots, albeit blameless ones), but rather a judgement of the system in which such listeners are hopelessly caught: 'their primitivism is not that of the undeveloped', he says, 'but that of the forcibly retarded'.[54] There was, I would argue, a similar kind of manipulative 'infantilization' at work on the part of the visual culture industry, and specifically the news media, in the aftermath of September 11th. It is difficult to deny that the spectacular image bombardment that followed the event was shaped to appeal to viewers' emotions rather than to critical thinking. The message conveyed was – rightly, up to a point – one of commemoration, focussing on loss and appealing in various ways to abstracted ideals such as the American spirit. Like Adorno's 'regressive listening', enforced 'regressive seeing' or naïveté in this respect was also facilitated by the promotion of fear, and when these respective messages had been established and driven home through persistent repetition, it was merely the next logical step to present revenge as a foregone conclusion.[55]

In *Afflicted Powers*, their study of the political forces at work in post–September 11th America, four members of the San Francisco-based Retort collective (Iain Boal, T.J. Clark, Joseph Matthews and Michael Watts) use the ideas of Guy Debord and the Situationists concerning 'the colonization of everyday life', and 'the society of the spectacle' to account for the problems that they see around them, summed up as social control and disintegration. They also argue that the matter of 'mastery in the realm of the image' has not been taken seriously enough in considering the political fallout of September 11th.[56] Guy Debord intended his notion of spectacle to be considered as a new form of, or stage in, the accumulation of capital. For him, this meant the reduction of more and more aspects of human life to the level of the market, and while this was initially understood not to be dependent upon any one mode of representation, it soon became associated above all with the dissemination of images and appearances. The 'colonization of everyday life', meanwhile, suggested the exertion of control over the realm of individual privacy by the dominant culture industry. The goal of Debord's analysis was to try to formulate resistance against these colonizing powers – a goal that somehow seemed possible in the 1960s. Debord was himself primarily concerned with the bearing that this rule of appearances had on politics, specifically state formation and surveillance. In their book, the Retort group revisits Debord's spectacle, stressing that it does not only, as it has come to be misread, refer to disembodied representations, but specifically to the 'exertion of social power'.[57] To quote Debord himself, writing in 1967:

> The spectacle is not a collection of images; rather, it is a social relationship between people that is mediated by images. The spectacle cannot be understood either as a deliberate distortion of the visual world or as a product of the technology of the mass dissemination of images. It is far better viewed as a *weltanschauung* that has been actualised, translated into the material realm – a world view transformed into an objective force.[58]

Retort conclude from this that America is a 'spectacular state' – one in which capital, as Debord forewarned, has accumulated so vastly that it has itself become an image.[59] This is the premise that explains the true implications of the September 11th attacks: the stakes of the 'image-war', America's actions and reactions in its wake and the bankruptcy of its rationale for actual war:

> [We are experiencing in the United States] a monstrous political deployment of (and entrapment in) the apparatus of a modern, not to say hyper-modern, production of appearances. Interests and imagery collide... Mistakes or overreach in the management of the image-world have immediate political consequences... and outright defeat in the war of images is something no present-day hegemon can tolerate.[60]

The state's deeper and deeper involvement in this internal culture industry means that it has come to 'live or die by its investment in, and control of, the field of images', now more than ever before.[61] If America is fundamentally a spectacular state, then its response – not only in terms of its subsequent foreign policy (which Retort has scrutinized), but first, and even more fundamentally, in the September 11th attacks' representation by its visual culture industry – can also be called a dazzling mobilization of the spectacular: a world view transformed into an objective force. The overvisibility of certain controlled imagery combined with the invisibility of other views served to deflect public attention onto the sentimental, the redemptive, the aesthetic, the dramatic and the sublime, with the overall effect of disarming genuine political engagement.[62] This is a bold claim to make, but it has its historical precedents; one of which is the American press coverage of the 1991 Gulf War. Elaine Scarry has identified this episode as a case of the deliberate critical disempowerment of the American people by means of the news media. In the process leading up to this conflict, neither of the constitutional requirements for war – a formal declaration of war and the consultation of the population – was met.[63] Because the president effectively acted alone, the people's authority, and therefore their responsibility to other populations, was forfeited, and civic power lost. Scarry details this sequence of events, explaining that it was made possible specifically by inviting the population to perform what she calls a 'mimesis of deliberation', meaning effectively that they were distracted. News audiences were encouraged, for example, to engage in debates about sideline issues of much lesser importance including the personal affairs of political figures involved in directing the war and the focus tending towards more immediate, trivial or 'exciting' news content.[64] It was unsurprising, Scarry says, that what followed was 'a general inattention to political events', whereby Americans became 'inattentive to the grave subjects that are our actual responsibility to oversee'.[65] 'Inattention' in this instance seemed to mean not a disregard for or disinterest in the military action itself, but in the difficult political questions regarding its justification, efficacy and consequences. By a process of paternalistic distraction, the Gulf War could continue to be ongoing front-page news, seemingly without these issues being addressed at all. Directly recalling Adorno's terms, 'the population', Scarry says, was 'infantilised and marginalized'.

One of the best the diversionary news stories of the Gulf War period was the imagery of the war itself. Dazzling, mesmerizing and most importantly, entertaining, the extraordinarily hi-tech video-game-like spectacle presented on the nightly news ensured that Americans watched in 'fascinated immobility', but actual loss of life was not part of the story. Debord warned that when this kind of diversionary spectacle becomes the news, populations lose both sight and ownership of political responsibility because 'all that was once directly lived has become mere representation'.[66] Seeming to offer a warning to post–September 11th America six years in advance, Scarry concludes: 'when the government commits itself to theatrical spectacle, the possibility of opposition disappears and dissent becomes impossible.'[67] The suspension of critical engagement with issues of foreign policy, domestic human rights and war in early twenty-first-century America was not a product of deflection or distraction towards more trivial issues (this would have been impossible), but of the overplaying, through photographs, of the in-built spectacle of the September 11th attack itself. The deflection of emphasis was towards an exclusively visual and emotional understanding of the event. 'The problem', in the words of Susan Sontag, 'is not that people remember through photographs, but that they remember only the photographs', and this inevitably 'eclipses other forms of understanding, and remembering.'[68]

The same *New York Times* article that noted a sharp increase in support for the president in the aftermath of September 11th went on to report that, on October 25th 2001, the House of Representatives and the Senate voted overwhelmingly to grant the government sweeping new powers to 'root out terrorism' with a bill that allowed immigrants to be held without charge and citizens' privacy breached in unprecedented ways.[69] The terrorists' actions had enabled George W. Bush to unite the United States behind him, quieting questions about the legitimacy of his presidency, and to reinforce a political and military sensibility that claimed a moral obligation to police the world. Instead of reflection in the face of America's vulnerability, the administration sought to turn all thoughts to revenge. Distress was channelled in support of political and military interests, and a path was cleared for war. Putting it even more forcefully, the Retort group concludes that 'unanswerable lies have succeeded in eliminating public opinion'.[70] Again, they cite Debord:

> once one controls the mechanism which operates the only form of social verification to be universally recognised, one can say what one likes... Spectacular power can similarly deny whatever it wishes to, once, or three times over, and change the subject: knowing full well there is no danger of riposte, in its own space or any other.[71]

Research into public opinion carried out during the Gulf War gives a clue as to why no riposte emerged to the denials or distractions surrounding that conflict. It seems that, presumably because the reality was so unpleasant or unsettling, many Americans were content to be mesmerized by the mysterious pictures.[72] 'Most people did not want to reason about the war'; John Taylor writes, 'they wanted to be numbed, and have responsibility taken from them. Giving up on reason and embracing generalised national hopes and desires is central to patriotism; it helps war leaders to stir up enthusiasm in the population and disguises or dismisses the dangers.'[73] The post–September 11th spectacle provided the US government with both a public distraction from the impending loss of life in Iraq, if not that which had already taken place at Ground Zero, and a cue for a huge, nationwide surge in patriotism. Michelle Fine wrote at that time of 'the long reach of ideology bleeding into conscious and unconscious thought and talk. You can't be in New York, New Jersey, the United States without hearing personal testimonies wrapped in thickly accepted nationalist discourse'.[74] Implicit in this discourse was, it seems, a tacit un-questioning, just as the *New York Times* had reported the judgement faced by those who dared to question the choices of the president or the reasoning behind the attacks themselves. But, such questions, in public discourse at least, were not raised often, because they had already been so effectively choked by the deluge of simplifying photographs and rhetoric. Among the most seriously oversimplified concepts, as Jacques Derrida has pointed out, was terrorism itself. 'Politically speaking', he noted in the very earliest days following the attacks, 'the more slippery a concept, the easier it is to appropriate it opportunistically... the most powerful and destructive appropriation of terrorism is precisely its use as a self-evident concept by all the parties involved.'[75]

Perhaps the most direct and forceful intervention in the public's interpretation of the September 11th attacks by the US government was *After September 11: Images from Ground Zero*; a touring exhibition of photographs presented by the US Department of State and Bureau of Educational and Cultural Affairs, launched in February 2004. Twenty-two sets of prints by photographer Joel Meyerowitz toured 135 venues in sixty-four countries, including the Afghanistan National Art Gallery in Kabul. The photographs were selected by the Department of

State to show 'the true human and physical dimensions' of the attacks' aftermath.[76] Meyerowitz's work is the only existing photographic record of the Ground Zero clean-up site. Almost immediately after the collapse of the towers, the area was fenced off, classified as a crime scene and closed to all photographers, until, with sponsorship from the Museum of the State of New York, Meyerowitz succeeded in gaining access on 13 September. Already an award-winning photographer with a record of solo exhibitions at the Museum of Modern Art, the Art Institute of Chicago, the San Francisco Museum of Modern Art, the Boston Museum of Fine Art and others outside the United States, Meyerowitz has been most celebrated as a photographer of street life and landscapes, and for his early pioneering use of colour in both genres. History will likely show, however, that the Ground Zero archive is the work for which he will be most remembered by the American public.

He introduces *Aftermath*, the publication that followed this project, by saying, 'I saw what I needed to do. To me, no photographs meant no history. I decided at that moment that I would find my way in and make an archive for the City of New York.'[77] Clearly understanding his task in terms of national record and commemoration, Meyerowitz describes himself as being influenced by the state-commissioned documentary photographers of the Farm Security Administration in the 1920s, which was both nationally significant and 'socially useful'.[78] True to this intention, his huge archive of Ground Zero images is now a freely accessible digital resource held at the Museum of the City of New York. In a second historical comparison, he also likens himself to Mathew Brady, another celebrated photographer of his day who, with the express blessing of the Lincoln administration, famously gained access to photograph the Union encampments and battlefields of the American Civil War. This comparison is, for Meyerowitz, seemingly based upon a notion of the photographer's responsibility to record catastrophic national events and to both shape and safeguard 'public memory'.[79]

In 1985, Alan Trachtenberg called the American Civil War 'the first significant crisis in modern history to occur within the memorializing gaze of a camera', writing that it represented, specifically in Brady's work, the first case of widely accepted 'historicism-by-photography, [the] notion that historical knowledge declares its true value by its photographability'.[80] This he also defines as the 'historicizing ideology' of photography. It could be said, borrowing Trachtenberg's words, that the September 11th attacks were the first significant crisis in modern history to occur *for* the memorializing gaze of the camera, and that its inherent and intentional photographability gave it more power than would otherwise have been imaginable. Along with many others who photographed the event and its aftermath, Meyerowitz expresses a belief in the 'historicizing-by-photography' that Trachtenberg attributes to photographers and audiences of the nineteenth century, showing that this acceptance of photography's role in the shaping of public memory has almost as long a history as photography itself. His efforts to win access and his subsequent toiling for nine months to create an archive that he saw as his national duty fit Meyerowitz, like Brady before him, into what might be called an American tradition of the national hero photographer. Journalism has long required the creation of star witnesses: brave, skilled and privileged in their access to conflict and catastrophe, whether promoted by the patronage of figures in authority, or (even better) working alone as unilateral renegades in pursuit of the truth. With comparable status to those engaged in combat or rescue operations, but on a uniquely reified level, these photographers are immersed in the action, and yet transcend it. As specialized witnesses, they are endowed not only with bravery but with the prestigious autonomy of the artist. *LIFE* magazine's commemorative book, titled *One Nation: America Remembers September 11, 2001*, compiling highlights of its own coverage of the period following September 11th, features a ten-page section devoted to James Nachtwey, one such celebrated figure. Nachtwey is well known as a war photographer, and the *LIFE* profile shows how this almost mythic prestige was transferred onto the task of photographing the 2001 attacks:

> You might say that he travels the globe as a professional photographer – perhaps the world's preeminent chronicler of war – but Nachtwey feels he goes as a witness... So he's never home, but he is always in the right place at the right time to record eerily beautiful images of violence and injustice... Nachtwey is regularly moved by what he sees, but while he lets emotion dictate which scene might be effective – which picture is most worth taking – he never lets it disrupt the task in hand. He worked through the day until it was dark, at times dodging debris, constantly piecing together the story.[81]

Again, the photographer is a warrior in a war zone. And again, this star status seems to come with a view, not least in the photographer's own mind, of his work as having real national significance for posterity. Confirming Trachtenberg's remarks about the accepted historicizing value of photography, Nachtwey reminisces that 'I started to think the pictures would serve to document a crucial historical watershed'.[82]

In times of particular crisis, it seems that the association of photography with courageous action does not apply only to privileged 'hero photographers', it was also a startlingly automatic one for ordinary members of the public caught up in the attack on the World Trade Center. In numerous eyewitness accounts, running to the scene with a camera was described in the same terms as running there with a first-aid kit or a shovel. One contributor to the *September 11 Photo*

Project, an exhibition of vernacular photographic memorials staged in Manhattan shortly after the attacks, recalls his immediate reaction to news: 'rather than watch from the safety of my window, I grabbed my camera and headed to the street.'[83] Another writes, 'I am a nurse and I knew I had to go there. I rollerbladed four miles downtown to the WTC with my medical kit and camera.'[84] Meyerowitz himself, whose photographic project carried the same sense of urgency as these amateur photographers but with the added weight of his official sanction and his pre-existing creative eminence, says of his project:

> It is a privilege to work at Ground Zero. Everyone who works there has been transformed by the spirituality of the place. The camaraderie among the workers in the zone reminds me of the stories we've heard about the World Wars, where men and women are thrown together by a common cause, share tragedies and victories, and are forever bound to one another by their effort.[85]

Again, taking pictures is equated naturally with helping in the rescue effort. A publicity portrait taken by Timothy Greenfield-Sanders shows Meyerowitz in the midst of 'the zone', looking intently at the viewer, holding his huge mahogany box camera and folded tripod casually over his shoulder in the same manner as a clean-up worker might sling his shovel on a break from digging (or a soldier his rifle). Heroism, and specifically the comparison with warfare, became a standard way of valorizing not just the military action that followed the attacks, but the very work of cleaning up the rubble. Here, the photographer claims this same mantle of military heroism for himself, elevating it even further by virtue of his artistic gift, his sophisticated photographic paraphernalia and his patriotic rhetoric.

An obvious difference between Mathew Brady's record and Meyerowitz's is that, unlike *Aftermath*, in Brady's photographs (most of which were actually taken by a team of lesser-known photographers under Brady's direction, including Timothy H. O'Sullivan) we are confronted with visible human remains, most famously in an image of the fallen at Gettysburg which came to be titled, 'A Harvest of Death' (Figure 1.6). Despite claims in the exhibition's companion publication that Meyerowitz's collection of photographs illustrates the event's human dimensions, the only direct acknowledgement of the loss of life is a single picture captioned, 'Bringing Out the Dead': a floodlit nocturnal scene in which a group of workers carry some recovered remains, the only visible sign of which is a corner of the flag in which they are draped. The rest is darkness. Almost every photograph is centred around firefighters, rescue workers and the ethereal ruins of the destroyed twin towers. Whereas in Meyerowitz's photographs there is only architectural destruction to signify loss of life, Brady shows the aftermath of battle in open fields where there was no falling rubble to obscure the dead. On seeing these photographs in 1863, Oliver Wendell Holmes wrote of an impulse to 'bury them in the recesses

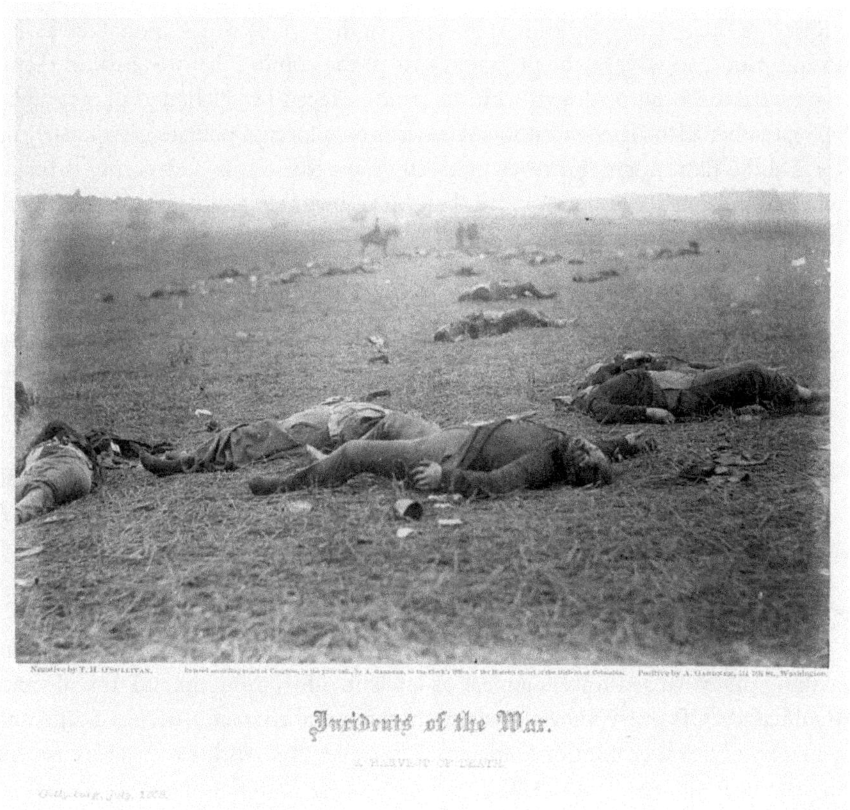

Figure 1.6 'Incidents of the War. A Harvest of Death', Gettysburg, July 1863. Photo by Timothy H. O'Sullivan. Library of Congress, Prints & Photographs Division, Civil War Photographs [LC-B8184-7964-A].

of our cabinet as we would have buried the mutilated remains of the dead they too visibly represented'.[86] Burying is an important concept here. In his *Camera Lucida*, Roland Barthes examines the modern Western tendency to bury death and quickly hide it from consciousness by hiding it from view.[87] Perhaps if the bodies of September 11th victims had been made visible to the public, the response would have been similarly to 'bury' and banish them instead of holding the photographic record in such prominence. Seemingly much less squeamish than modern audiences, viewers flocked to see Brady's pictures of human destruction and paid money for them. However grim, the corpses in these photographs remained easier to confront than slavery, the primary cause of the conflict that was behind them. Again, parallels can be drawn with the truths effaced by celebrated photographs of September 11th. The notion that America's own foreign policies, particularly in the Middle East, might, however indirectly, have led to this destruction is much more complicated and unattractive than Meyerowitz's magnificent account. One reviewer of *Aftermath* writes:

> Meyerowitz doesn't resort to the heart wrenching, the lachrymose, the obvious, the stuff of Eyewitness News ... Both the pictures and the text are understated, avoiding too the mawkish sentimentality that has come to define our collective public recollection of the fall and its physical and emotional aftermath ... Thankfully, Meyerowitz's purpose bears none of the shameless opportunism of politicians, the tabloids and local TV news. None of what novelist Philip Roth controversially called the 'kitschification of 3,000 peoples' deaths.' You'll find no hero worship in *Aftermath*, though there are plenty of heroes present.[88]

As an accomplished landscape photographer, Meyerowitz succeeds in making the collapsed towers appear as ancient ruins, monumental in scale and significance. Of course, they also claim monumental characteristics in a different sense: the book's promotional material describes the work as 'an elegy to the thousands who lost their lives'.[89] These are photographic monuments as well as monumental photographs. And as well as the epic depiction of space, Meyerowitz's characteristic landscape style also has a bearing on the images' capturing of time, which is well suited to their ideological inference. In a deeply critical indictment of the work, which he has no qualms about calling propaganda, Liam Kennedy has argued that the 'gravitas' of these images is achieved in part because Meyerowitz captures 'extended moments rather than decisive moments', which invites empathetic contemplation as the only response.[90] This is not the frozen snapshot style that by necessity characterizes so many other photographs of the 'action' of September 11th, but a controlled, stable depiction of the sustained passage of time in a single frame. There is no chaos here, no elusive meaning. Meaning appears stable, steady and easily grasped.

Though framed as the only documentary record of the clean-up operation, the photographs have less in common with the American documentary tradition than they do with history painting, and specifically in several cases, scenes of the sublime drama of the sea. One image, 'Welders in South Tower' is a wide-angle nocturnal scene showing a small group of metalworkers amongst the very last standing remnants of the building. Rising above the horizon of the pit's boundary the surrounding buildings are cast in deep black-blues and greens, against which the welders' fire is tiny but brilliant. In many of his pictures, the photographer makes atmospheric use of rising smoke, steam or spray from fire-hoses. In this image, steam or smoke – it could be either – catches the light and picks out architectural details, both highlighting and obscuring, like a watercolour wash, or sea-spray. It creates a plane of its own amongst the other receding layers in the image, all of which are in perfect focus and redolent with textural detail. The human figures are somewhere in the middle distance, both dwarfed and anchored by the hot halo of their work, which seems to keep them from drowning in the expanse of twisted rubble that encroaches on them in dark waves. This picture above all evokes the shipwrecks, storms and naval battles of J.M.W. Turner, in which man struggles in noble contention with the sublime power of the elements.[91] It makes sense that these photographs should find their historical reference point not in the fleeting here-and-now of documentary photography but the paintings of Turner and the Romantics: an art of transcendence, mythic hubris and eternal truths. Meyerowitz says that his goal 'was not to make "pretty" pictures of the destruction but to record – with meticulous archival precision – what happened … it was not about making Art,' though he does admit that many of the images 'revealed an accidental beauty'.[92] Some have dared to describe the act of terrorism at the World Trade Center as 'the greatest work of art that is possible in the whole cosmos' (Karlheinz Stockhausen), and the perpetrators as 'brilliant' (Norman Mailer) and 'death artists' (Jonathan Franzen).[93] After the spectacle of the attack had passed, the site was not beautiful. It was a mass graveyard. Many images of the area, made by professional photographers like Gilles Peress and Susan Meiselas, as well as the majesterial ruins of Joel Meyerowitz, are formally beautiful, though it has seemed sacrilegious to say so (and so they are called surreal). The photographic artistry that can transform the horrific and the unseeable in these scenes is part of the commercial appeal of commemorative publications like *Aftermath* and *LIFE*'s *One Nation* book.

The *After September 11* exhibition was presented as a kind of corrective, intended to reveal to audiences around the world the unmediated reality of what Americans had been through, and the accompanying catalogue publication seemed designed to instruct audiences in how to react. Alongside reproductions of Meyerowitz's photographs, the catalogue features many images of people, including some who had participated in the clean-up, looking at the exhibition at its various locations, contemplating the pictures alone or in groups. In the same vein as photographs of politicians surveying the scene itself, this seems to be a paternalistic lesson in how to look. Though not strictly what Adorno had in mind, here is the culture industry's infantilizing agenda: a symbolic intervention in the processes of witnessing and understanding. But, the overriding problem with this exhibition was much more urgent than the question of how much visual trauma viewers could tolerate, or exactly what they saw. At its launch event, the secretary of state made a speech that betrayed a startling leap from the grief invoked by these photographs, to military retaliation:

> September eleventh was a very personal experience for each of us. Each of us remembers where we were when we first learned of the attacks. Each of us remembers our initial chilling impressions and our response. These images remind me that our country, our people and our families are very precious and that we must do all we can to protect them from the scourge of terrorism ... It gave us a sense of purpose and vision as a people, showed the world what Americans were made of, and *gave us the opportunity* to lead a worldwide coalition to go after not only the perpetrators of these attacks, but to go after terrorists around the world.[94] (italics added)

In his address at the National Cathedral on 15 September 2001, President Bush made a similar link, telling the congregation, 'our unity is a kinship of grief, and a steadfast resolve to prevail against our enemies. And this unity against terror is now extending across the world'.[95] Again, the causal association between grief and militarism was taken to be a foregone conclusion. Like the photographs, it spoke for itself. The text of the president's National Cathedral address was reproduced in the *After September 11* exhibition catalogue, further cementing the connection between these pictures and war. Identifying Meyerowitz's work as the archetype of what he calls 'late photography', David Campany has argued that such images, as well as being ideal vehicles for mass mourning, can foster 'political withdrawal' precisely because of their profound stillness and silence. The dangerous truism that such imagery speaks for itself can, he says, 'easily flatter the ideological paralysis of those who gaze at it with a lack of social or political will to make sense of its circumstance'.[96] Meyerowitz's photographs were part of a state apparatus that capitalized on this ideological paralysis, and that had the power not only to cement whatever meanings it chose to invest in them, but to underwrite the authority of these meanings and promote them around the world.

The American media's presentation of September 11th can at best be called incomplete in its abundance. While a good deal of writing, discussion and debate did take place in the aftermath of this event, its overwhelming presentation was visual, and specifically photographic, amounting to a spectacle of such force that it paralysed critical dissent. In Adornian terms, this enforced regressive seeing was paradoxically entrenched by the autonomy of the press and the impression of total, unimpeded visibility. Public engagement was swept aside by 'public memory', and the dazzled, grieving American people forfeited the ability to see, beyond their own borders and the present moment, the deaths to come. As well as in the loss of human life and the material destruction, this attack was a spectacular blow to America within the symbolic economy of spectacle on which the state itself is based. America's leaders knew better than anyone that such an act of image-engineering was itself a piece of statecraft and a devastating political blow. As the Retort group argues, when an image-based state is defeated in the image-world as America was, it is obliged to come up with an answer. And so, the US media struggled, using all the redemptive narratives, emotive plotlines and visual cues at its disposal to try to manage the fallout of its symbolic defeat. Years later, the state is still 'flailing blindly in the face of an image it cannot exorcize, and trying desperately to convert the defeat back into terms it can respond to'.[97] The primary location for this attempted symbolic riposte has been Iraq. But, not only was that campaign a disaster in conventional military terms, it has also, despite the construction of triumphal photo opportunities (the fall of Saddam's statue and Bush's flight-deck victory declaration coming most obviously to mind, both of which were of course countered by the far greater impact of 'the Abu Ghraib photographs'), failed to produce a vision that could reassert America's status in the economy of images. Further, the endless repetition, within its own media machine, of the defeat itself has not only had the effect of undermining the psychological recovery of its population as I will go on to argue, but also of simply reiterating the crushing point again and again. In Retort's words, 'where, in the end, is the image the war machine has been looking for – the one to put paid to the September haunting? … The Towers keep falling.'[98]

2 FOREVER SEARED: THE TRAUMA OF PHOTOGRAPHIC SEEING

On 13 September 2001, the *San Francisco Chronicle* attempted to sum up the state of the American psyche:

> This week's frontal assault on America is a collective trauma unlike any other in any of our lifetimes… We need to acknowledge our trauma. We need to treat this emotional wound. We owe it to the victims, we owe it to ourselves as we look for the resiliency to reconstitute our everyday lives after a jolt of unprecedented madness. Retaliation must not be the extent of our attempt at catharsis.[1]

For most who watched this attack happen on television and, later, saw it in innumerable still photographs, there was no direct exposure to death, as not even the live television broadcasts had shown any human destruction other than indistinct victims falling from the towers at a distance. For them, the task was one of bearing witness to the fact that the event happened, and the second-hand knowledge that many people died. When journalists began discussing the psychological fallout resulting from the attacks, many wrote about it in terms of the shock of lost security, suggesting that in this, there was no lesser trauma for those watching from the other end of the country than for those in Lower Manhattan. Two excerpts, one from the *San Francisco Chronicle* and the other from the *Chicago Tribune*, illustrate how the trauma suffered by those present at the scene seemed diminished in comparison to this different, more widespread effect:

> Everything has changed. There was a more innocent time, little more than 48 hours ago, when this phrase was hyperbole… Our national psyche changed the instant terrorists crashed the first of four planes that killed thousands Tuesday,

deepening our sense of vulnerability and altering our relationship to the world in ways we don't fully understand.[2]

When the smoke cleared from the collapsed World Trade Center towers, everything had changed. It was as if someone had yanked a cord and the walls of America fell away. Suddenly, we understood the unimaginable truth: we are as naked and vulnerable as any country. Our security, with its military might and vast network of intelligence agents, is as illusory as a Hollywood set.[3]

The ubiquitous and mostly unquestioned use of the word 'trauma' in discussion of September 11th by the mainstream American news media is symptomatic of what has been called a 'post-traumatic turn' in psychoanalytic and sociological discourse since the late twentieth century.[4] This term describes the point at which psychotherapy came to supersede psychoanalysis as a cultural phenomenon of theoretical and even political interest, began, it is argued, around 1980, when post-traumatic stress disorder was first codified as a psychological disorder.[5] Following this moment, trauma studies became a recognized academic discipline, and trauma (along with psychotherapy) became a cultural discourse within the humanities where previously it had been the preserve of science. The background to the many news headlines describing September 11th as a traumatic event was the recent founding of academic programmes in trauma studies across America that helped to provide a language with which to talk about such catastrophic events in the press and elsewhere.[6] Trauma is now a matter of broad popular cultural concern. So much so, that some professionals within the field have criticized the casual public overuse of the term and declared that America has become 'overpsychologized'.[7] The condition of trauma, whether understood in terms of its rigorous professional definitions *or* its knee-jerk overuse, is a factor that greatly complicates the historicizing ideologies and political apparatuses surrounding September 11th.

In recent years, trauma theory has largely departed from the work of Sigmund Freud, but his legacy endures if only as the first to map out the territory of the unconscious and to establish the central factors within the structure of the traumatic experience as memory, repetition and belatedness.[8] In this chapter and subsequent ones, my rationale in focussing on Freud (and also on Jacques Lacan), in addition to more recent developments within trauma theory, is primarily that his work enables us to go back to first principles, understanding the symbolic structures of the unconscious in the deepest and most fundamental terms. Having looked in the previous chapter at the attacks' initial media presentation primarily by way of an Adornian critique that positions audiences as marginalized victims, we move on to consider the psychological phenomena that were associated with this position. I argue that alongside the ideological force of the images, a different force was also at work, which made its impact before any political readings or interpretations could take shape. I want first to establish the particular characterization of trauma as it occurs within the experience of seeing September 11th via the remove of images, looking to a range of sources to ask whether trauma is an appropriate term to use in the first place; who was traumatized; and how, and subsequently to set out the ways in which the media's representation of the event created new problems both for trauma theory and for traumatized subjects themselves.[9] Jürgen Habermas has called September 11th the 'first historic world event', meaning that it was visible, unedited and live, to a world audience as it was happening, making the world public a 'universal eyewitness'.[10] For him, the unprecedented singularity of September 11th lay in the unedited 'real-ness' of its media portrayal. According to David Hazinski, head of a broadcast news initiative at the University of Georgia's telecommunications department, more than two billion people watched the attack happen in real time or very soon after.[11] Robert Pledge, head of the Contact Press Images photo agency, notes that this was due largely to the time of day at which it took place: 'During all major events in the recent past, Tiananmen Square, the Gulf war, the Iraq invasion – there's always a part of the world that's in the dark. But this could be seen at once, anywhere, in both hemispheres, any latitude, any culture, throughout the world, live – something that we've never had happen before.'[12] Though the presentation of this event was, as I have argued, subsequently very carefully managed, it was explosively different from any other in its immediate initial worldwide dissemination, and it was on this level essentially unmanageable not only for the press but for the psyche also. This must be considered a new kind of traumatic experience – one that challenges the basis of trauma theory as it has existed up to this point.

Freud's engagement with trauma began during his clinical training at l'Hôpital Pitié-Salpêtrière in Paris between October 1885 and February 1886. His early insights, which remain the central puzzle for trauma theory in recent decades, concerned the process by which traumatic experiences disrupt the normal flow of memory and cognition. These are experiences of which, he writes, 'no memory can as a rule be recovered', and which 'were not understood at the time but which were *subsequently* understood and interpreted'.[13] Based on this model, Jean LaPlanche and Jean-Bertrand Pontalis in their seminal guide to psychoanalytic language later defined trauma as 'an influx of excitations that is excessive by the standards of the subject's tolerance and capacity to master such excitations and work them out psychically'.[14] This means that for the subject, rather than being able to integrate memories of the traumatic incident into their normal narrative history as they would other kinds of memory, the traumatic memory is inaccessible and un-integrated, yet it can recur or reappear beyond their control. Some memories are simply too forceful, too far beyond the understanding of the subject to be integrated properly, so these experiences become abnormally lodged within the subject's psyche in such a way that they can only be recovered belatedly. Adopting the word 'trauma' (originally derived from the Greek, meaning to pierce or wound) from physical medicine and applying it instead, the mind carries implications of invasive shock and violence, as well as potentially lasting injury. Psychologist Judith Lewis Herman provides a further definition based in clinical practice:

> Unlike commonplace misfortunes, traumatic events generally involve threats to life or bodily integrity, or a close personal encounter with violence and death. They confront human beings with the extremities of helplessness and terror, and evoke the responses of catastrophe. According to the Comprehensive Textbook of Psychiatry, the common denominator of psychological trauma is a feeling of 'intense fear, helplessness, loss of control, and threat of annihilation'.[15]

Developing this idea, Liza Saltzman and Eric Rosenberg emphasize the fact that trauma brings with it a profound questioning of human relationships, experience and identity and creates 'a state of existential crisis'. It destroys the subject's assumptions about 'the safety of the world, the positive value of the self, and the meaningful order of creation'.[16] This definition is their starting point for an application of the principles of trauma to questions about art and visual culture. This combination of a Freudian foundation, Herman's clinical, therapeutic definition of trauma as a metaphorical blow to the psyche and Saltzman and Rosenberg's 'existential crisis' impacting a wider society or culture's sense of identity forms the basis for my argument here.

If most Americans were never directly exposed to the trauma of September 11th in terms of threat to their own personal safety, and particularly given the general invisibility of bodies and death itself in the media coverage of the attacks, can we really say that they were traumatized at all, or just shaken and scared? For some commentators and trauma theorists (including Zelizer, Saltzman and Rosenberg), it is accepted as self-evident that September 11th counts as a traumatic experience for the national civilian population. I agree that it does indeed count as such, but not that this should be taken as self-evident. Is there such a thing as collective trauma, and how does it differ from individual trauma? Might not this be as problematic an assumption as that carried within the term 'collective memory'? According to sociologist Kai Erikson, who has studied the traumatizing effects of natural disasters, accidents and criminal atrocities on community groups, attributing collective or community trauma is on one level simply a matter of extending the metaphor of bodily wounds to the tissues of social life. The social body can be damaged in the same way as the individual body or mind, leading to a group identity or ethos that is 'different from (and more than) the sum of the private wounds that make it up'.[17] This is easy enough to accept when we are talking about, say, a town in which every family has been touched by the effects of an earthquake, or about the immediate locality of New York City post-September 11th. But, Erikson goes further, suggesting that collective trauma can be extended to the wider community, to those who were not directly 'wounded' but whose experience was vicarious. 'Events of local origins can have consequences that reach across huge distances', he says and – writing some years before September 2001 – goes on to claim that occasionally conditions are such that 'news of it is broadcast so quickly and so widely that it becomes a moment in everyone's history, a datum in everyone's store of knowledge'.[18] In this case, this effect was felt intuitively by so many people across the country and even the globe that it explains not only the immediate and widespread use of the word 'trauma', but the easy move from this to the idea of collective memory. In the previous chapter, I argued that collective memory is an ideology that has been supported by photography's supposedly self-evident mode of address. Here again though, the self-evident and the intuitive easily segue into more dangerous territory. Comparable to the previous discussion about heroes, one such danger is in the slippage between recognizing oneself as having been traumatized and calling oneself a 'victim'. This too was an immediate and widespread reaction. One *San Francisco Chronicle* article claimed, 'it makes no difference if no one we knew could possibly have been hurt in New York: the sense of danger permeated every house, every neighbourhood in the country. We were all hurt, in one way or the other.'[19] Dominick LaCapra discusses the pitfalls of claiming second-hand trauma for oneself in this way, using the same terms as if one has been personally injured or bereaved. Addressing the problem of 'vicarious victimhood', he stresses that with respect to trauma and its representation, it is crucial to maintain the distinction between victims and subjects: '"Victim" is not a psychological category. It is, in variable ways, a social, political, and ethical category. Victims of certain events will in all likelihood be traumatised by them, and not being traumatised would itself call for explanation. But not everyone traumatised by events is a victim.'[20] LaCapra, whose work is broadly concerned with 'the generalisation of trauma or its transformation into the sublime', notes a pervading tendency within Western Christian and Romantic traditions to glamorize melancholy, suffering and self-victimization.[21] The association of suffering with sublime heights of revelation and even redemption is important to resist. Writing with specific reference to commemoration of the Holocaust, he explains:

> Notably for those born later, these events may, through a kind of posttraumatic effect, prompt a generalised hyperbolic or exorbitant style that at times becomes indiscriminate and verges on a paradoxically bland sensationalism, which may undermine critical judgement and obscure, or provide too one-sided a resolution of, the problem of the actual and desirable relations between excess and normative limits.[22]

Here, echoing Adorno, is another warning against distraction and too-easy recourse to the emotive and the spectacular. This time the emphasis is less political and more ethical. But it is also, I suggest, psychological. In 2001, the kind of generalized hyperbole of which LaCapra warns provided 'too one-sided a resolution' not only of September 11th as 'evil' or 'war', but also of the psychological disturbance that it engendered. Patrick Reardon of the *Chicago Tribune* was one of the journalists who immediately turned to the language of trauma in analysing what was happening across the country:

> A Los Angeles-based psychologist and an expert in the field of trauma and disaster psychology, said, 'You don't have to be there and you don't have to know someone there to feel the impact of this penetration into our safety and security.' Indeed, he said, there is vicarious trauma that many Americans are likely to suffer *from having watched* Tuesday's events and from recognizing how much less safe they are than they thought.[23] (italics added)

The 'public trauma' of September 11th came, for the most part, as the result of *witnessing* – from the images that were seen. Seeing was obviously part of the trauma for those present at Ground Zero, but in their case, it came with a real threat to bodily safety and surroundings. The rest of the country, faced primarily with a visually orientated experience and no embodied threat, was subject to something different.

Spencer Platt's photograph of the second plane's explosion engulfing the South Tower (Figure 1.1) was taken from the Brooklyn Bridge as he was making his way towards the unfolding story, instinctively trying to get as close as he could. He was not where he wanted to be, but the perfection of this photograph – its frontal viewpoint, captured from exactly the right distance at exactly the right instant, arranged as if the fire and smoke were superimposed onto a tourist postcard view of the World Trade Center – ensured its place in news reports on television and in print all over the world as fast as Getty could distribute it. There are other photographs of this moment and thereabouts, and film footage of it was broadcast live around the world, but that footage could not hold in such fine detail the impossible inferno of the fireball, the choking black of the huge hole in the adjacent tower or, maybe most stunning of all, every tiny splinter of red-hot metal and glass that had begun to rain down like glitter towards the street below. In Platt's picture, all of this is exquisitely frozen in high definition for all time. Watching the plane approach the tower frame by frame on film and seeing that fireball appear for the first or the hundredth time, one knew that this was a world-changing news event (see Figure 1.2). This photograph, though, presents the decisive moment in a level of shattering detail that video footage could not, and captures it from a privileged viewpoint that was not accessible to most of those who were present on the ground, but was closer than most of the video cameras that caught it. For these reasons, it holds a particular kind of terror that resides very specifically in its character as a frozen spectacle, and that is not comparable to other registers of experience. This is what was meant by one reporter who wrote, 'we will never be the same again… [the sight of the second plane's impact is] an image forever seared onto our memories.'[24]

Of course, this is a traumatic image not just because it is spectacular, but because its spectacle both signifies and obscures the deaths of thousands of people. For E. Ann Kaplan, the possibility of being traumatized by images is tied directly to empathy towards other human beings. She posits three kinds of empathic response engendered through 'mediatized' or secondary exposure to traumatic events, specifically through the viewing of images:[25] first, 'empty empathy' (which is closely related, it seems, to the condition of compassion fatigue, in which a surplus of pathos in images quickly leads to detachment and a loss of engagement for the viewer); second, 'witnessing' ('a response that may change the viewer in a positive, pro-social manner, and that… involves ethics'); and third, 'vicarious trauma' ('a response in which the viewer is shocked to the extent of being emotionally over-aroused; that is, the empathic response to an image of a catastrophe may be so strong and personally painful that the individual turns away, thinks distracting thoughts, unable to endure the feelings aroused').[26] Each of these depends on both the context of viewing and the aesthetic form of the image itself. Kaplan's view is that, specifically within the category of vicarious trauma, the viewing of certain images under certain conditions can indeed have a traumatizing effect. Leaving aside for the time being the tendency to turn away and seek distraction from such images, this definition certainly applies to the photographs and viewing conditions surrounding September 11th, as experienced by viewers who were not present at the scene. Vicarious trauma seems to leave little room for empathy because its effect upon the viewer themselves is so overwhelming, but it does begin with empathy and would be impossible without it. It is empathy with the victims in the towers that lies at the root of the vicarious trauma engendered by pictures like Platt's, even though we cannot see them, and even though the triggering mechanism of its impact is, we might say, aesthetic. This kind of witnessing, Kaplan writes, 'is necessary for national traumas. People as collectively responsible require structures within which often silently endured traumatic experiences can be "spoken" or imaged'.[27]

The possibility of different kinds of trauma, as introduced by Kaplan, Kai Erikson and others, allows us to see the seemingly hyperbolic statements of the journalists quoted above as indicative of a community traumatized in its own right. This is not just sensationalism, vicarious victimhood or second-hand assimilation of the experiences of those present at Ground Zero. It is its very own kind of terror. It is fair to say that the 'national psyche changed' on that day, and that America's relationship to the world was altered in ways that it did not fully understand. These characteristics, such as the threat of annihilation, existential crisis and the destruction of a subject's assumptions about 'the safety of the world, the positive value of the self, and the meaningful order of creation', indicate that though this is, formally speaking, a different kind of trauma from that of an individual or a direct witness of death itself, according to the definitions of Herman, Erikson, Saltzman, Rosenberg and others, it is trauma nonetheless.[28] And, the possibility for this broadened definition is entirely due to the attack's appearance in images.

For Saltzman and Rosenberg, the most important characteristic of traumatic memory, and its central puzzle, is its elusive, mysterious visual character:

> We are convinced of the centrality of pictures, of the visual, or, more specifically, artistic production and practice, to such negotiations. The formulation of trauma as a discourse is predicated upon metaphors of visuality and image as unavoidable carriers of the unrepresentable. From primal scene to flashback to screen memory to the dream, much of the language deployed to speak trauma's character is emphatically, if not exclusively, visual. It may even be argued that the very form taken by trauma as a phenomenon is only, however asymptomatically or not, understood as or when pictured. The inability to frame trauma in and of itself lends the form almost naturally to a process of visualization as expiation.[29]

In the wake of September 11th, many Americans gravitated towards photographs, collecting them and focussing on them as a way of coming to terms with the facts. Photography was, to say the least, a highly significant agent in the event's assimilation. We have considered some of the ways, in fact, in which the event was itself an image: its power residing primarily within its symbolic function. It was a spectacular gesture designed to cause maximum damage in being *seen*, as well as in material and human destruction. So, it should not be surprising that seeing was also understood to be part of the process of recovery. Reflecting on the impact that photography had in his own vicarious experience of September 11th, one blogger explained, 'I will never be able to describe September 11th as fully as these pictures. And yet, for as powerful and moving as these pictures are, they will never be able to describe the experience nor tell the complete story of those who were there.'[30] This is a feeling that was shared by photojournalist Gilles Peress: when a set of his pictures appeared in a commemorative exhibition by fellow Magnum photographers at the New York Historical Society, he chose to display only one caption: 'I don't trust words. I trust pictures.'[31] It was a widespread sentiment: that while images may have been inadequate to represent what happened, they did a better job than words. So, images, and especially photographs, were at the centre of countless different attempts to come to terms with the attack and express the memory of what it was like to watch it unfold: to 'be there' in time if not in space.

To begin to interrogate this claim of the photograph's superior power of expression in response to trauma and its rightful displacement of words, we come to Freud and Lacan. In his development of Freud's foundational work on trauma, Jacques Lacan makes significant departures that might suggest a fundamental parting between the two thinkers based on the dichotomy between words and images. On the one hand, Freud can be understood, in his 1899 work 'Screen Memories', for example, to argue that representation, specifically in the form of associated 'mnemic images', provides a key to remembering something that is important but absent (or 'omitted').[32] Through effective analysis, representation can, albeit indirectly, act as the initial pointer that alerts the subject (or the analyst) to the originating cause of the trauma. Have been confronted directly, this can then be assimilated as part of a process of remembering and 'working through'.[33] In this way, the correct handling of images retained in the psyche can be understood, in this early stage of Freud's thought at least, as playing a necessary role in recovery. There is a similar principle at work in his famous analysis of the so-called Wolf Man.[34] In this case, the centrality of images is made particularly concrete, as the patient makes actual drawings, recording the strange images seen in his dreams, which Freud then uses as the key to uncovering the cause of the neurosis. The 'Screen Memories' essay is littered with references to 'scenes', 'impressions' and 'reproducible mnemic images', and cases like the Wolf Man's indicate that for Freud, the unconscious, consisting of memory traces from the experiences and traumas of early childhood, is associated strongly with non-linguistic, spatially oriented phenomena that offer themselves to the analyst for interpretation.

For Lacan, on the other hand, trauma and representation of any kind can be read as mutually exclusive, because trauma, as the *tuché* or missed encounter with the 'real', is by definition totally elusive and impossible to grasp.[35] Instead, it repeats. The closest that trauma comes to being representable at all is through the cycle of symptoms that are its only outlet, and which must be tackled using language in the process of analysis. But, it would be too simplistic to see Freud and Lacan as polar opposites in this regard – Freud asserting that the unconscious is constituted by images which are in turn the only means to recovery from trauma, and Lacan proposing a linguistic key instead. While Lacan's fundamental privileging of the role of language (as any signifying system that is based on differential relations) in the unconscious is quite clear, Freud's attitude to images is much more ambiguous.

Though he does seem to place more of an emphasis on the recollection of pictorial phenomena than his successor, as the pioneer of the 'talking cure', there can be no doubt that Freud saw words as the tools of his work. ('Nothing', he said in 1916, 'takes place in a psychoanalytic treatment but an exchange of words'.[36]) For Freud, the only moment in which the visual takes the upper hand in the development of the psyche is in the revelation of sexual difference. While, for Lacan, it is the reflexive recognition of the child's own body that is most significant in the formation of the ego, for Freud, the key moment is the primal scene, and the child's first sight of the female sexual organ. Other than that, he tends to downplay the visual, and in the instances where it seems undeniably important (such as the 'Screen Memories' essay and his work with the Wolf Man), he does not seem altogether comfortable with this. When dealing with dreams, for example, he prefers to dwell on their linguistic description and interpretation rather than granting any significance to their impact or affect as visual objects that might somehow exceed language:

> If we reflect that the means of representation in dreams are principally visual images and not words, we shall see that it is even more appropriate to compare dreams with a system of writing than with a language. In fact the interpretation of dreams is completely analogous to the decipherment of an ancient pictographic script such as Egyptian hieroglyphics.[37]

This statement, while on one level appearing entirely contradictory, indicates that while dreams may indeed be constituted by 'visual images and not words', Freud's goal is always as quickly as possible to take these visual images and turn them into linguistic ones.[38] Here, and at various other stages throughout his long career, he seems to wrestle with this same tension: recognition on the one hand that images form an important constitutive part of unconscious activity, but on the other, wariness of their power. Take, for example, this statement from *Moses and Monotheism*, written in 1937:

> The strongest compulsive influence arises from impressions ... at a time when [the child's] psychical apparatus [is] not yet completely receptive. [This] fact cannot be doubted; but it is so puzzling that we may make it more comprehensible by comparing it with a photographic exposure which can be developed after any interval of time and transformed into a picture.[39]

Here is Freud articulating the 'belatedness' that is now accepted as a key characteristic of traumatic memory, expressed perfectly in the metaphor of the photographic process. Ulrich Baer has taken this central metaphor and developed it into a thorough schema that contributes to the understanding of both photography and trauma itself. Freud's observation is that, as in the taking of a photograph, the traumatic event is not assimilated or experienced fully at the time of its occurrence, but only belatedly in its repeated possession (or 'developing') by the one who experiences it. Baer draws from this the suggestion that photography, considered as a structural analogy, can provide a special understanding of these unremembered but unforgettable experiences:

> Because trauma blocks routine mental processes from converting an experience into memory or forgetting, it parallels the defining structure of photography, which also traps an event during its occurrence while blocking its transformation into memory ... The fact that traumatic experiences recur and that they attain meaning only at and through this belated repetition – like

negatives that harbour an image until they are printed and emerge from the developing vats – does not invalidate their realness but should compel us to reconsider the relations between memory and reality.[40]

Photographers working in situations of extreme horror have attested to this process in very practical terms, at times identifying with it so strongly that their own experience seems to elide with that of the camera. Of her time spent working in Russia during the Second World War, Margaret Bourke-White wrote that she would 'consider focus and light values and the technique of photography, in as impersonal a way as though I were making an abstract camera composition. The blind[ness] lasts as long as it is needed – while I am actually operating the camera. Days later, when I developed the negatives, I was surprised to find that I could not bring myself to look at the films. I had to have someone else handle and sort them for me.'[41] Similarly, Lee Miller spoke of not truly seeing the scenes that she encountered at Nazi death camps until after her photographs were developed.[42] Speaking as a non-professional photographer, literature professor and New Yorker, Marianne Hirsch has written of her experience taking photographs in Lower Manhattan in the early aftermath of the September 11th attacks, describing it as a kind of automated seeing without understanding. Because she was operating in a state of shock, the meaning and even formal content of her pictures (made as a purely personal response to the event) was deferred, waiting to be developed and properly seen at a later time.[43] On the level of wider cultural experience, the belatedness embodied by Thomas Hoepker's photograph of Brooklyn onlookers has operated similarly. Where it was once 'too confusing' to be seen at all, it has now risen to a level of cultural consciousness at which it is understood to be, as Jonathan Jones writes in the *Guardian*, 'a picture about history, and about memory'.[44]

The 'developing' aspect of this metaphor is obviously tied to the analogue or chemical photography process, but I see no reason why it should not apply to the digital as well. The digital photograph is visible instantly, but its taking can still be a detached and 'automated' process, as anyone observing tourists at a famous landmark or beauty spot will know. Baer's outworking of Freud's thought focuses on the striking parallel between those moments arrested mechanically by photography and those arrested experientially by the traumatized psyche: moments that bypass normal cognition and memory. In his early writings, Freud uses the metaphor of the camera to explain the unconscious as the place where bits of memory are stored until they are developed into conscious memories.[45] He later qualifies this though, and the ambiguous embracing and subsequent disavowal of the camera metaphor leaves us wondering about the relationship between photography and trauma in Freud's mind, and how literally he invites us to take it.[46] Freud's formative experience of working with 'hysterics' under Jean Martin Charcot at l'Hôpital Pitié-Salpêtrière involved photography in the most direct and clinical of ways. A central component of Charcot's research was the attempt to capture the manifestations of traumatic symptoms – specifically bodily contortions and facial expressions – in photographs.[47] The study of hysterical symptoms, which Freud and Josef Breuer later liken, in their *Studies on Hysteria*, to 'a pictographic script which has become intelligible after the discovery of a few bilingual inscriptions', can, as noted previously, be seen as a kind of foundation for Freud's subsequent understanding of trauma.[48] The emphasis on picturing or representation at this early stage in his training – both in the contemporary understanding of hysteria itself and in the photographic method of its observation – is surely significant for the later development of his theory. At the very least, he seems confused by the mystery of trauma's capturing, not fully in images, but not in words either. Ulrich Baer's way of resolving this is to say that trauma, as 'a disorder of memory and time', occupies a space *between* the visual and the verbal.[49]

Given the metaphorical correlation between photography and the mysteries of trauma's structure and character, what happens when there is, in an event like September 11th, such a strong connection between the experience of the trauma and the practice of photography itself? Or, in other words, when for so many people the photographs *were* the experience and the mode of its witnessing, as well as the means for attempted catharsis, remembrance or recovery? Baer describes his work on trauma and photography as being outside of both historicist and formalist analysis. It is, he claims, not concerned primarily with the politicization of the context or viewing of the image itself, nor with its formal qualities, but with something else entirely. In addition to Charcot's photography of hysteria, he also discusses the work of American photographer Mikael Levin and a set of slides taken between 1942 and 1945 by a Nazi official in the Łódź ghetto. In examining these specific bodies of photographic work, he does not focus on the historical or narrative contexts in which they are set but treats them as objects which 'isolate experiences that remained apart from lived reality at the time of their occurrence'.[50] He is using these photographs not as tools to recover the past, but as illustrations of 'the constitutive breakdown of context' staged by both traumatic experiences and the taking of photographs.[51] Their historical specificity is crucial to their value, but they are not documents, they are symbols. Similarly, in discussing the picturing of September 11th, Baer's approach is useful only if we remember carefully to separate the formal process of photography from its content. (Recognizing the power of Spencer Platt's photograph of the exploding towers means seeing it as the eruption of an experienced moment rather than just a record of visual information.) Postmodern theory has, he points out, tended to displace attention from the photographic image to its extra-pictorial dimensions, which can be productive but can also miss the remaining fact that images have force because they are images. It is easy to bypass the essential mystery that makes a photograph what it is when we seek to use it merely as a descriptive window into the past or as an illustration of a particular narrative. Photographs offer encounter as well as information. It can be difficult to account for this – it is the enduring problem (indeed the defining problem for the theoretical study of images of all kinds) of talking about pictures using words. The discourse of trauma theory, being, as Baer puts it, somewhere between the two, means that it might be useful at this impasse. He suggests that it can testify to, if not really explain, 'what assails the self from within without constituting a proper experience'.[52]

Freud says that the reason why repressed traumatic memories do not go away without a commitment to effective psychoanalysis is that what cannot be properly remembered cannot be left behind. The neurotic repeats instead of remembering: 'the patient does not *remember* anything of what he has forgotten and repressed, but *acts it out*. He reproduces it not as a memory but as an action; he *repeats* it.'[53] This is the repetition-compulsion. Repetitive acting out is the avoidance of working through, or the unwillingness to remember. In the course of ordinary experiences, memory integration happens naturally. But, memories of experiences that are extraordinary, frightening or traumatic, while having intense psychic impact, become, as we have seen above, unintelligible. They are un-integrated; consigned to the psyche in such a way that they are very difficult to recall at will but manifest themselves in other, often involuntary, ways. These memories can give rise to symptoms, often in the form of repetitive behaviours that were the raw material of many of Freud's recorded cases. Specifically, he noted that behind the apparently destructive compulsion to repeat is an urgent need to master the trauma: in one way or another, the painful memory is relived again and again in order to create retrospective anxiety, until a sufficient defence has been built that it can be better coped with the 'next time'. Unfortunately, this defence is often so effective that it serves to impede the process of recovery or even normal life. Freud explains: 'The patient brings out of the armoury of the past the weapons with which he defends himself against the progress of the treatment – weapons which we must wrest from him one by one.'[54]

Working through, on the other hand, is the clarification and integration into the fabric of the mind of that which was previously warded off by the repetition process. It is remembering as catharsis. When all of the patient's defensive mechanisms and 'weapons' have been disarmed and they have suffered the pain of confrontation with their memories, then true progress can be made. How can we reconcile the compulsion to look at images of the September 11th attacks with an unwillingness to remember, or with the avoidance of working through? Endless volumes of information, repetition of disturbing imagery, determined encounters with the full range of visible horror are precisely what many people seemed to gravitate towards in the aftermath of the attacks. In the context of an 'overpsychologized' culture, many seemed almost obsessed with facing, looking, remembering and working through their emotions, which raises the question of how successfully this can be achieved through repeated looking at photographs. In Baer's view, the structural analogy of the photographic process can help us to understand the behaviour of traumatic memory, but photographs themselves do not help us towards the constructive remembering of traumatic events. Despite the enduring compulsion to try to make sense of photographs, to contemplate them and to use them as tools to help recover and organize memories, they still help us to understand the nature of trauma itself better than they help us to understand narrative history.[55] For those who collect, focus, fixate and rely on them in this way, the relationship to photographs will thus have more in common with Freud's process of 'acting out' than 'working through' or real remembering. They become the defensive weapons in an armoury, which must be 'wrested' from us 'one by one' if we are to move on as individuals or as a society. This problematic fixation with photographs is also exacerbated by the factor of external repetition, with the endless reappearance of (the same or similar) photographs and moving images in the media following the attacks. Just as, for many bewildered children who watched the repeated television footage, the event did seem to happen again and again to more and more buildings across the city, the photographic images continually repeat, and so the traumatic encounter is perpetuated.

Repetition is not the same as remembering. There is a sense in which the repetition of moving and still images aided understanding and helped witnesses to come to terms with the enormity of what they had seen. When the first plane hit the North Tower at 8.46 a.m. that Tuesday morning, onlookers thought it was a horrifying mistake. But, at 9.03 a.m., when the second plane hit the second tower, the truth was confirmed that this was a deliberate act of terrorism. No accident could have happened twice in exactly this same way. In this case, repetition verified the true character of the situation by making the first act intelligible. But, it was also this initial repetition that allowed not only understanding, but trauma to 'sink in', rooting it into witnesses' consciousness in its improbable and horrifying truth. The most arresting and spectacular photographs we have of this event, including Spencer Platt's fireball scene, would not exist if the first impact had not alerted some of the best photographers in America to the breaking story and compelled them to go downtown with their cameras. The second plane's impact made the first intelligible, but in this sense, it was the first that made the second visible to the world. The fact that it took a second, delayed, repetitive enactment (or reproduction) to seal its status simply adds another layer to the complex story of this event's traumatic character. Repetition was already built in to the event even before photography began to compound it. As one reporter put it on 12 September under the headline, 'Mesmerizing Scenes of Hell', 'the repeated sight... is now sealed in the national memory bank'.[56] If the image, seen and then repeated, *is* the trauma, and if with each repeated viewing the trauma is acted out again and again, looking again at photographs cannot possibly be the cure.

'Language and its structure', writes Lacan, 'exist prior to the moment at which each subject at a certain point in his mental development makes his entry into it.'[57] The realm of psychic phenomena which he calls 'the symbolic' consists of systems of signifiers that form networks to which we have little conscious access but which govern our lives completely. They organize our world, the very texture of which is symbolic.[58] The most prominent of these symbolic systems is language. Lacan suggests that the unconscious is itself structured like a language and constituted by a series of chains of signifying elements. His way of accounting for the process that Freud calls 'acting out' is to say that when the unconscious is confronted with a traumatic experience, that experience becomes fixed in a signifying chain that manifests itself as a symptom:

> The double-triggered mechanism of metaphor is the very mechanism by which the symptom, in the analytic sense, is determined. Between the enigmatic signifier of the ... trauma and the term that is substituted for it in an actual signifying chain there passes the spark that fixes in a symptom the signification inaccessible to the conscious subject in which that symptom may be resolved – a symptom being a metaphor in which flesh or function is taken as a signifying element.[59]

If the symptom has a structural relation to a linguistic metaphor, it is through this language that the patient (or the traumatized witness) communicates their experience – 'the patient cries out through his symptom'. When the symptom is physiological, we might even say that this is the body or the 'flesh' trying to speak. So, the linguistic chain must, through language, be deciphered for an alleviation of the symptom to take place: 'the symptom resolves itself entirely in an analysis of language, because the symptom is itself structured like a language.'[60] This idea of ridding the body of symptoms through language was Freud's. He discovered that identifying the disturbing event that caused a symptom, and talking about it, could alleviate the symptom. But, trauma by its nature is an 'affront to understanding'. In Lacanian terms, it lies outside of the symbolic order, of all that we can name, understand or adequately describe using language. Hence, survivors of traumatic events are very often unable to name or express their experience in speech. This principle is well recognized by patients, clinicians and contemporary theorists of trauma. Judith Lewis Herman ascribes it not only to survivors or victims but to witnesses, saying that it can be difficult for them, 'to see more than a few fragments of the picture at one time, to retain all the pieces, and to fit them together. It is even more difficult to find a language that conveys fully and persuasively what one has seen.'[61]

A recurring theme of the newspaper coverage of the attacks from around the United States in the week following September 11th was precisely the overwhelming force of pictures and the failure of words. On 12 September, the

New York Times said that 'mere words were inadequate vessels to contain the sense of shock and horror that people felt'.[62] And, on the thirteenth:

> Language failed this week. 'Beyond comprehension', 'beyond our worst imaginings', 'beyond belief' – these were the phrases heard again and again in the last two days. As people struggled to describe the events of Tuesday morning, they reached for metaphors and analogies that might capture the horror of what they had seen ... words felt devalued and inadequate ... Inevitably, many witnesses and television commentators turned to film analogies to describe what they had seen.[63]

Also, in the *New York Times* on the twelfth, Caryn James gave her analysis of President Bush's immediate reaction to the attacks, giving special weight to its visual and verbal dimensions. Her article begins with an already typical account of the defining nature of the day's pictures:

> In this visual era, the incredible live images, replayed throughout the day until their reality sunk in, defined the events ... The images were terrifying to watch, yet the coverage was strangely reassuring simply because it existed with such immediacy, even when detailed information was scarce. [64]

She goes on to describe the president's first television appearance of the day, at 9.30 a.m., surrounded by the Florida schoolchildren with whom he had been reading a storybook when he first learned what was happening, as the 'least comforting moments in the day'. It was, however, 'more reassuring than the taped statement later from the Air Force base in Louisiana'. The reason for this, she says, is that 'the audio was not working when some networks first played the tape, creating the impression that things were not under control as much as he said'.[65] Without the coherent words that were required by the nation at that moment, the image of a silenced, worried president, moving his lips without making any sound, did more to distress than to comfort. But, more distressing still, according to James, were the moments when the president himself was not only silent but invisible, leaving citizens to form their own troubling mental images: 'Through the day, some of the most harrowing reports told viewers what they did not know: where the president was. The unseen image of Mr Bush meeting with advisers "in a bunker" was almost as chilling as the violence onscreen.'[66]

Like numerous other reporters, James judges the president's later 8.30 p.m. Oval Office speech inadequate, but 'what mattered was that he was visible, live from the Oval Office, offering a sense of stability and a sense of a future'.[67] Her article ends with a summary that 'the day's coverage had already shown that words had less impact than live pictures in this tragedy'.[68] Here is the same tension that would later be expressed by many who sought to use images as a way to grasp and recover from the event: that while pictures are inadequate, they are at least better than words. This is applied not only to the retrospective attempt at emotional recovery, but also the immediate imperative to understand what had just occurred – to 'get to grips with it' in the first moments. The less obvious point of James's article seems to be that both words *and* images were essential. When one or both was missing, or when they were inappropriately proportioned, the result was distress and disruption in the process of understanding.

Before much time had passed, it became clear to some that, unlike other atrocities for which a single iconic image has come to stand, the huge number of photographs of this event – so many similar but slightly different images – meant that September 11th would not be so easily summed up. On 16 September, Christopher Knight of the *Los Angeles Times* offered impressive insight into the absence of such an 'icon', considering the chaos still surrounding the subject at the time of his writing. Central to his conclusion was, again, the relationship between words and pictures. He pointed out the distinctiveness of the September 11th image-event in its disruption of this relationship, due largely to its immediate media representation:

> Typically, words precede the creation of iconic images. A story is told, then a picture forms. What is an icon, after all, but art's equivalent of the word made flesh? But the word comes first. Icons illustrate existing faith and doctrine, which is often inchoate until the picture comes along and suddenly sorts out the disarray. Then, a gathering critical mass of people sees the image and collectively knows, 'That's it!' ... Perhaps that remains possible here, since the inchoate still characterises so much of this ongoing event.[69]

Pictures give form to ideas, whether these are abstract ideas of faith and doctrine or events that have happened to other people in faraway places. And they achieve this authority, Knight argues, by a process of accumulation: the greater the number of people who recognize a picture to be iconic of something, the stronger the potency of the icon and the greater its cultural resonance. In this case though, there was a hitch:

> ... in the terrorist assault this week, the typical sequence was reversed. Pictures proceeded language [sic]. The stories were being told simultaneously with the arrival of the image flood – and in many cases only by the pictures themselves. We stared at them in an inescapable condition of disbelief, as language sputtered and words struggled to keep up.[70]

The absence of a single icon that would stand for the whole event is due to a disruption in continuity. There could be no icon, not only because the protocol of understanding was disrupted, but because there were just too many images. Knight's own conclusion was that, at least for the time being, this was not such a bad thing:

> ... for icons also simplify. They're a visual form of cliché. The story that erupted last week is complex, and established doctrines need re-examination and revision. It may just be too soon for icons yet.[71]

Robert Hariman and John Louis Lucaites are less dismissive of the role that icons play in public life. Rather than just simplifying, icons – defined for them as images that represent historically significant events, activate a strong emotional identification or response and are reproduced across a wide range of media and contexts – contribute to civic discourse by communicating 'social knowledge' in a way that 'exceeds words'.[72] For them, the emotive power of iconic images is tied to political agency because the act of seeing 'activates one's own sense of social awareness. Critical reason is intertwined with social reflection'.[73] This may be true, and Hariman and Luciates's book on the subject remains the most full and convincing account of the role that iconic photographs play in civil democratic society, in the American context at least. But, the point that Christopher Knight makes in his *LA Times* article is that because of this event's overwhelmingly immediate dissemination – the effects of what Paul Virilio would call its exposure – the possibility of any kind of public icon being identified in the first place was foreclosed. While the very first stages of the 'image flood' occurred via television, accompanied by 'sputtering' and 'struggling' commentary, it was from among the subsequent deluge of still, silent photographs that an icon might have emerged (although it is not clear, when Knight says 'pictures', whether he means moving, still or both). This basic point about the real-time broadcast of the event had already been made elsewhere. Knight, however, takes a further step, considering the precise consequences of this immediacy for our usual way of taking in information through words and pictures. He observes that these two forms have a usual protocol or temporal succession on which our understanding depends. The nature of traumatic experiences is, as we have seen, that they are characteristically disintegrated from any kind of narrative flow. This leads us, in looking at any of the many hundreds of photographs taken in lower Manhattan on that day, to confront, in Ulrich Baer's words, 'photography's tremendous potential to capture such experiences without integrating them into a mitigating context'.[74] In his essay exploring the extent to which Richard Drew's 'Falling Man' photograph can be called an icon, Rob Kroes puts it more simply, stating that photographs are not just distinct from language or without language, but 'before language', and it is this prefiguring or pre-empting of context that gives photographs their power to 'compress' or 'concentrate' meaning, experience and time, and thus to become iconic.[75] The problem here, though, is that the disjointed and temporally isolated nature of the traumatic experience is matched and exacerbated by the temporally isolated nature of the photographed moment. Kroes's argument, in line with that of Hariman and Lucaites (whose position is made clear in title of their book on iconic images: *No Caption Needed*), is that the pre-linguistic character of photographs is what gives them their iconic power, allowing us the feeling that they 'have done the work of memory for us'. But, when the pictures of something so far outside our frame of reference come before the words that explain it, not only do we struggle to place it within our immediate symbolic frame of reference, but the wider frame of reference by which we might designate 'icons' breaks down too. As the years have gone by, certain photographs, like Drew's 'Falling Man', have risen to the top of the pile and been put forward as icons that might stand for the event. Notably though, this has not been a spontaneous process. Each of them has been accompanied by arguments and deliberations (like Rob Kroes's) in which the nature of icons is wrestled with, the impact and representative significance of individual pictures is weighed up and the conclusion is more of a tentative question than a statement: 'could this be *the* 9/11 icon?' There are many forceful, widely reproduced and instantly recognizable photographs of September 11th, but when it comes to 'iconicity', none so far has reached the level of tacit consensus.

Several decades ago, Susan Sontag pointed to the protocol of assimilation that might be required for images to be integrated into public life in the kind of constructive manner that Hariman and Lucaites describe, taking it as given that 'the contribution of photography always follows the naming of the event'.[76] Furthermore, she goes on, 'without a politics, photographs of the slaughter-bench of history will most likely be experienced as, simply, unreal or as a demoralizing emotional blow'.[77] When such a catastrophe is presented in the first instance without a context (a politics) to explain it, the effect is simply emotionally crippling. The word cannot be made flesh if the flesh comes first. Nor can the flesh perform the function of the word. To return to Lacan's notion that the symptom is a metaphor, it seems that in the first hours following the September 11th attacks, a similar malfunction occurred. At this moment in history, the trauma was sealed and the symptom was fixed in its signifying chain.[78]

As well as repetition and the succession of words and pictures, another temporal factor in the behaviour of traumatic memory is belatedness. Saltzman and Rosenberg, again, provide a useful summary:

> Trauma … in its classic formation … remains dependent on an economy of belatedness that is the psychic space in which the overwhelming might be held. It is in the possibility of such a space that representation can emerge as some kind of version of the traumatic. Without representation, in all its deferral, trauma implies an absolute form that we would never know. In other words, the naming of trauma would be denied, and loss would be beyond

> management. In its instance of portrayal, 9/11 collapsed the difference between event and its representation, implying the evisceration of adaptation to the circumstances of trauma by way of the very visual culture that accounted for it in the first place.[79]

In an argument that seems to go against the evidence laid out so far, the suggestion here is that it is in belated representation, or some kind of image-making, that the key to traumatic memory lies. Through representation, we can hope to 'return' in a productive way to the traumatic experience and somehow redress the malfunction by which it has become inaccessible. In other words, our own visual memory of an event cannot help us, but pictures of it can: providing the visual recall that we need from an external source. This seems to be a more complex way of arguing that the trauma of September 11th *was* essentially in its representation, and so images can in a literal way return us to it. But, this is a misleading view of the nature of representation. It may be through representation that the necessary shards of traumatic experience with which to begin a recovery process can be retrieved; it may even be, more specifically, via the model of photography as Ulrich Baer suggests. But, just as the key to Baer's model is, as it were, in the form of the photograph rather than its content, so the idea of particular pictures or concrete representational objects as the way to recovery is misleading. Saltzman and Rosenberg are not actually guilty of this mistake. Their main point here, rather, concerns the 'economy of belatedness' that defines trauma's structure and the disruption of this economy that took place in the media representation of September 11th. Because the traumatizing event was depicted instantly, simultaneously and repeatedly, it was severed from the belated, on which the assimilation of the traumatic depends. We could say that in the 'normal' course of a traumatic event, memories are sealed off in a state of deferral for our own protection – they must be 'belated' and encountered at a later time because experiencing them in their fullness all at once would be fatal for the mind. (Lee Miller would not have been able to carry on with her assignment if she had truly 'seen' the sights of the Nazi death camp through her viewfinder as she worked.) But, on September 11th, the instant, endless television replays and repeated photographs destroyed the possibility of belatedness. The image was immediately everywhere and unavoidable. Because of the way in which it was represented, it was not *re*presented at all – it was just *presented*, again and again. This, then, was a new kind of trauma, the memory of which could never be properly integrated. Virilio, too, has pointed to this absence of representation in the event in favour of presentation, going further by not only identifying this as a distinctive factor of the September 11th attack, but that it heralds the end of representation in modern real-time televised media in general. He calls the event an iconoclastic phenomenon, on two levels. First, in the iconoclasm of representation: the attack was on the World Trade Center, the image of capitalism that had to be smashed. And, second, in its constant, homogenized worldwide replay:

> We were not informed, we were frozen in front of a single message generalized on a world-wide scale. This tele-presence in reality is an iconoclasm of real presence, because we only saw one thing … In that case, we only had one eye, a 'big optic' on the global scale. This single big optic. Solitary vision is an iconoclasm of presentation.[80]

Virilio claims that this signals the end of the age of representation and gives way to a new era of perpetual presentation. The modern media machine no longer provides representations of things, it no longer *re*ports or *re*presents; it simply presents what is there, in eternally simultaneous real time. He calls this a 'pollution of distances', because presentation which bypasses representation constitutes a loss of the distance that is necessary for real subjectivity to come into play, just as the distance between the eyes is necessary for binocular vision. This loss of distance corresponds with the collapse of the economy of belatedness: it is in the instant and continuing repetition (though *re*petition may be the wrong word) of the image that the trauma is perpetuated, and through which, the hope of successful assimilation or recovery is also collapsed. In order to comprehend it, we need space, distance from the image, which we did not have. The very work of witnessing then turns into the experience of trauma, as opposed to its mode of therapy. Or, as Saltzman and Rosenberg put it, the continual presentation of the image becomes perpetually 'the overwhelming and unavoidable instant of its occurrence'.[81]

Just as, for Freud, 'acting out' is not a conscious activity, and recognition of its destructive effect is overpowered by the stronger compulsion to repeat, nationwide (and even worldwide) witnesses of the September 11th attacks acted on a compulsion to return again and again not to words but to pictures, enacting a repeated confrontation with them that ostensibly served, as in the acting-out process, to meet a deep need. As the *Chicago Tribune* reported on the day:

> ABC at one point Tuesday offered an image of New Yorkers in Manhattan's Times Square, safely away from the point of attack on the island, standing in awed, respectful silence, looking up at the giant TV screens broadcasting network coverage … The people were unable to hear what was being said, but the pictures were enough.[82]

Like witnesses and survivors of other traumatic events, people in New York and, in a different way, those far beyond underwent a traumatizing process on that day, which destabilized their sense of security and reality and their relation to the rest of the world. The disruption of visual memory was a constitutive part of this process.

Added to this memory disruption (which in trauma theory terms could be called conventional), the 'pollution of distances' occasioned by its immediate, repetitive and predominantly visual dissemination both deepened and complicated it as a memory. It introduced a problem of levels in the classification of communal trauma and of attributing psychological damage to a subject whose 'psyche' is not an individual mind or even that of a clearly defined group of victims, but a new entity linked very closely to a technological mode of presentation that does not obey even the enigmatic spatial or temporal 'rules' that trauma theory has managed to identify. What we can be sure of is the following: that this trauma was firmly based in the visual, falling outside any symbolic order of understanding or articulation, and was commonly perceived as 'unspeakable'; that its integral and then subsequent repetition was key to both the understanding and the further traumatizing of its viewers; and finally, that the trauma caused had as much to do with national security and status for the wider population as with the death or bereavement of members of the immediate New York or Washington communities. Beyond these more-or-less stable facts, there was a vacuum. The split second following the South Tower's impact – when the world suddenly knew what it saw – was wide open. Before the crashing deluge of images, the rush of interpretation, the diagnosis of national trauma and the talk of war, there were two clouds of smoke, the bright blue sky and silence.

3 BUILDINGS MADE FLESH: NOTIONS OF THE UNCANNY AND THE REAL

Seeing the attacks of September 11th 2001 unfold on television news, many viewers reported thinking that what they were seeing was a hoax or a somehow-familiar movie sequence.[1] Long afterwards, the language used to describe the experience of first- or second-hand witnesses indicated that this sense of illusion never quite disappeared – the scenes were so improbable as to appear strangely familiar, smashing the accepted boundaries of lived experience and transgressing into the realm of half-remembered nightmare. In an essay written in 1919, Sigmund Freud writes that there are some occurrences in which 'the distinction between imagination and reality is effaced, and when something that we have hitherto regarded as imaginary appears before us in reality'.[2] The name he gives to this invasion is 'the uncanny': an elusive and mysterious category of feeling whose characteristics pervade the language used to talk about the September 11th attacks from their very first moments. I will argue here that the concept of uncanniness provides a link between the historicizing ideologies in which the visual phenomena of the attacks are implicated and the psychosocial effects of trauma, grief and fear.

For Freud, the concept of the uncanny is a way of accounting for a very particular kind of anxiety. His essay on this subject differs from much of his other writing because it is, in part, a work of literary criticism: with characteristic psychoanalytic depth, he probes not just the minds of patients, but a work of fiction – an 1816 short story by E.T.A. Hoffmann called 'The Sandman' – from which he draws a range of themes that contribute to what might be called a social approach to psychoanalysis. Completed shortly after the end of the First World War, the essay incorporates numerous observations on the nature of anxiety and shock that Freud had perhaps been unable to discuss elsewhere (for example in his studies of so-called shell shock) because they fell beyond the realm of the strictly clinical.[3] He begins laying out his thesis on the uncanny by acknowledging it to be a rare subject area in which psychoanalysis and aesthetics – here taken to mean 'the theory of the qualities of feeling' – overlap.[4] Freud suggests that there is a primitive part of our minds that persists when rationalizing what is beyond our understanding, attaching transcendent or even magical meanings to the things that trouble us because they cannot be classified within our usual symbolic frames of reference. As a theoretical approach to what might be called the aesthetics of anxiety, the concept of the uncanny is uniquely placed to help us understand how images and sensory experiences are linked to the widespread anxiety and trauma surrounding the case of September 11th. Specifically, I will show that this concept, along with that of the Lacanian 'real', which we will come to later, reinforces the link between the ideological readings of September 11th photography that have been presented in the first chapter, and the psychological ones discussed in the second.

Recurring throughout the whole of 'The Uncanny', present on all levels from the narrative details of Hoffmann's story itself to the subtlest of Freud's own descriptive metaphors, are the distinct but related themes of vision and the eyes: there is the phenomenon of the 'evil eye', references to the universal delusion of being watched (which can itself become 'discernible to the physician's eye') and the repeated binary of darkness and light.[5] Beyond all these, though, is the most villainous hallmark of 'the Sandman': that he tears out children's eyes. Freud identifies this immediately as pointing towards the first characteristic of uncanniness: 'the feeling of something uncanny is directly attached to ... the idea of being robbed of one's eyes', or, by association, being forced to look at certain things.[6] He claims that in his psychoanalytic experience, dreams or myths about going blind are related to the fear of castration, and that for children in particular, 'the fear of damaging or losing one's eyes is a terrible one'.[7] The significance of eyes in the story of September 11th – looking, witnessing and spectacle – has already been demonstrated, as has the unusual tendency of the news media at the time, and particularly newspapers, to show photographs of people looking on in horror without actually picturing the scene at which they look (Figure I.1). In such pictures, witnesses can often be seen either covering their mouths as if enacting the unspeakable nature of the sight or covering their eyes as if protecting them from it. Five days after the attacks, *Los Angeles Times* art critic Christopher Knight wrote that the 'eye-popping avalanche' and 'visual overload' of pictures had already been 'burned into our collective consciousness'.[8] Metaphors of the destruction of the public's 'collective' eyes, 'popping' and 'burning', reminiscent of the Sandman story, recall the deep, primitive and apparently universal blindness-anxiety that exists just beyond our conscious minds. Distinct from the specifically traumatizing effect that the images themselves may have had, this amounts to just one level of several on which the events of September 11th can be read as 'uncanny'.

The German word that Freud uses – *unheimlich* – can be literally translated as 'unhomely'. Because of this direct link to ideas of home and domestic space, the concept of the uncanny has played a particular role within theories and discussions of architecture. Most prominently, Anthony Vidler writes that the uncanny 'found its metaphorical home in architecture'. Specifically, he suggests, the uncanniest of all architecture is found in the city, where, 'what was once walled and intimate, the confirmation of community… has been rendered strange by the spatial incursions of modernity'.[9] Cities are, for Vidler, unhomely at the best of times. But, the archetypal modern metropolis has always been New York City, and the archetypal uncanny architecture was the World Trade Center. For almost thirty years, its twin towers dominated the New York City's skyline. To many New Yorkers, the cityscape was unthinkable without them, as towering anchors and symbols of home; iconic, unmistakable and eternal, they put the rest of the city in its place. But, even before they were built, the towers were also widely hated. Not only did they represent a 'spatial incursion' on the existing community of Lower Manhattan by displacing the businesses and homes razed to make space for them, but they were seen by many as inherently alienating on account of their size – so vast that it seemed to bear no conceivable relation to the human bodies that would inhabit them. In 1970, three years before it was to open, architecture critic Lewis Mumford wrote that the World Trade Center was an example of the 'purposeless giantism and technological exhibitionism that are now eviscerating the living tissue of every great city'.[10] But, the truly uncanny destiny of these giant buildings was only fully realized in their destruction.

As if in answer to Mumford's image of living tissue, Susan Sontag writes that 'a cityscape is not made of flesh', but concedes that when catastrophe strikes, 'sheared-off buildings are almost as eloquent as bodies in the street'.[11] She is talking about the long-established photojournalistic tradition of substituting fallen bodies for fallen buildings. Where visceral human destruction is too graphic, too recent or too close to home for news editors to print, rubble has long stood in not just as a displacement, but as a direct metaphor for flesh. It was in the aftermath of September 11th, and particularly in the anthropomorphic fetishization that characterized the twin towers' commemoration, that this convention reached its historic apogee. I offer just three examples. The first is a photograph taken in Paterson, New Jersey, in 2004 by Jonathan Hyman, who has spent years photographing vernacular September 11th memorials in a project published under the title *Landscapes of 9/11*.[12] The photograph shows a polished granite headstone in a grassy cemetery. It appears to occupy a spacious, sunny plot, and some cut flowers have been laid at its base. There is no visible inscription on the stone; instead of any identifying name or dates, there is only the engraved image of the New York City's skyline, with the towers tall and proud in the centre. This is presumably the grave of a victim of the attacks, but the implication is that it is also, at least in part, a memorial to the twin towers themselves. The buildings, like loved human bodies, have been buried in the ground and laid to rest.

Second, on May 30th 2002, a ceremony at Ground Zero marked the end of the eight-and-a-half month clean-up operation with the removal of a 30-foot support girder – the 'last beam' – from the site. This final remnant was shrouded in the stars and stripes, decorated with a funerary wreath and, on the back of a flatbed truck, driven offsite via a route lined by an honour guard. Recalling the traditional burial of the unknown soldier, the symbolic substitution involved in this ceremony was so overt that it might more accurately be called a kind of transubstantiation.[13] In October 2006, Spencer Platt photographed a similar ceremony that was less formal but no less evocative, as the famous 'cross in the rubble' was removed from Ground Zero and taken to its new home outside nearby St. Peter's Church (Figure 3.1). Crowds watched as the steel relic, symbol of both human body and divine redemption, was carefully moved to its final resting place.

In a third example, also photographed by Jonathan Hyman, a sculpture commemorates the deaths of nine parishioners of a Brooklyn church. The memorial takes the form of a bronze figure of Christ, who holds lovingly in his hands a scaled-down replica of the towers, with a fragment from the actual buildings' remains mounted on a stone at his feet.[14] It is interesting to imagine how this memorial gesture, or either of these others, might be read by someone unaware of the towers' destruction in a terrorist attack: Jesus Christ cradling the values of world trade and global capitalism, the things that the buildings used to signify. The intended message is presumably that the lost inhabitants are held forever within the love of God and possibly to associate their suffering with his own. But, we cannot see these victims – only the buildings that both contain them and stand in for them.

Beginning with the work of Marcus Vitruvius, Anthony Vidler has traced the ways in which the form and dimensions of the human body have underpinned architectural theory and practice since the first-century B.C. Leonardo DaVinci's famous illustration of Vitruvius's treatise on architecture (Figure 3.2) shows the ideal male figure, his outstretched limbs contained within the circle and the square, as the measure of perfect geometrical proportion. The implication is that the built environment is at its most beautiful, functional and valuable when it takes its cue from the human body that inhabits it.[15] The twin towers broke these rules in the extreme. They were so vast that not only did they dwarf the human body, but they could not even be accommodated by the embodied human eye. At 110 stories high, the towers could only be apprehended in full from a great distance (a view that featured in many of the thousands of photographs and postcards used in commemorative gestures once they were gone). Up close at ground level, their form was so dramatically foreshortened and distorted that the result was a dizzying, physically felt kind of visual confrontation.

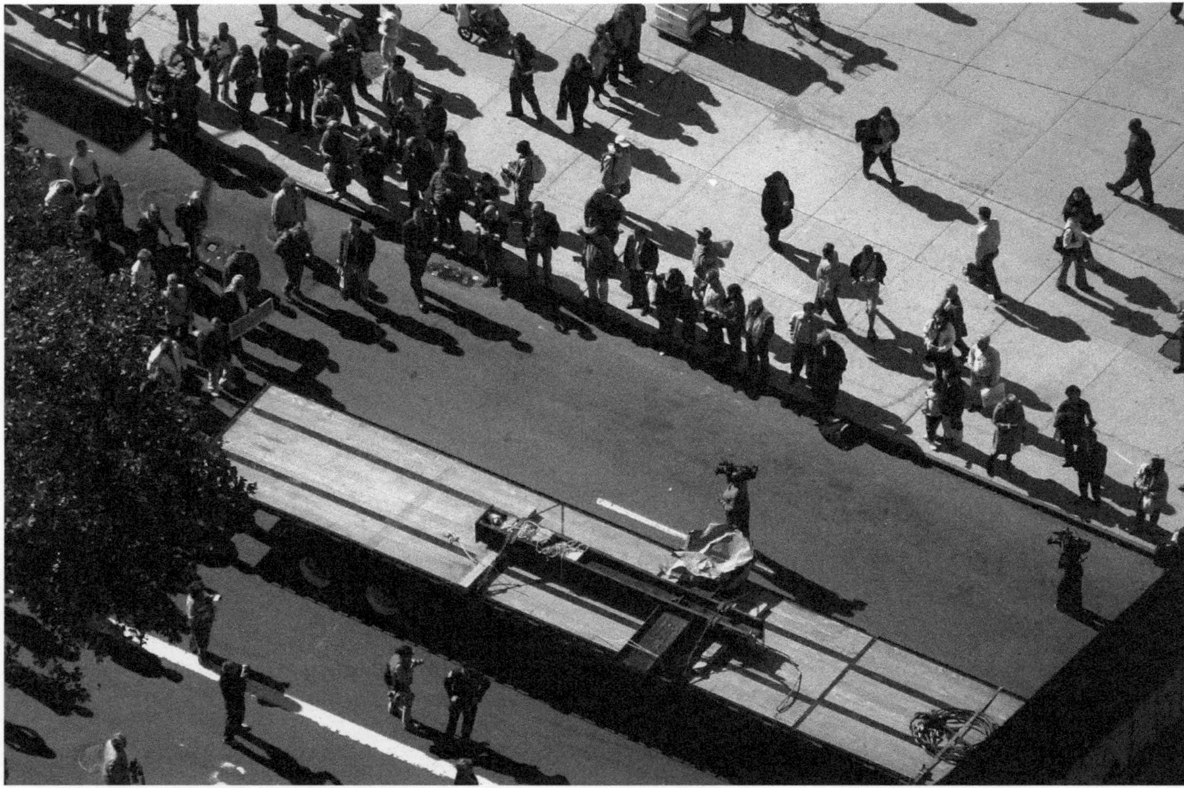

Figure 3.1 Workers move the cross-shaped steel beam that was found in the rubble of the World Trade Center to St. Peter's Church in New York City, October 5th 2006. Photo by Spencer Platt, Getty Images.

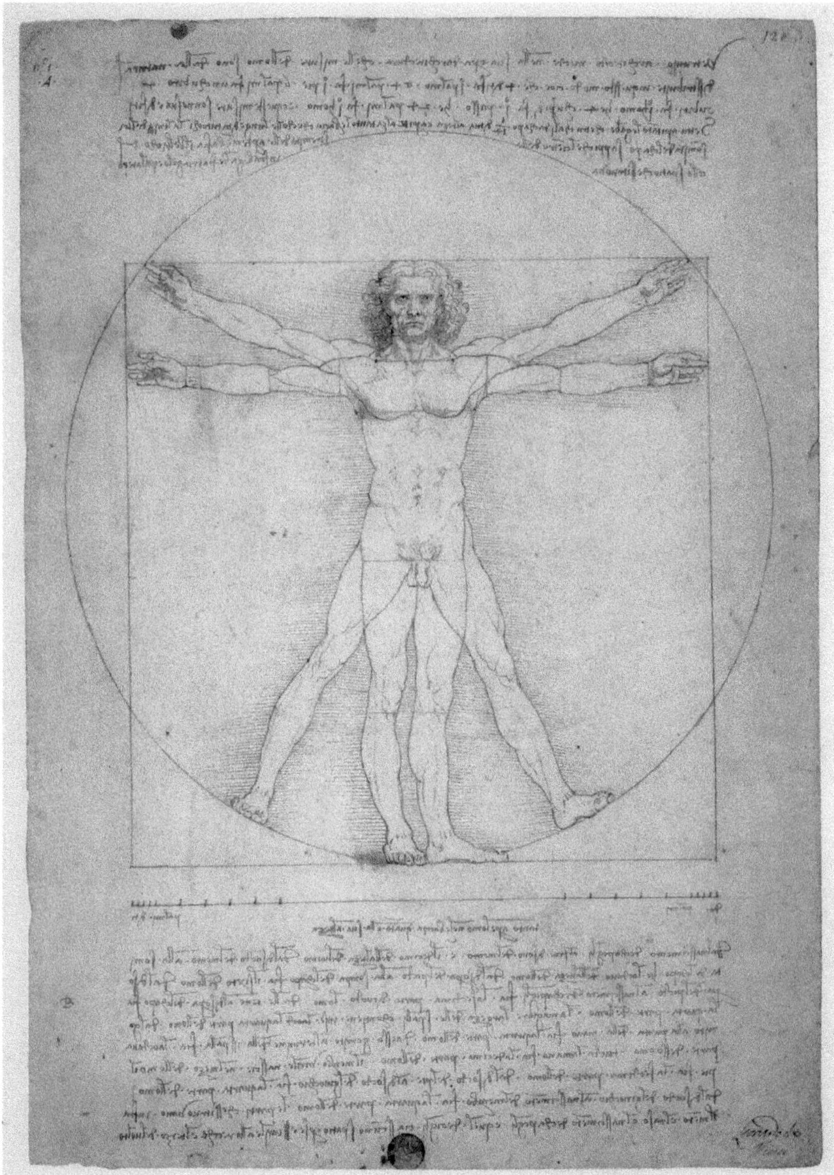

Figure 3.2 *Vitruvian Man* by Leonardo da Vinci, circa 1490. Gallerie dell'Accademia, Venice.

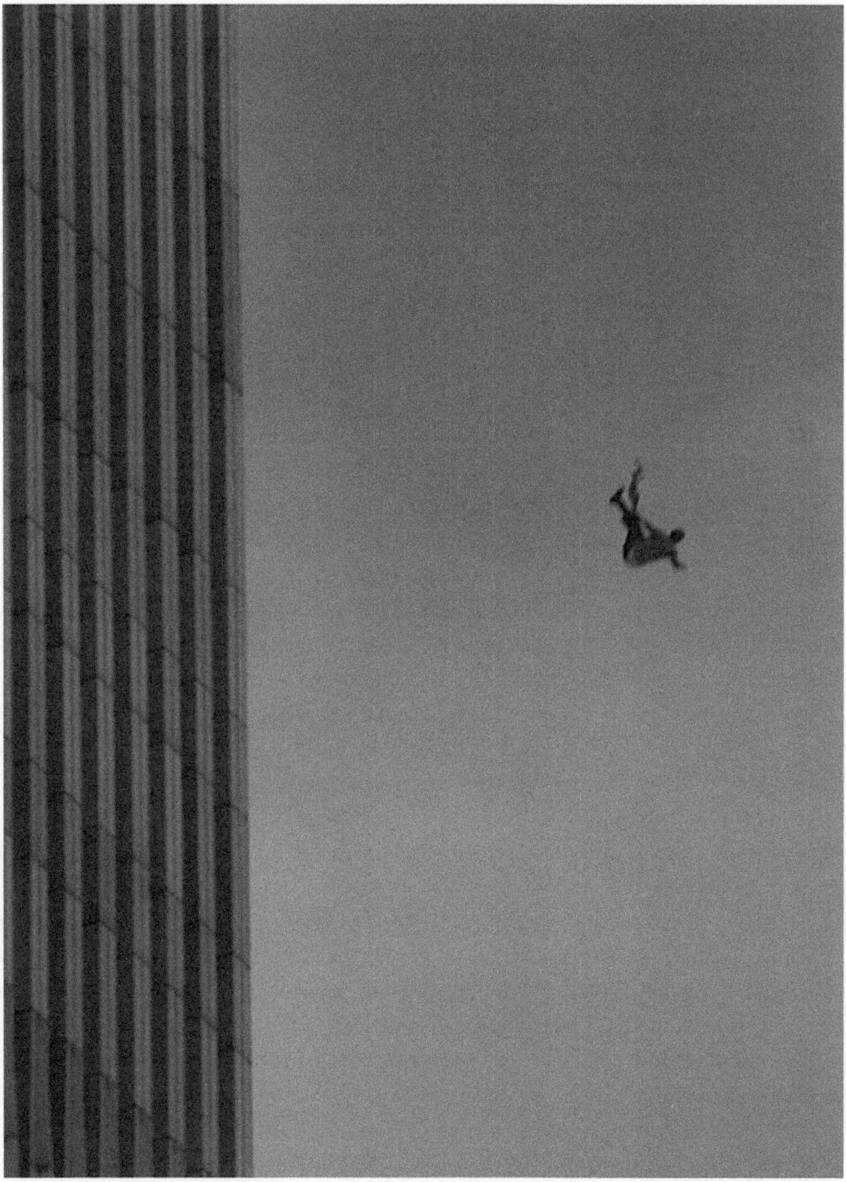

Figure 3.3 A person falls to his death from the World Trade Center, September 11th 2001. Photo by Jose Jimenez, Primera Hora/Getty Images.

As well as in Lyle Oweko's famous *TIME* cover photograph, this is equally and dramatically illustrated in a manner of speaking by another of the most famous September 11th press photographs, Richard Drew's 'Falling Man'. If DaVinci's drawing shows the Vitruvian ideal – the human body inscribed and centred as the organizing principle of the built environment – Drew's picture (and to a lesser extent any number of other photographs showing victims who died by falling, such as Figure 3.3) shows body and building as utterly incompatible. If the photographer had zoomed out far enough to picture the tower in its entirety, the falling figure would be all but invisible. And so, he has had to reduce the building to an abstracted series of Op-Art-style geometric forms that assault and confuse the eye.[16] Vitruvian man is grounded, centred, contained and in harmony. The 'jumper' tumbles through oblivion, dwarfed, lost, ejected and without bearing. He has an equally striking but completely different relationship to the geometry of space. His space has been, to say the least, 'rendered strange'.

Conversely, one of the reasons why 'the cross in the rubble' so captured the imagination of the grieving public may be that it is not, as such, a man-made structure. It is a monument that was not built, but which emerged spontaneously, springing by some mysterious organic process out of the architecture. Ever since it was first built, somewhere within that giant alien edifice this fragment of redemption was waiting to be found – born out of its destruction. And, it is hard to overlook the fact that it was on a perfectly, uncannily, human scale. Platt's photograph of the removal of the cross (Figure 3.1), its own solemn deposition scene, identifies it with any and all of the watching people by exactly aligning their shadows with the angle at which it lies on the flatbed truck. Every person in the crowd is alive, but each carries with them a dark double, cast by the harsh sunlight on the ground: the dead who could have been. The city is full of ghosts, and this cross stands for all of us – sanctification for the dead and for the living, either hope or just *memento mori*.

Another phenomenon in the lexicon of uncanniness that is implicated in readings of the September 11th attacks is the double. The uncanny character of the double, *doppelgänger*, or twin, is traced back by Freud to a primitive impulse of self-preservation and defence against the destruction of the ego. Culturally, for Freud, the common use of twins in literature (and subsequently film and other artistic practices) to signify strangeness or evil is rooted in deeply held desire to maintain a power over death: the 'invention of doubling as a preservation against extinction'.[17] As long as there are two of me, I cannot die. Charting the conception, design process and materialization of the World Trade Center's 'twin towers', Terry Smith sees this primitive logic everywhere at work. He presents the story of the towers as a series of egotistical, capital-focussed overreaches, culminating in the building of not one, but two of the tallest buildings in the world. The objective in making the towers so big was from the beginning, he says, a shameless exercise not in practical function but the arrogant assertion of power.[18] The fact there were two of them was simply a blunt overstatement: 'they seemed to say: "Look, we can do this, and do it twice!" More, "We can do this again, endlessly, all over the world, wherever and whenever we wish!" '[19] From here, Smith argues, it is possible to trace the inevitable and very Freudian trauma that resulted when that 'preservation against extinction' was demolished. Freud says that confidence in the power of the double depends on a kind of childish fantasy, to be outgrown in the course of normal psychological development and life experience:

> Such ideas, however, have sprung from the soil of unbounded self-love, from the primary narcissism which dominates the mind of the child and of primitive man. But when this stage has been surmounted, the 'double' reverses its aspect. From having been an assurance of immortality, it becomes the uncanny harbinger of death.[20]

For the mature and psychologically balanced adult, the double no longer delivers assurance. Instead, it becomes a disturbance and a threat – a *memento mori*. In his account, Smith goes on to quote Joseph B. Juhasz, author of a commentary on Minoru Yamasaki, the towers' architect.[21] Writing in 1994, shortly after the unsuccessful first bombing attempt on the buildings, Juhasz reflects on what he sees as the buildings' inherent alienation of humanity, leading to its inevitable, almost in-built destruction:

> Of course, any 'stability' based on the suppression of open systems becomes an element in a drama which in its own terms must terminate in cataclysm. In an allegorical sense, the vast, twinned doubled ghostly presence of WTC presents a sepulchre from which ghosts will not rise as on the day of cataclysm as the resurrected dead, rather as a tombstone it prophecies the raising of Golems and Zombies.[22]

This is the kind of prophetic insight that, in the common modern usage of the word, is called 'uncanny', particularly, perhaps, in light of Jonathan Hyman's 'tombstone' picture, and the many images that circulated in the darker corners of the internet showing sightings of ghostly faces in the dust-clouds as the towers collapsed.[23]

If a transformation of the implication of 'doubling' from an assurance of immortality to a harbinger of death is part of a natural process of 'growing up', what does that lead us to conclude in the story of the twin towers and their destruction? In Freudian terms, and at a symbolic level, September 11th could be allegorically understood as a stage of psychological development; a kind of reality check, in which confident narcissistic self-love was cut short by the uncanny reminder of mortality and the arrival of fear. But for whom? Not just for the architects or developers of the towers, or even just for the citizens of New York City. Smith, Slavoj Žižek and many others have identified the towers of the World Trade Center as icons; symbols not only of the capitalism and free trade which were their daily business, but, particularly in their destruction, of America's security and power. The symbol that the towers became in their destruction was vastly more potent than that which they had been before. If the burning towers were, to the whole of America, a symbol of newfound vulnerability, mortality and fear, where previously there had been power, exceptionalism and a sense of indestructibility, then the subject of this psychological change should have been a whole nation.

Part of the significance of the double is in its appearance as the first, initial repetition of the same. The troubling force of the double, of the evil *doppelgänger*, for example, lies in its suggestion of all the other possible 'doubles' to come, in their endless repetition. Freud explains,

> in other words, there is a doubling, dividing and interchanging of the self. And finally there is the constant recurrence of the same thing – the repetition of the same features or character-traits or vicissitudes, of the same crimes, or even the same names through several consecutive generations.[24]

And so, the double attack on the double towers signalled a terrifying and endless reign of terror to come. The doubled arrogance of the 'twin towers' did not, in the end, ensure a defence against death. In fact, as I argued in the previous chapter, their 'doubleness' only served to seal the enormity of their destruction by creating the opportunity for a double defeat. Those first-hand witnesses of the first plane's impact may have seen it as a freak accident or a terrible mistake. The first strike came without warning, and so, pictures or footage of it are relatively rare. By and large, those who saw it did so because they were there in person and happened to be looking in the right direction. But, when the *second* plane crashed a *second* time in an almost *identical* way into the *second* tower, the networks' cameras were already in position and rolling, and the hordes of photographers had already made their way downtown. Unintentionally, the world's media was ready and waiting to catch, copy and disseminate the doubled attack that in turn foreshadowed terrorism's indefinite replication. This vague threat was the rationale for a 'homeland security' system that is still, as David Simpson wrote in 2006, 'projecting a war that can never end and a state of alert that can never be given over'.[25]

The uncanny refers to 'what is frightening – to what arouses dread and horror', but, as Freud goes on to say, not all frightening things can be called uncanny: 'one is curious to know what this common core is which allows us to distinguish as "uncanny" certain things which lie within the field of what is frightening.'[26] The conclusion he reaches is that 'the uncanny is that class of the frightening which leads us back to what is known of old and long familiar', and 'we are tempted to conclude that what is "uncanny" is frightening precisely because it is *not* known and familiar.'[27] So, the uncanny seems to represent a tension between the familiar and the unfamiliar: a frightening thing which leads us back to what we know, yet is new and alien in its uncanniness. Many attempts to describe the events of September 11th involved reference to video games or films that had been seen before – one of the most commonly mentioned was the 1996 film *Independence Day* – which were not necessarily traumatizing in themselves (because most viewers can identify them as fiction), but which served as a frame of reference, both for the improbable appearance of the attacks and for their possible implications which in the first instance could only be imagined.[28] In one of many press examples from the earliest days following the attacks, a *Chicago Tribune* article described them as 'surreal' and 'like a toy or a video game', and quoted CBS anchor Dan Rather assuring television viewers, 'this is an actual photograph, not just a graphic made up by us'.[29] In another, from the *New York Times* on 13 September, Michiko Kakutani wrote:

> In a culture besotted with disaster movies, there was an initial sense of déjà vu and disbelief on the part of these spectators – the impulse to see what was happening as one of those digital special effects from the big screen ... It may seem trivialising – even obscene – to talk about movies in the same breath as this week's tragedy, but the fact that so many people did is a symptom of our inability to get our heads around this disaster, our inability to find real-life precedents, real-life analogies for what happened.[30]

In an uncanny encounter, something frightening that has been previously experienced and repressed *recurs*. This, Freud says, happens most commonly in relation to death and dead bodies, or the reappearance of spirits and ghosts.[31] This previously experienced frightening phenomenon is not necessarily a traumatic memory, but is just as likely to be an infantile fear or a 'primitive belief' of some kind.[32] Freud identifies the character of these familiar experiences as not only previous, recurring and anterior in origin, but also as springing from that which is patently imaginary or fictitious, again inviting the association with film:

> an uncanny effect is often and easily produced when the distinction between imagination and reality is effaced, as when something that we have hitherto regarded as imaginary appears before us in reality, or when a symbol takes over the full functions of the thing it symbolizes.[33]

On 13 September, discussion began in the American news media about the converse effect: the impact that the attacks would have on Hollywood, and specifically on upcoming US film releases.[34] Releases postponed on grounds of taste included *Collateral Damage* and *Big Trouble*, which were both identified as being too closely reminiscent of the real events of the previous few days.[35] *Collateral Damage*, due for release on October 5th, was postponed until February 8th 2002, apparently due to its storyline in which an American firefighter sets out on a 'personal battle' against terrorism following the killing of his wife and child. Scenes involving a terrorist plane hijacker were cut altogether, as was one of the film's promotional taglines: 'The war hits home'. In a film like *Collateral Damage*, just as on the real-life streets of New York City, the distinction between imagination and reality had been effaced (to use Freud's terms) to such a disorientating extent that the release of these scenes to the public at such a time was seen to be not only distasteful but irresponsible. Reality and fantasy were so closely aligned that it became unclear which was encroaching on which.

The 'compulsion to repeat' is a phenomenon given much attention by Freud in his work regarding the recovery from traumatic experience.[36] He identifies the uncanny as that which reminds us of this inner compulsion, which is 'powerful enough to overrule the pleasure principle', but at the same time draws us in such a way that the idea of pleasure cannot be fully ruled out.[37] This idea – that a kind of gratification is paradoxically at work in self-destructive behaviour – is later developed by Lacan, who formulates it in a different way, using the term *jouissance*. A complex concept, *jouissance*, refers to, among other things, the capacity of the unconscious mind to experience suffering as a kind of satisfaction.[38] It is the unattainable fulfilment of a drive manifest, for example, in the subject's tendency to return again and again to that which damages him. In fact, Lacan associates it at one point with a sado-masochistic complusion.[39] Given Freud's coupling of the repetitive tendency (later developed by Lacan as *jouissance*) with the uncanny, the repeated images of September 11th – among which we have already identified several registers of uncanniness – thus have yet another connection with it. Slavoj Žižek sums up the connection between this and *jouissance*:

> When, days after September 11 2001, our gaze was transfixed by the images of the plane hitting one of the WTC towers, we were all forced to experience what the 'compulsion to repeat' and *jouissance* beyond the pleasure principle are: we wanted to see it again and again; the same shots were repeated *ad nauseum*, and the uncanny satisfaction we got from it was *jouissance* at its purest.[40]

The need to see and see again was amply met by an endlessly repetitive deluge of photographs. Photographs in which death was everywhere present but invisible: the scene of death, the cause and frame-by-frame process of death, as well as the haunting missing-poster photographs of the smiling but presumed dead. This particular layer of uncanniness is the one Freud calls 'perhaps the most striking of all': 'many people experience the feeling in the highest degree in relation to death and dead bodies, to the return of the dead, and to spirits and ghosts.'[41] Many expressed a need to see again and again even the most disturbing of these pictures, but Žižek offers the troubling explanation that this in fact indicated not a need for confirmation, information or catharsis, but a drive to satisfaction – *jouissance* at its purest. The problem with attempting to make sense of the attacks by referring to disaster movies is that disaster movies are not just frightening, they are enjoyable. They are thrilling, exciting and (usually) ultimately satisfying, which is why audiences pay to consume them. When Žižek and others use the word 'fantasy' to account for these references, they are not just pointing out the evocation of fiction, but of desire. Sure enough, Freud acknowledges early on that his uncanny refers most often not to the outright horrific, but to that which is more uncomfortably, subtly strange – odd coincidences, déjà vu, creeping suspicions and paranoias – and often involves attraction as much as repulsion.

Susannah Radstone has argued that this inflection goes beyond Freud's definition of the uncanny and impacts a Freudian understanding of the traumatic, too:

> While contemporary trauma theory emphasizes the impact of shocking events in the production of psychic disturbance, Freudian-inspired psychoanalysis emphasised (and continues to emphasise), rather, the part played by the conflict that arises from unconscious *fantasy* – perhaps, but not necessarily, prompted by an event – in the emergence of symptoms.[42]

She is arguing here that designating September 11th as a trauma will have distinct implications depending on which definition of trauma you use. This potentially includes the suggestion of fantasy, which, like Lacan's *jouissance*, is always linked in the Freudian schema to sexual difference and desire.[43] Key to some of the more contemporary definitions of trauma explored in the previous chapter is that the victim is passive, put-upon and overwhelmed: this kind of trauma depends on the unimaginable happening to a mind that is totally unprepared. Radstone argues, however, that in a more authentically Freudian understanding of trauma, the victim is, even if only on the very deepest of unconscious levels, actively implicated on account of their fantasies (which may presumably be furnished by cinema). Far from an unexpected shock, this kind of trauma is predicated on the imagined taking place, and the mind being on some level very much prepared. Even more controversially, Radstone then suggests that this confrontation with forbidden fantasy can in fact be what makes some experiences traumatic: 'An event may prove traumatic, indeed, not because of its inherently shocking nature but due to the unbearable or forbidden fantasies that it prompts.'[44] Her understanding of the trauma of September 11th, then, would presumably involve the suggestion that it did not just compel us by reminding us of something we had seen before, but by giving us something that we wanted, and that the recognition of this was too much to bear. An easier interpretation to stomach, perhaps, is in the inherent converse of Radstone's theory: 'an event's traumatic impact may be linked to its *puncturing* of a fantasy that has previously sustained a sense of identity – national as well as individual'.[45] This is precisely the puncturing of national security and identity that I argued for in Chapter 1, and which is at the heart of an uncanny reading of the twin towers' collapse: the fantasy of preservation against death, violently ruptured and denied.

While the events of September 11th can be associated with the uncanny on several significant levels, at the same time, they evoke something beyond it: something more acute and radically destabilizing. There is a certain subtlety to the phenomena that Freud uses to exemplify uncanniness and to the language he uses. A 'feeling of uncanniness', he writes, can be provoked by such things as fictional stories, coincidences, twins, certain kinds of unfamiliarity, uncertainty, strangeness and of course latent desire.[46] But, for those watching the events of September 11th, even at great and mediated distances, this was not just a strange, unsettling or *unheimlich* experience. It was, to use Dominic LaCapra's term, a 'limit-event'.[47] It was not subtle, but it was brutal, violent, explicit and larger-than-life. This undermines any simple reading of it as uncanny. LaCapra explains (using language not unlike Freud's) the notion of the 'limit-event', with reference again to the Holocaust:

> Extremely traumatic series of events beggar the imagination, and such events often involve the literalization of metaphor as one's wildest dreams or most hellish nightmares seem to be realised or even exceeded by brute facts. Such facts go beyond the imagination's powers of representation. Indeed, when things of an unimaginable magnitude actually occur and phantasms seem to run rampant in 'ordinary' reality, what is there for the imagination to do?[48]

Notwithstanding its levels of cinematic prophecy and possible primitive wish-fulfilment, September 11th was still beyond imagination. It was on many levels uncanny, but at the same time, it demands to be understood within the framework of a more forceful notion: that of the Lacanian 'real'. Of Jacques Lacan's three registers of subjectivity – the real, the symbolic and the imaginary orders – the real, reformulated several times in the course of his work, refers broadly to that which resists symbolization.[49] What is ordinarily called 'reality' would, for Lacan, be defined as an amalgam of the symbolic and the imaginary orders, while the order of the real encompasses everything that is excluded from this: the margins of what is without meaning and which we fail to situate. The real lies beyond our symbolic system for naming, categorizing and understanding. A blunt example of this problem is the frequent evocation of film and video games in accounting for September 11th. As frames of reference for such a limit-event, these categories came close, but not close enough. The experience of seeing the attacks was still beyond the scope of the symbolic: it was 'refused in the symbolic order'.[50] A similar principle applies in this case to the widespread usage of the word 'surreal'. The surreal is not a synonym for either the Freudian uncanny or the Lacanian real, but the use of the word by so many people points towards a dimension of this experience that has characteristics in common with both concepts. 'Surreal', in this context, evokes the inexplicable, the dreamlike and that which is beyond understanding or adequate description because it is in excess of reality. It is both a breakdown of and a confirmation of the known. It is also used as a way of avoiding the word 'beautiful', but this we return to later.

The connection between the Freudian uncanny and the Lacanian real is not one of equivalence but of emergence. The uncanny is by no account the same thing as the real but can be understood as the instance of its emergence into the imaginary order as the familiar breaks down. In instances of uncanniness like those explored here, the real emerges unbidden, fractures and disturbs. Mladen Dolar says that it 'spring[s] up at the most awkward times, both as an irruption of the unexpected and with clockwork precision, totally unpredictable and predictable in one.'[51] Lacan's own term for this kind of encounter with the real, however, is the *tuché*, and for him, it is specifically associated with the experience of trauma:

> The function of the tuché, of the real as encounter – the encounter in so far as it may be missed, in so far as it is essentially the missed encounter – first presented itself in the history of psycho-analysis in a form that was in itself already enough to arouse our attention, in trauma. Is it not remarkable that at the origin of the psychoanalytic experience, the real should have presented itself in the form of that which is unassimilable in it – in the form of the trauma.[52]

For Lacan, the traumatic experience is a missed encounter with the real: it is 'the real that eludes us'.[53] Like the traumatic memory, the traumatic experience cannot be represented: only repeated. And so, at each juncture and level on which September 11th invites the interpretation of uncanniness, we are confronted with the ungraspable, unnameable devastation of the real. But, at each of these points, we also miss it. And, this is perhaps the true root of our trauma.

As we have seen, for the American culture industry and the systems of its administration, these qualities – the ungraspable, the unnameable, the unassimilable (or, recalling the words of Donald Rumsfeld, the 'unknown unknowns') – could not be tolerated. A system of naming and identification had to be found: a framing ideology to account for the uncanny, which was too close to pleasure, and the real, which was outside all capacity for representation, let alone redemption. This ideology, as we saw in Chapter 1, took on various guises, but the one that could do the best job of laying the uncanny to rest was religion.

The prevalence of religious iconography throughout the media's representation of September 11th cannot be ignored. From the mysterious 'cross in the rubble' to more subtle and apparently unintentional formal references to Western Christian art that crop up in many of the most widely reproduced photographs, a transcendental, redemptive interpretation of the attacks can be read into their visual character at almost every stage. Long before the substitution of bodies with other transubstantiative symbols became a photojournalistic convention, it was a religious doctrine: the sacrament of Holy Communion predicated on the substitution of Christ's body and blood with bread and wine. This is the gesture by which the faithful celebrate the ultimate redemption of suffering and accounting for sin. Its message, on which the whole of Christian theology rests, is that Christ's violent death has a meaning in which all can share, and which points towards hope and salvation. To use another term of Dominick LaCapra's, this is the ultimate 'redemptive narrative' – a system of meaning which, whether or not we ascribe to it within its religious context, we must be careful not to transfer to other realms where it represents too easy a resolution of the irredeemable.[54] LaCapra argues that while the construction of basic factual narrative is an integral part of working through and moving forward after a limit-event, there are types of narrative that can have the opposite effect. 'Redemptive' or 'totalizing' narratives are those that attempt to construct a system of meaning around catastrophic events in which all details are accounted for under a glorifying, hopeful or moral framework. Redemptive narratives fit into an Adornian system of public 'infantilization' because they are comforting but false. LaCapra is writing with particular reference to the Holocaust, but a simple example of this tendency within the context of September 11th is the declaration that its victims did not die in vain. Just as it is perfectly possible to have respect for the memory of these people without resorting to the assertion that they are 'heroes', it is important not to indulge ourselves by ascribing a higher meaning to their deaths. Most died horrible, ignoble and utterly senseless deaths, and to claim otherwise is not only fantastical, but unethical and symptomatic of the wider system of simplistic ideological narratives (of patriotism, good and evil, etc.) put forward by the Bush administration at the time and carried forward by large sections of the media. Ulrich Baer, also writing about the Holocaust, says that 'any restorative narrative of good overcoming evil, of the triumph of the human spirit … in short, the culture industry's redemptive version of the Holocaust – would amount to "false witnessing" '.[55] The parallels are clear.

Consistent with the form in which almost all information about September 11th was disseminated, the message of the event's religious redemption has been most effectively transmitted not in words but in images. Susan Sontag has remarked in general terms that the spectacular is intrinsically implicated in the religious narratives through which Western viewers have learned to understand suffering. In other words, photographers do not need to make deliberate reference to Christian iconography in order for their images of catastrophe to be read in this way, because this interpretation is already there in our consciousness.[56] Sometimes, though, the association is made explicit. The most well-known example of this in the case of September 11th was the immediate labelling of a photograph by Shannon Stapleton of the body of Father Mychal Judge as 'The Ground Zero Pietà'. The picture shows Judge, a Franciscan friar, Catholic priest and fire house chaplain, being carried unconscious on a metal chair by three uniformed men and two civilians, having become the first certified casualty of the Ground Zero attack. The group emerges through a cloud of dust that obscures their surroundings, framed with a compositional skill that we recognize because we have been primed to do so by centuries of religious art, and specifically the topos of the Christian Pietà. Even though this image breaks with American photojournalistic convention by showing a dead body (or one very close to death), the distress of this is counterbalanced both by its religious echo and by the altruism, determination and unity of the men bearing Father Judge's body. It is also made more palatable (in the editorial sense discussed in Chapter 1) by the fact that none of his injuries are visible. The religious resonance of the image is made more forceful, of course, by the fact that the victim is a priest, and this fact might also explain to a large extent why it was so quickly given an overtly religious caption, but there is perhaps no better example of the compulsion to use photography as a means of organizing chaos and rationalizing hopelessness. As Robert Hariman and John Louis Lucaites write, 'the religious metaphor in the label "icon" works because of how, by staring into the image, one senses a higher power unfolding and is lifted up into awe, reaffirmed in one's relationship to that power, and moved to act accordingly'.[57] For them, the uplifting effect of 'awe' is what secures the place of such images in the public imagination. I argue that in this particular image, and in others, a more prosaic effect of direct interpretation is also at play: the reading of a redemptive narrative that comes straight from religious doctrine, explicitly aligning the death of Christ with the dead of Ground Zero.

From among Jonathan Hyman's body of work depicting vernacular September 11th commemorations across America, there is a particular set of memorial symbols that brings together the iconography of the twin towers, bodies and religious redemption in a different and most literal way. In the two examples of Hyman's work discussed earlier, buildings have been turned symbolically into bodies: marked on a gravestone as if buried in the ground and held in the arms of Christ in the place of the human victims. But, within the visual language of commemorative tattoos, the places are reversed, as bodies instead bear the symbol of the buildings, inscribed on the skin of those left behind. In his travels, Hyman has photographed many such tattoos, observing that, within the wider history of tattooing in American culture, they are as much about identification and belonging as memorializing, and that submission to the physical pain of their inscription is

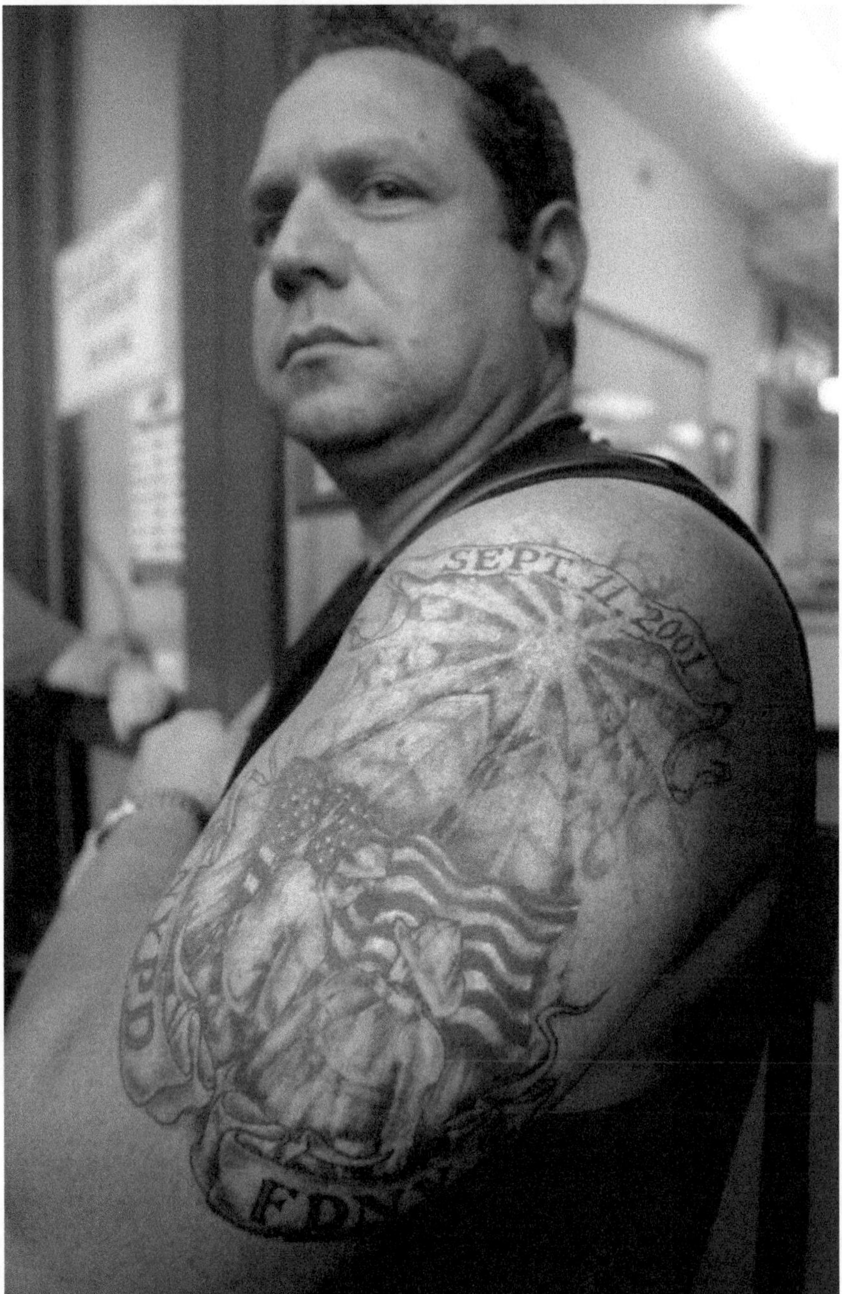

Figure 3.4 Seattle Police officer Steve Borkan displays his September 11th memorial tattoo near Ground Zero prior to the official memorial ceremony, 11 September 2002. Photo by Mario Tama, Getty Images.

often an important part of their symbolism.[58] One such tattoo (a typical example, photographed by Mario Tama, Figure 3.4), on the arm of Seattle police officer Steve Borkan, places the twin towers within the narratives of both religious redemption and military heroism. At the base are two uniformed figures – a NYPD officer and a firefighter – and a banner of stars and stripes, above which the dramatically foreshortened towers rise, framed by billowing clouds and rays of light. As Hyman puts it, in this and many similar tattoos and murals, 'the towers do something many desire for themselves in the moment of death. They go to heaven'.[59] Not only has the symbolic history and meaning of the buildings been utterly transformed, but their scale, too. No longer alienating giants, they are now visually contained within the scrolling inscription typical of tattoo iconography and arranged in harmony with the beams of benevolent heavenly light. The unhomely towers have been redeemed, inscribed on the skin as a sacrificial act of solidarity, a badge of honour, and a living, breathing memorial. By the appropriation of imagery, the flesh speaks its trauma.

The experience of seeing September 11th happen (specifically on television at the time, but also later, in still and moving images) corresponds with Freud's conception of the uncanny in at least four significant ways: it was the invasion of reality by fantasy; it was the return of the uncannily familiar from past cinematic 'experience'; it involved the element of repetition on several levels; and it was fundamentally a function of vision. Paradoxically, however, while the experience did involve the recurrence of the familiar, its smashing of familiar frames of reference and its magnitude also associate it with an emergence of the Lacanian order of the real, beyond integration or categorization. Lacan describes such an 'irruption' in the subject's psyche as

> a sudden emergence of a total strangeness that will progressively bring on a radical submersion of all his categories to the point of forcing him into a veritable reshaping of his world... A requirement of the symbolic order, through being able to be integrated into what has already been put into play in the dialectical movement on which the subject has lived, brings about a serial disintegration, a removal of the woof from the tapestry.[60]

Lacan is describing the destabilizing of the self that can result from an irruption of the real, and the overwhelming need to find resolution for this. The terms he uses – the 'radical submersion of categories', the 'reshaping' of the subject's world and the 'serial disintegration' or 'removal of the woof from the tapestry' – all align with testimonies of post–September 11th trauma commonly recounted in the press and elsewhere. One of the necessary patterns by which traumatized individuals and groups attempted to reshape their world was through gradual and varied processes of mourning. This we will come back to in subsequent chapters. But, this limit-event was so extreme that even before mourning could begin, its uncanniness had to be accounted for within the public imagination. Even in more ordinary historical circumstances, write Hariman and Lucaites, exponential increases in information availability mean that 'public memory becomes organized around a very few quasi-religious images' which can reflect 'either a scarcity of images or the reverse: an overabundance that has to be ignored if one is to function at all'.[61] Again, for them, the implications of the 'quasi-religious' are more generalized, meaning a kind of formal or aesthetic transcendence rather than an interpretive framework in which these images might be read. But, the effect is still, as they argue, a defence against the intolerable.

Ideology, such as that implicated in the misuse of religious doctrine, is very often constituted by the attempt to explain away the uncanny, which Freud says is in the first place a means of accounting for what our primitive psyches have repressed and cannot confront. Mladen Dolar explains:

> The uncanny is always at stake in ideology – ideology perhaps basically consists of a social attempt to integrate the uncanny, to make it bearable, to assign it a place, and the criticism of ideology is caught in the same framework if it tries to reduce it to another kind of content or to make the content conscious and explicit.[62]

But, this aim is both unrealistic – being, after all, an ideology – and impossible. The critical analysis of such ideology, though, as Dolar argues, must be open to the same accusation as it in turn tries to 'explain away' the uncanny not by invoking further ideology, but by ideology's concrete or 'truthful' unmasking. In tackling the questions of how people in the United States, prompted, directed and informed by the powers of government and media, have dealt with their uncanny *memento mori* and their fear; how their psyches may have been injured; and the nature of the mourning that has ensued, we must try to avoid such reductive conclusions. Like the uncanny, there is a limit to the full interpretation of ideology, too. That is why psychoanalysis, balancing as it does the project of interpretation with a respect for the subjective and inscrutable nature of human behaviour, recurs as the most appropriate framework for considering the causes and effects of both. There is no getting away from the fact that psychoanalysis has somewhat fallen from favour in the past few decades on both the therapeutic, clinical level, and that of its higher, more conceptual or societal application. If both Freud and Lacan have been superseded, why return to their accounts of psychoanalysis? The first answer is that it is the territory of trauma: in the mediated presentation of September 11th, the visual came before the verbal, and this temporal disintegration corresponds to the structure of traumatic experience itself. Only psychoanalysis provides the language for this. The more fundamental reason, though, is that psychoanalysis is the only adequate response to the web of political manipulations involved. It is the only discourse that can begin to address the full impact of the full range of factors operating in this process, from the moment of the trauma, to the misuse of images, to the damage of individual psyches, to the devastation of countries, and back again. Because the truly shattering impact of September 11th was not how many people it killed or how much physical destruction it caused, but how it was understood. The real damage was done, as in all acts of terrorism, not on the ground or in the sky but in the psyche. Everything that has been done since, in the name of retribution on the one hand or commemoration on the other, has been done on the basis of its *interpretation*: its reading and analysis. To unravel the web of cause and effect that has sprawled outwards from that moment, the psyche is the starting point.

4 RECLAIMING THE IMAGERY THAT HAUNTED US: RECOVERY, COMMUNITY AND REMEMBRANCE

Even before the towers had come down, the hunger for photographs was voracious. Across America and far beyond, people trawled breaking news reports trying to build up a clearer picture of the sequence of events, gradually filling in the blanks of disbelief and passing rumour. Then, detailed illustrated newspaper and magazine editions appeared, with special supplements devoted to photographic accounts of what it was 'really like' and what 'really happened'. Photographs seemed to offer the best hope of grasping the truth, just as, through the hundreds of 'missing' posters displayed throughout the streets of Manhattan, friends and relatives searched, mostly in vain, for hope of life. Then, gradually, people began to respond with their own photographic gestures of various kinds, by taking pictures or appropriating those made by others and attaching new contexts and meanings to them. As well as being visual objects that offered a cathartic encounter with the moment, and documents of what had taken place, photographs came to take on a further complex role, as vehicles for self-expression: focal points around which communities could gather and begin to rebuild.

As the language of trauma had characterized so much of the public discourse around the event in its early aftermath, so the term 'bearing witness' began also to gain currency as a kind of self-evident truism, particularly in connection with photography. It became clear that 'witnessing' involved more than just passive seeing: in many cases going far beyond this into elaborate ritual acts of collection, display, ownership, interpretation and sharing. Photographs were brought together in memorial projects that prioritized independence, non-partisanship and the personal rather than the political. A co-curator of probably the most famous of these projects, *Here is New York: A Democracy of Photographs*, describes his motivation: 'in order to come to grips with all of the imagery that was haunting us, it was essential, we thought, to reclaim it from the media and stare at it without flinching.'[1] Barbie Zelizer suggests that such collective photographic movements are a typical response to public trauma and have existed in one form or another for almost as long as photography itself: 'photography, and the ritual practices it involves, helps individuals establish moral accountability in a way that helps them move on, and in so doing they reinstate the collective after traumatic events temporarily shatter its boundaries.'[2] Collective recovery from traumatic public events begins with the individual making sense of what has happened with respect to their own personal identity. Then, the scope of this process widens as the individuals connect with one another and that identity becomes shared. Photography so often plays a role at this point because photographs allow others to see what we have seen, even through someone else's camera. The centrality of photographs in individual and collective attempts to come to terms with the events of September 11th is clear even before we begin to discuss these projects in any detail. What is more complicated, though, is the question of how such uses of photographs by individuals might fit within the historicizing ideologies that pervaded the more formal public photographic record. How does the dominance of 'public memory', and specifically the struggle to subsume the intolerable uncanniness of this event, affect the task faced by individuals as they negotiate their personal memories? In light of the power of these historicizing ideologies, is any truly autonomous photographic gesture really possible?

Figure 4.1 shows a blurred and indistinct view of the Manhattan skyline following the collapse of the World Trade Center. To the right, we see fingers holding up a Polaroid print of the burning towers just after they were hit. The two images, the smaller one superimposed on to the larger, make up a kind of 'before and after' view. The scene in the background shows the absence of the towers that stood in this spot when the Polaroid picture was taken. This is one of the thousands of pictures submitted by members of the public to *Here is New York*, an open-submission photography exhibition organized in the weeks after September 11th in a small shop-front at 166 Prince Street in Manhattan, and it represents in a particularly potent way the logic and meaning of the project as a whole. The Polaroid print is much more distinct and clearly focussed than the larger, background one, and is held by a hand – presumably the hand that took it. For many people, the experience of that time was chaotic, hazy and difficult to grasp. But photographs are easier to grasp, both physically and psychologically. And so, the holding and collecting of photographs became essential. As well as providing a space for self-expression and allowing images to be viewed in privacy and stillness at the viewer's own pace, individual or public collections of photographs provide the additional function of ownership, offering people the means to gather their experiences in discrete collections, hold them in their hands (or hard drives) and put a name to them. This sense of ownership and agency, the logic goes, contributes to the

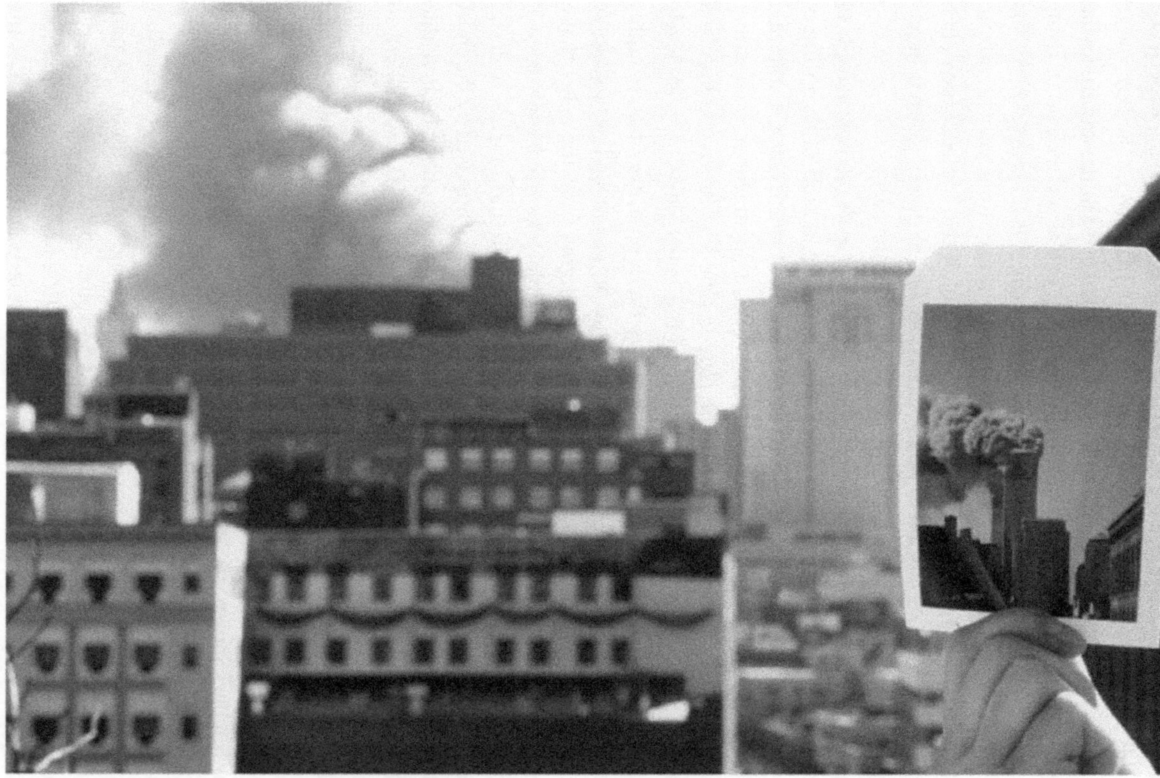

Figure 4.1 Hand holding a Polaroid photograph of the burning World Trade Center against the New York skyline, September 11th 2001. Photo by unknown photographer, *Here is New York* archive.

healing process. Many witnesses have talked in a personal way about grasping the event through photographs, saying that looking through many images was a constructive way of processing and integrating what was happening at that time. If photography is an attempt to gain power over the world – if it is, in the words of Susan Sontag, 'a defence against anxiety, and … a way of certifying experience' – then this particular photograph enacts a doubling of that effect.[3] The Polaroid in the hand was taken at an earlier time, and it holds the key to understanding what is going on in the 'present' of the rest of the image. It explains the cloud of rising dust, telling the story of what was there before and why it is no longer there. The picture is an attempt to hold back the overwhelming tide of time: very literally to 'get to grips' with what is happening, stage by stage. But, it also conflates the stages, collapsing them into one instant of hopelessness. As well as power, death is here – suspended simultaneously in the future, the present and the past.

Displayed in the small Prince Street exhibition space with many hundreds of others, this picture stood as a document of a document, a kind of recording of one person's confused journey through the events. Like the title of the exhibition itself, it says, 'Look, here is what we have seen. We must document and remember it.' The implicit evidentiary function of the *Here is New York* project, epitomized by this particular photograph but applicable to the entire collection, is closely connected to its subsequent form and status as the largest ever photographic archive dedicated to a single event. Allan Sekula has argued that all photographic practice involves an intrinsic 'archival ambition', springing from the belief that a collection of photographs of a subject represents reliable, possessed knowledge of the truth of that subject.[4] 'Archival projects typically manifest a compulsive desire for completeness,' he writes, 'a faith in an ultimate coherence imposed by the sheer quantity of acquisitions.'[5] *Here is New York* has become a vast public archive that identifies itself as such, but this archival ambition or impulse is also evident in countless other individual and shared memorial projects where the collection and display of photographs represents a desire for coherence, completeness and truth. The group of photo editors and photographers who conceived *Here is New York* associate this ideal of collective or collected truth directly with democracy. Curator Michael Shulan, again, explains:

> The guiding principle of *Here is New York* is simple: if one photograph tells a story, thousands of photographs not only tell thousands of stories but perhaps begin to tell *the* story if they are allowed to speak for themselves, to each other, and to the viewer directly – not framed either by glass, metal or wood, or by preconception or editorial comment. In the political sphere it is the principle, after all, which America's Founding Fathers advanced when they developed the notion of democracy – that wisdom lies not in the vision and will of any one individual, or small group of individuals, but in the collective vision of us all.[6]

In this distinctly American vision of democracy, in which collective vision goes hand in hand with resolute autonomy and individualism, the specific presentation of the photographs – naked and 'unmediated' – is of central significance. Exhibited in the shop-front space as uniform, equally sized inkjet prints hung from wires by bulldog clips, their unframing is ideological as well as literal. This is a direct gesture of resistance against the metanarratives that so quickly came to characterize the wider public record of September 11th. There is an attempt to seize a kind of power over the events by photographing and containing them in pictures, but this mastery, and the authority claimed by the exhibition as a whole, is emotional rather than political or ideological. Behind each of these pictures is a personal narrative, not a master narrative.

Margaret Olin has considered this distinction, saying that the exhibition raised a broader question about narratives within American consciousness at that time. Writing about the ideas of 'democracy' and 'levelling' that were prioritized in the project, she says that 'the prenarrative confusion out of which its levelling occurred was partly responsible for the bewildering effect of the exhibition … as though a new society were born out of the destruction. Yet a narrative existed, because the visitors all knew it.'[7] The curators' strategy of affording equal prominence to all views, and the deliberate resistance to narrative coherence, led, unsurprisingly, to an overwhelming confusion of visual information, which notably did not involve words. Seemingly, in order to intensify the confrontation between images and viewers, the refusal to display any captions alongside the photographs was another gesture designed to leave the images unframed, open to autonomous interpretation and response. It is possible, though, that this simply amounted to same kind of debilitating image overload that was being presented by the media. As previously discussed, words were sidelined there too, with the effect of disabling critical engagement and predetermining public interpretation in some dangerous ways. In the case of *Here is New York*, the intention was exactly the opposite of this, and yet, as Olin says, the narrative of which its participants and viewers were all too aware was effectively washed over with an incoherent spectacle that may have done more harm than good. Olin also points out that while most of the photographs in the exhibition were submitted by 'ordinary people', many were also the work of professional photographers and had already appeared in newspapers – or, more to the point perhaps, looked very much like those that had appeared. How, then, was this exhibition so different from 'the media' that it sought to resist? The fact is, perhaps, that the aggregate picture presented by the mainstream media was so all-consuming that there were no points of view left for individuals to claim as their own. Most interestingly of all, for a project that was hailed as so open and democratic, in which no photographer's work was supposedly turned away, and where we might therefore have expected to see a range of imagery from which the press shied away – namely that of the injured and dead – exactly the same narrow categories and omissions can be observed here as in the nation's newspapers and illustrated magazines. As Olin asks, if this is a 'democracy', then what are we voting on? And, if all these images represented some kind of consensus of truth, where were the dissenting voices?

How can we account for the paradox of this project's absolutely democratic, individual resistance to institutional control, and its apparently total adherence to the norms of those institutions? Michel Foucault writes:

> I'd like to underline the fact that the state's power (and that's one of the reasons for its strength) is both an individualizing and a totalizing form of power. Never, I think, in the history of human societies ... has there been such a tricky combination in the same political structures of individualization techniques and of totalization procedures.[8]

His answer is the same as that observed in Chapter 1: in a modern society such as ours, power is not enforced from above but circulates in such a way that individuals come to internalize it and adhere to its priorities voluntarily, whether they are picture editors at major regional newspaper desks, amateur photographers or neither of these. In each case, the wide-open space for individual expression (or discretion) is countered by a totalizing power that makes any choice a predetermined one. On this point, he is in agreement with Adorno: the individual is free to decide but is made unaware of the narrowness of options from which they choose. Foucault stops short of using the term 'illusion' (which is rooted in the Marxist tradition that he aims, unlike Adorno, so fundamentally to resist), but in the process he describes there is certainly a kind of magic trick at work:

> I don't think that we should consider the 'modern state' as an entity that was developed above individuals, ignoring what they are and even their very existence, but, on the contrary, as a very sophisticated structure in which individuals can be integrated, under one condition: that this individuality would be shaped in a new form, and submitted to a set of very specific patterns.[9]

In his own discussion of the paradox of control through individualism – whereby 'the need which might resist central control has already been suppressed by the control of the individual consciousness' – Adorno is more concerned than Foucault with the issue of consumption.[10] This, then, brings us to consider what happened when *Here is New York*, at first a free and public platform, was transformed into a saleable commodity. The exhibition's companion publication appeared a year after the attacks: 864 pages long, containing 868 of the more than 5,000 images originally submitted by 3,000 photographers; the creators of the book state that it is edited not to show the 'best' or the 'strongest', but to give a representative sense of the collection. The book's (now defunct) website also claimed that it is 'the most comprehensive record of the events'.[11] The rather disorientating effect of leafing through this book even briefly is the result of the editors' conscious attempt to recreate an experience not only of seeing the exhibition, but of being in New York at the time of the attack. According to the editorial commentary, the photographs are so numerous because this is the best way of approximating a sensory experience of 'being there'. The book offers the opportunity to own something of this experience: to hold it in one's hands, bound in a heavy, solid volume that also comes, as if to emphasize the ideals of possession and containment, in its own box.

In discussing the challenges involved in reproducing a photographic archive in the form of a book, Allan Sekula says that there are two conventional approaches available to an editor. The first is to present the photographs as historical documents: a transparent means to positivist knowledge. The photographs in this case are seen not as an interpretation of history, but as its direct representation: documents of immutable truth.[12] The type of history presented in this approach is a kind of pictorial spectacle-history through which the viewer is invited to trust the camera above any other historical apparatus or testimony. The criterion of truth here is not logical argument, but transparent experience, as the viewer's gaze is guided to focus on the emotive and the experiential as an irrefutable explanation of history, no matter how aesthetically striking the pictures themselves may be. This is the category into which, for example, Joel Meyerowitz's *Aftermath* squarely fits. The second approach is to present photographs consciously as aesthetic objects, as ends in themselves, or artworks, valued not for their transparency but their subjectivity. The removal of the images from their initial archival context is part of what invites the viewer to this kind of interpretation of an image. *Here is New York* is a case in point of the difficulty, faced by anyone responsible for presenting an archive in published form, of choosing between these two approaches. The book is visually arresting, lavishly produced and expensive to buy. Many of the images are aesthetically accomplished, well composed and atmospheric (recalling many witnesses' description of the event as being 'movie-like'). For several years after its publication, individual prints continued to be available, just as they were throughout the run of the original exhibition, to buy for a profit to be donated to charity.[13] With this end in mind, many of the images were manipulated using Photoshop, and the mix of sources – professional, amateur, high-tech camera, disposable camera, camera-phone – are all tidily conformed to the same format, colour-corrected and uniformly printed. All this gives the impression, despite the quite overwhelming force of the photographs' content, of a product created for coherent aesthetic effect and intended to be a commodity in a commercial transaction.

Shulan writes that *Here is New York* was 'not an art exhibition in the conventional sense – partly an impromptu memorial, partly a rescue effort and partly a testimonial of support for those who were actually doing the rescuing – it became a rallying point for the neighbourhood and the community at large'.[14]

This last point was the basis for another exhibition-turned-commemorative book, created by Wall Street executive, SoHo resident and amateur photographer Michael Feldschuh. The motivation for *The September 11 Photo Project* was the preservation of the many ephemeral shrine-like creations that were, by 20 September, otherwise being destroyed by the elements or removed from the streets by the New York authorities. To allow them to be safely displayed and seen, Feldschuh created an exhibition space that was designed 'to capture the essence' of these thousands of ad-hoc memorials.[15] It opened on October 13th 2001 at 26 Wooster Street, a large gallery close to Ground Zero. Material was displayed using very similar means to those of the *Here is New York* exhibition, but this time using original prints and written documents rather than scanned versions. The overall impression of *The September 11 Photo Project* exhibition was thus somewhat more eclectic, with a strong emphasis on inclusiveness. As in *Here is New York*, the curators insisted that 'no submission is better or worse than any other'.[16] The exhibited material, comprising both photography and other matter such as drawings and hand-written notes, was grouped by contributor rather than theme or chronology and presented as a seamless series. Nothing in the exhibition was for sale, though the accompanying commemorative book was.[17] The book reflects the exhibition's style, with full-page reproductions of photographs and handwritten papers, as well as installation views. Contributors' own captions and personal statements are included, such as 'I took this photograph in SoHo on West Broadway shortly after the second tower collapsed. The thing that strikes me now is the very different, immediate reactions to the disaster: horror and disbelief, and panic.'[18] The aim of *The September 11 Photo Project* was to give prominence to the kind of personal point of view that would otherwise have been invisible or literally swept away. For Feldschuh and the exhibition's organizers (in common, again, with those of *Here is New York*), the inherent value of such points of view is taken to be self-evident. In contrast to the work of the celebrated 'hero-photographer', this material belongs to the specifically twenty-first-century category of user-generated content, carrying the assumption that each person's subjectivity counts and is of interest. In this context, however, the material carries the additional stated weight of witness-bearing and contributing to the healing process. Both showing (of contributed content) and seeing (by visitors) were perceived to be essential aspects of this process, as was the exhibition's policy of making sure that no voice was stifled, and no individual denied the opportunity to benefit from the project's therapeutic effect:

> When a human being is confronted with pure evil, sometimes the only course of action is to bear witness. From the first moments of the attacks on September 11, people felt compelled to start recording what they saw and thought ... No one person can completely understand the events and implications of that day, but through a collective eye, the views of many may lead to a new understanding for all.[19]

As well as the ideas of Foucault and Adorno regarding the illusion of free individual expression, the concept of collective memory is key to understanding the role of projects like this one and *Here is New York*. Sontag's warning that there is no such thing – only collective instruction – should be borne in mind when considering the seeming autonomy of such projects, which is convincing, especially given the inclusion of apparently anti-establishment messages of pacifism (and, notably, identification with the suffering Afghan population[20]). But, as collections of material like this come to be exhibited and preserved in museums and other institutions, becoming public archives charged with the function of reminding, the ultimate effect is always about more than just memory.

For Foucault, power is fluid and participatory, permeating society via a network by which each individual is always both its subject and its object in different ways and in different contexts. Everyone is subject to 'power/knowledge', even those who are ostensibly the most powerful members of a society. Power is, essentially, not a commodity to be borne or wielded by any distinct person or group: it is productive, discursive and relational. This picture of the circulation of power contradicts the notion that the dissemination of ideas after September 11th (or any other event in the public eye) constitutes a 'top-down' ideological exercise imposed upon a population lacking any agency of its own. Even the largest broadcast and print media corporations are implicated in complex flows of power that defy their traditional one-way models of communication. But, the apparatus that embodies Foucault's vision more perfectly than any other, founded on the principles of counter-hegemonic, horizontal, relational, multi-directional information streams, is of course the 'net'.[21] In what could be taken as a direct riposte to Adorno, or indeed Marx, whose theory of ideology states that the powerful minority within a society imposes upon its subjects a false image of reality that is contrary to their interests and must be exposed as such, Foucault explains that 'power is not to be taken as a phenomenon of one individual's consolidated and homogenous domination over others, or that of one group or class over others'.[22] For him, the exertion of power is much more subtle and complex. His theory accounts much better for a society whose mechanisms of influence are epitomized by the circulation, ubiquity and individuating power of the World Wide Web. Of course, this formulation and Adorno's are not mutually exclusive: a crucial factor shared by both is the centrality of a carefully cultivated illusion of individuality or 'individualization' which also, in ways that neither of them could have anticipated, lies at the heart of twenty-first-century digital life.

Out of the unprecedented demands that the September 11th attacks placed on online news platforms, whole new ways of reporting and accessing information were forged. In the first instance, many of the major news websites crashed due to overwhelming traffic, and those that stayed online did not necessarily have answers to the questions of what had happened, why or how. So, people turned instead to eyewitness blogs, forums and message boards. Local blogs were particularly important in providing links to independent journalistic sources and information pages that might otherwise have been inaccessible or difficult to find, acting as portals that were uniquely placed to link communities together. Media theorist Stuart Allan writes that this was a critical moment from which members of the public were encouraged to 'be the media' in a new 'collective form of collaborative newsgathering' that was consistent with the ethos of the World Wide Web as cooperative, flexible and dynamic.[23] In the 'patriotic frenzy' following the attacks, he says, it was also online that voices of dissent – militant, pacifist or simply sceptical – could most clearly be heard. Overall, Allan argues, vernacular uses of the internet in response to this event disrupted the power relations by which the media has conventionally been governed.[24] Over subsequent years, a number of other high-profile violent events seemed to demonstrate the enduring influence of this disruption. After the London transport system was attacked in a series of coordinated citywide suicide bombings on July 7th 2005, for example, newspapers and agencies made immediate appeals to members of the public for photographs, because the (mostly underground) scenes had been inaccessible to professional photojournalists. As unfolding news of the bombings circulated faster on message boards and blogs than anywhere else, it was remarked in the *Times* that 'the "citizen journalist" has truly come of age'.[25] It seemed that since September 11th the power of newsgathering had begun to change hands.

As well as information, though, the web offered connection. Allan quotes one woman as saying that in addition to there being always 'someone to listen' as she struggled to process her feelings about the attacks, she found 'the sheer volume of material on the internet to be a comfort of sorts', because somewhere out there, there might ultimately be 'some semblance of an answer to this ugly mess'.[26] The combination of connectivity and individualization offered by the internet made it a natural forum for people to share their experiences. 'More than news,' wrote Amy Harmon of the *New York Times* on the day after the attacks, 'what people all over the world craved in the wake of yesterday's terrorist attacks was connection to each other, and many of them found that most easily achieved by going online.'[27] Similarly, that same day, the *Los Angeles Times* reported that as websites attached to major national newspaper and television stations became overloaded and inaccessible in the rush for reliable information, smaller, individually produced web pages and chat rooms became the sources not only of information but of reassurance and community.[28] Then, all over the United States in the days and weeks following, people collected their thoughts and feelings, turning them outwards for the world to see via blogs and personal web pages. And at the heart of many of these, as the primary vehicle for expressions of grief and remembrance, were photographs. In collective photography projects like *Here is New York* and *The September 11th Photo Project*, most people participated by taking and presenting their own pictures. But, for creators of memorial web pages living in cities and towns across America far away from the scene of the attacks, this was not an option, and so their September 11th galleries consist of appropriated photographs, gathered from news sources and re-framed as tributes to the dead.

These memorial sites are difficult to quantify and study in a formal way. Some research has been done, however, thanks in part to the work of *The September 11 Web Archive*, a project that attempted to capture and archive for posterity as much September 11th-related web content as possible in the period up to December 2001.[29] One study of web-based memorializing, carried out by communications scholars Kirsten Foot, Barbara Warnick and Steven M. Schneider, confirms that the number of such vernacular websites created in response to the attacks was in the high hundreds if not thousands.[30] The conclusions they draw with regard to the social and psychological function of these sites seem to be concurrent with the small amount of other analytical work that has been carried out on this material, mostly in the academic fields of communication and rhetoric.[31] Broadly speaking, Foot, Warnick and Schneider see it as representing 'a version of the past which, when taken in concert with other versions, can provide a variegated picture of the forms of social action and reaction that marked post–September 11th events – and this picture contributes to our present understanding of how these events were experienced and understood'.[32]

Belonging to the increasingly indistinct category of personal blogs, these memorial sites tend to be designed and maintained by private members of the public, usually from a platform of free downloadable software that is widely available and easy to use. Most are discrete, static pages: carefully presented one-off creations rather than being integrated directly into blogs or social media profiles that change over time. However, they are usually attached to such blog-style sites – local community sites, family histories, profiles or hobby pages. Two examples of this, still live at the time of writing in 2014, are memorials by Thomas W. Krafft, whose page is an offshoot of a community website based in the town of Crowley, Louisiana, and another attached to a Mustang car enthusiast's site, called 'Stangbangers'.[33] Both of these pages, in a format common to countless others, feature an introductory paragraph followed by a gallery of photographs that are either presented full size or as 'thumbnails' that can be enlarged by the viewer. Beyond the introductory header, text plays a very marginal role. This kind of memorial site offers special insight into the uses of appropriated photographs as vehicles for expression and mourning and demonstrates what happens when the kinds of photographs discussed in previous chapters make a transition from one context to another, moving in a quite literal way through what Foucault calls a 'net-like organisation'.[34]

In the introduction to his page, Thomas Krafft tells us a lot about his selection and use of photographs. He explains that his memorial was created, in part, out of a concern that he might somehow forget the images of that day and writes about the difficult relationship between words and images, recounting an anecdote about a moment of silent confrontation with an Arab man ('from *that* region of the world') shortly after the attacks. The nervous communication between them, he explains, however filled with emotion, could only be wordless. Finally, he writes, 'I will never be able to describe September 11th as fully as these pictures. And yet, for as powerful and moving as these pictures are, they will never be able to describe the experience nor tell the complete story of those who were there.' Similarly, the Stangbangers memorial page is introduced with personal, autobiographical recollections about where the author and his wife were at the time, and what they felt. Typically, there is a sense that their collected images stand for much that could not be said. They 'speak for themselves' or at least for these particular people, who felt that 'there was nothing to say. We would never be the same.'

The sixty-five photographs displayed on Thomas Krafft's page include many familiar views: the collision of the planes, the fiery towers, dust-covered people making their way through the streets, firefighters in the rubble. Most of them have been cut and pasted from mainstream news websites (CNN.com, NBC.com and others), mixing views of the Ground Zero at the time of the attacks with images taken much later. Krafft describes his gallery simply as 'a collection of photos I've found since September 11th.' Other similar sites feature a mix of 'straight' photojournalistic images and those that have been creatively manipulated in various ways, superimposed with text or even special moving effects as animated GIF files. It is clear in each of these cases, however, that the intent is not factual documentation, but a very different function. The presentation of these photographs, together with the text that introduces them, demonstrates a desire to preserve not just the memory of the lost, but a sense of the chaos and pain that marked the original experience, as if this is just as valuable. There are often pseudo-philosophical, religious and especially patriotic conclusions as to the meaning of and appropriate response to the events, and to the images themselves, but the dominant message seems to be something like, 'this is not a time to enter into political debate, but to reflect on the human cost of this tragedy and join together in mourning. We must never forget how awful it felt when we first saw these images.' So, the images are said to communicate for themselves the fullness of what happened. It seems important that a kind of bravery is required in looking at them, and that this bravery or bearing witness is in itself a tribute to those who died. However, another set of intentions is also evident, as site creators appropriate the photographs they collect and 'make meaning' out of them in different ways, whether by manipulating the images themselves or designing the sequence and surrounding context in which they appear. The original selection process of editing and deciding which images to include in their particular collection, of course, also reflects the creator's own view of the events. For example, Thomas Krafft lays out his apparently un-manipulated photographs as plainly as he can, stating that they speak for themselves, yet he has also deliberately designed his site in accordance with particular religious iconographic conventions associated with death and remembrance: against a black background and preceding the main photographic content of the site there are images of a lighted candle, a person in a posture of prayer and happy portraits of victims as their loved ones would wish to remember them. Presumably, all of this framing helps him to make sense of the other images' content. There is a visible tension between the impulse to preserve a sense of disorder and even pain and to exert normalizing control over what has happened. This is an exercise not only in bearing witness and paying tribute, but also in personal psychological recovery. Krafft acknowledges this to an extent when he says that for him, it is about making sure that he does not forget.

In his work on cyberspace and culture, Kevin Robins has analysed some of the social and interpersonal implications of internet use in the early twenty-first century. He questions prevalent utopian attitudes regarding the connectedness that the web offers and examines the ways in which people really relate to one another and the wider world as manifest online.[35] Broadly speaking, Robins argues that the internet, while in some ways potentially life-enhancing, can in this sense actually regress its users' consciousness as human subjects by cutting them off more and more, first, from relationships with one another, and second, from the necessary pain and chaos of the world. Certain kinds of web-based interaction can serve to insulate individuals within idealized spaces where confrontation, differences of opinion and engagement with real-world political events are easily avoided. Limiting our social interaction to these virtual spaces, he suggests, serves our natural tendency to avoid pain.[36] On first impressions, it would seem that the kind of interactivity involved in September 11th memorial websites might go against this view. They illustrate what happens when the pain of the real world feels inescapable and indicate a desire not to avoid it, but to confront and even embrace it as a form of catharsis which reaches outwards towards others. Technology cannot in this case be used to transcend pain but is used as a tool in coming to terms with it – to choose, in the words of Michael Shulan, to 'stare without flinching'.[37] The declaration made again and again on these sites, as in myriad other commemorative gestures from tattoos to school murals, 'we will remember', indicates that cyberspace is in this instance being used for the opposite function to that which Robins suggests: both to hold on to pain rather than escaping it and to join together as a remembering community. Furthermore, as a direct response to a series of terrorist attacks at which, as one *New York Times* reporter put it, 'the whole nation – to a degree the whole world – shook', these memorials arguably do constitute a dramatic encroaching of the political and social world onto the supposedly utopian order of cyberspace.[38] On the other hand, digital manipulation of images and mediation of the contexts in which they appear (like Krafft's framing schema of pseudo-religious iconography) betray the more typical tendency to use technology as a way of managing the chaos of the real world. Digital photography and easy image-editing software greatly increase individuals' power to alter what is unacceptable, and the internet provides ample raw material for this as well as a platform for these mediated views to be publicly displayed and mutually validated. (One very widely circulated example of this kind of editing is a photograph of a firefighter at Ground Zero, seated with his head bowed in despair, comforted on either side by angels which have been superimposed onto the scene.) When photographs are appropriated in this way, from the subtlest re-framing to the crudest, the events are recreated, their meaninglessness tempered and brought in line with a metanarrative that makes sense. Most significantly of all perhaps, the photographs featured in these memorial websites almost all come directly from mainstream news sources, and we have already seen how in the context of their original appearance, the most widely circulated of these are very often already invested with particular ideological readings.

The second part of Robins's critique of utopian attitudes to internet technology, beyond its capacity to cocoon us from the 'real world', concerns its tendency to cut users off from one another and damage their capacity for authentic community. Foot, Warnick and Schneider argue that September 11th web-based memorials contradict this claim too. They draw very optimistic conclusions about these sites as restorative social spaces, saying that they have had 'both immediate and long-term social consequences'. Specifically, 'in the immediate aftermath of the attacks, they made it possible for a worldwide, bereaved community to participate in the pathos of the event.'[39] Initial participation in the pathos of an event though, while meaningful, is not necessarily the same as 'long-term social consequence', but the communal dimension of this kind of online activity does seem to be significant, just as it was for projects like *Here is New York*. For many web-based memorial creators like Thomas Krafft, a large part of the attempted psychological benefit of the project consists in reaching outward via their site to a wider grieving community. Some sites are involved in collectives, or webrings, where users connect and promote one another. Even for those that do not do this though, interaction is fundamental to their form if only by virtue of the fact that they are online: they are public facing rather than private tributes. The presence of an audience, even when this is only implicit and hypothetical, is central to the exercise. This is why many of the sites are called 'galleries', rather than, say, 'albums' or 'collections'.

Judith Lewis Herman emphasizes the importance of community and mutual support in a subject's recovery from any trauma:

> Sharing the traumatic experience with others is a precondition for the restitution of a sense of a meaningful world. In this process, the survivor seeks assistance not only from those closest to her (/him) but also from the wider community. The response of the community has a powerful influence on the ultimate resolution of the trauma. Restoration of the breach between the traumatized person and the community depends, first, upon public acknowledgment of the traumatic event and, second, upon some form of community action.[40]

Sharing personal feelings in a space that is seen as both public and supportive, like a collective of linked memorial pages, allows for this kind of process to happen. The function of this space is, as it were, to invite others to bear witness to their witnessing – a corporate, reciprocal act of mutual validation through looking at pictures. Public acknowledgement, though, is just one of Herman's prerequisites for recovery. The other is 'some form of community action'. Communities in the 'real world' are often exclusive, segregated and limited by geographical distance, while the internet has demonstrable power to connect diverse groups of people and offer the potential to form alliances that are politically effective. Online platforms have provided the means for political unity and activism on a variety of high-profile occasions, from the 2003 anti-war protest movement to the 'Arab Spring'. In these contexts, disparate people found online the means to express shared values and to communicate with one another, resulting in manifest action in the public sphere. It may be helpful, though, to distinguish here between communities and networks: many kinds of online connectivity exists which does not attempt to replicate community as such, but simply to achieve a common goal or to identify with one another on the basis of specific interests. September 11th is an event with dramatic political implications, but photographic memorial websites do not generally engage with these issues. While often expressly patriotic, and in many ways deeply politicized, such websites are for the most part not overtly partisan, refraining from comment on party or international politics. Varying degrees of support or distain are shown for the American administration and its policies, but the overwhelming tone is conservative, in solemn remembrance of the victims. The emphasis is human rather than political, and where a virtual 'community' is called together, the goal is not any particular action (except an 'act of remembrance'), but emotional solidarity and support.

In *Afflicted Powers*, members of the Retort group describe the global anti-war protests of February and March 2003 as the physical manifestation of an existing 'digital multitude', accumulated over the preceding years and intensified during the final few months leading up to the impending war in Iraq.[41] Existing patterns of resistance had, they say, made effective use of cyberspace, and much of the energy that characterized these protests came from the realization of these virtual groups as physically present and united crowds – 'an *image* of refusal become a reality'.[42] Ultimately, however, they conclude that this same cyber technology had realized the anti-war movement's potential not only for political assembly and activism, but as 'the perfect instrumentation of "spectacular" dispersal, isolation, and derealisation – the machinery of a *self-administered* dreamworld'.[43] Even as cyberspace accommodated both the virtual and 'real' accumulation of a community of protest and action, its deep implication within Western culture's commitment to spectacle meant that the internet's capacity to isolate and atomize inevitably foreclosed any possibility for unity or political effectiveness that it might foster. The Retort group also point out, however, that this does not apply universally. The 'webmeisters of revolutionary Islam', they suggest, unlike those in the Western world, have always had a much firmer grasp of how the language of images can be used for political influence.[44] Within the Iraqi resistance movement, too, sites like Albasrah.net present photographs as evidence of injustices allegedly perpetrated by US occupying forces, in page after page of what are tellingly called 'facts in pictures'. The page is remarkably similar in its layout to Thomas Krafft's September 11th memorial and others like it: row upon row of thumbnail photographs, minimally captioned, given to speak for themselves. Taken side by side, these two websites are as good an illustration as any of a post–September 11th image-war.

In several important ways, the events of September 11th represented a turning point for the traditional power structures that govern America's media landscape, and the capacity of individuals to appropriate and construct the representation of events is demonstrated in small ways all over the World Wide Web, including the reclaiming of photography in memorial websites. However, despite the fundamental connection between media control and political agency, they are not the same thing. September 11th memorial sites are only independent or autonomous creations in so far as they are compiled from a large but essentially homogenous body of images and points of view, the interpretations of which have been narrowly predetermined by the American press in the first place. Slavoj Žižek writes in the introduction to his critical account of post–September 11th political discourse, 'you're free to decide, on condition that you make the right choice'.[45] The great paradox in this instance, though, is that the choices have already been made for you, and yet the great array of photographic material combined with the wide-open creative space of the internet still gives the impression of freedom.

Images, like any other form of information in Foucault's power/discourse model, move around in clusters and networks, always in flux of signification, always connected. As they shift from one context to another, their meanings evolve, and an image that has one kind of power in one location will command a completely different kind of power when seen in a new place and put to a new use. A photograph that was first framed as 'breaking news' becomes a tribute to the dead or a timeless focal point for remembrance; an American photographer's picture of the burning World Trade Center towers is used as propaganda on an extremist Islamic website; and an image of people somewhere in the Muslim world celebrating the attack as a victory is condemned in the West.[46] Birgit Richard writes that when this shift in signification happens to enough images at once, such as through the proliferation of memorial gallery sites, a new kind of cultural practice is forged and the network itself changes. In these instances, 'new connective knots [are formed] that can be interpreted as a sign of how a society tries to cope with its loss.'[47] This means that as well as trying to analyse and understand particular images, there is an urgency to interpret these new knots and clusters that offer insight into a society's behaviour or values at a particular time.

On the internet, this is made a little easier because these sites of accumulation are literal, and connected collections of images devoted to making sense of events like September 11th are signs that can, with careful analysis, reveal much about the culture from which they emerge. Foucault himself asserts the importance of trying to differentiate between the various networks to which phenomena belong, identify their relationships and deconstruct their systems of influence. When these phenomena are images, the work involved is a kind of visual literacy: looking and questioning, directed not just at the many hundreds of visible images in the post–September 11th media environment, but the invisible ones which they imply (such as pictures of dead bodies). These skills of recognition and interpretation become more and more important as the capacity for images to 'move' in this way between digital spaces increases, and as these spaces load them with such a diverse and unstable range of meanings.

An enduring concern within Foucault's work is the techniques used in attempts to gain power over a subject (or text) by observing and therefore knowing it, like the prisoners who are controlled by the normative gaze of the all-seeing Panopticon.[48] He urges us to examine how power operates within, through and as discourse by considering the apparatuses through which it moves. One example of this kind of apparatus is the Panopticon prison. Another is the archive. Before the internet began, subtly and distinctly, to change our understanding of what a photographic archive is, Allan Sekula defined it as simply 'a quantitative ensemble of images': a commodity owned by an institution or an individual who had the right, whether it was accessible to the wider public or not, to organize and make use of a particular set of photographic prints or negatives in whatever way they saw fit.[49] It was a collection of photographs around a particular theme or subject, which, Sekula said, implicated a very particular attitude to the appropriation of images that may even be called intrinsic to all photographic practice. He argued that 'archival projects typically manifest a compulsive desire for completeness, a faith in an ultimate coherence imposed by the sheer quantity of acquisitions.'[50] Whatever their function, the management of archives is always a question of power and desire and can never be neutral. The collections of photographs featured in memorial websites, and, more broadly, the vast online pool from which they are sourced in the first place, constitute an archive of a kind that stretches the boundaries of this definition. The internet-based September 11th archive – the fluid, informally organized but easily searchable repository of freely circulating photographs open to use and appropriation by anyone, copyright notwithstanding – differs in significant ways from Sekula's original formulation, but his main point, that archives represent a compulsive desire for completeness and a faith in 'ultimate coherence' based on 'sheer quantity', is absolutely applicable.

Defining the digital public record of September 11th as an archive in itself opens it up to another level of Foucauldian reading, in that the archive is for him exactly the kind of apparatus that invariably upholds the state's interests, whether directly or indirectly. The examples that he uses to expound his ideas about this kind of power in the fullest detail are those of discipline and punishment. It is easy to see that, for example, a police photography archive is a system designed for observation and recording that is directly related to power and control. It is an archetypal apparatus of photographic knowledge by which power is held and exercised. Developing Foucault's ideas along the specific lines of photographic examples like this, John Tagg argues that photographic archives of other kinds, presumably including the *Here is New York* archive, Joel Meyerowitz's *World Trade Center Archive* and the wider, less formalized web-based September 11th 'archive', can also be said to represent the 'emerging apparatuses of a new and more penetrating form of the state'.[51] This online September 11th archive fits Foucault's model of power not only because of its 'penetrating' net-like structure, but more significantly because of its participatory, individuating character and the fact that in spite of the potential for fluid and contingent signification, in many cases the dominant readings hold on and persist even as the photographs move. According to this model, everyone has access to the power of such images, and everyone is potentially in control of their uses and effects, but the catch is that the individual is thus not only an agent of power, but a part of its mechanism: he or she becomes power's vehicle. Subjects do not wield power. Power, rather, produces subjects: 'the individual, that is, is not the *vis-à-vis* of power', says Foucault, 'it is, I believe, one of its prime effects.'[52] As individuals appropriate and use photographs, they themselves become part of the apparatus. The creator of the Stangbangers memorial page had access to the entire archive of September 11th photography available on the internet. And, yet, the first thirteen photographs on his page show only minor variations of exactly the same scene. Thomas Krafft, too, could have chosen a set of pictures that reflected something of his own recollection of the events in all its nuance and personal idiosyncrasy, but instead he chose only the most ubiquitous press photographs, five of which have already been discussed in this book. What this implies, of course, is that his own recollection of the event is not constituted by a unique personal viewpoint at all, but by these very pictures, which were what he saw at the time and have become his memories. Adorno's formulation of this principle states that 'freedom to choose an ideology – since ideology always reflects economic coercion – everywhere proves to be freedom to choose what is always the same'.[53]

How does this kind of coercion square with the politics of American individualism and freedom that is so often bound up in the patriotic rhetoric of memorial sites like these? The unprecedented scope that the internet offers for freedom of expression has led some to call it a definitively American medium. Its individualizing power has been seen to characterize modern American subjectivity in a way that seems in fact to lend itself very well to a Foucauldian interpretation of internet use. Howard Rheingold is credited with coining the term 'virtual community', in a book which he subtitles *Homesteading on the Electronic Frontier*, and Ziauddin Sardar has aligned cyberspace with American mythology in a more critical way by calling it 'the American dream writ large'. Like Rheingold, he too recognizes how fittingly the metaphors of pioneering, conquering and colonizing can describe forms of online activity.[54] Seen in Foucauldian terms, however, this promise of the internet as a frontier to be freely explored and claimed in the pursuit of self-realization is counterbalanced by a totalizing power that both negates and relies entirely upon it. The totalizing power that he has in mind 'cannot be exercised without knowing the inside of people's minds, without exploring their souls, without making them reveal their innermost secrets. It implies a knowledge of the conscience and an ability to direct it.'[55] The conditions for this are ideal in a social space that so many people now habitually use precisely to reveal their innermost secrets, expose their souls and, in a manner so homogenized that it becomes a paradox, to assert their individuality. This is the same space in which the vast September 11th photography archive operates, exercising its influence in a fluid, relational, circulating network that gives the impression of infinite perspectives but is really limited to a narrow few, and which by its coherence as an evolving but discrete photographic archive is inevitably implicated within the totalizing power of the state. The free circulation of these images, and their appropriation in such intimate and seemingly individual expressions of the inner lives of its users, gives this network its peculiar influence. The kind of subjectivity into which this apparatus forces its users, Foucault argues, must be 'refused':

> Maybe the target nowadays is not to discover what we are but to refuse what we are. We have to imagine and to build up what we could be to get rid of this kind of political 'double bind', which is the simultaneous individualization and totalization of modern power structures. The conclusion would be that the political, ethical, social, philosophical problem of our days is not to try to liberate the individual from the state, and from the state's institutions, but to liberate us both from the state and from the type of individualization linked to the state. We have to promote new forms of subjectivity through the refusal of this kind of individuality that has been imposed on us for several centuries.[56]

But how? What, in this context, might a more genuinely autonomous use of images, or of the internet itself, look like? The appropriation of photographs in September 11th memorial websites is motivated by a need to make sense, or meaning, out of a senseless tragedy. But in practice, the re-contextualization of these images in self-styled tributes motivated by specific emotional or political concerns constitutes not only a search *for*, but a co-production *of* new meaning. As each website producer collects photographs from news sources and places them within the context of their own chosen iconographic conventions and framing concepts, their meaning changes from documentary news photography to something else. The photographs remain exactly the same, but new meaning is generated because he or she has now taken ownership of them. In this way, the photographs can be seen as commodities, and the site producer can be called a consumer.

As we've already seen, Marxist warnings about top-down ideological manipulation in capitalist society are undermined by a model that conceives the circulation of power as being layered and multi-directional rather than imposed from above.[57] This revised model understands that consumers are no longer passive, and commodities can diverge from their specified paths acquiring new meanings through different kinds of active consumption. Furthermore, as the nature of capitalism fundamentally changes from a system based on manufactured goods to one constituted primarily by information that cannot be so straightforwardly quantified or monetized, the possibilities for subjects' agency are opened up in new ways, such that the definition of 'commodity' itself needs to be rethought. 'Mature capitalism', writes John Roberts, is distinguished by 'the reign of the commodity-as-image and the commodity-as-sound', as 'the life of the commodity expands into all areas of human production and consumption.' And, all this takes the form, he says, (recalling Foucault) of 'an interlacing system'.[58] The fact that money does not change hands within this system when individuals acquire the commodity-as-image for their own use is beside the point. So powerful is this form of capital, accumulated as Debord warned to the point at which it has colonized every corner of psychic experience and made it subject to economic coercion, that it begins to encompass phenomena that could never, under the old paradigm, be commodified as private property – such as memory, or even mourning.

Marita Sturken has presented a detailed and rather damning argument that in late capitalist America, mourning has become a form of consumption, and in particular, 'the terrorist attacks of 9/11 produced a frenzied consumer response to the fear of terrorism'.[59] She says that in the buying and selling of everything from enhanced security systems to Ground Zero souvenirs, consumption became a way of asserting both comfort and innocence, which also allowed for a complete disavowal of any idea of the United States as an imperialist aggressor. According to Sturken's argument, the consumption of photographs can be likened to a kind of historical tourism, the position of the tourist being always one of innocent detachment. History is packaged to create 'cathartic' experiences, removed, consumable, naïve and artificial. Thus, the appropriation and use of photographs for memorial purposes would be for her a means of expressing sorrow without any of the hard work of political critique.[60] This, as we have seen, is exactly the framework in which many of these photographs were originally presented: a dazzling visual force that disabled critical engagement by way of a spectacle that largely served to keep politics at arm's length. As well as the prevailing interpretations of images themselves, this effect, too, has been transferred wholesale into individuals' supposedly autonomous memorial expressions.

According to the Marxist model, subjects always theoretically had agency at two points within the capitalist system of consumption: the choice of what to consume and the choice of what to do with it.[61] Or, as Stuart Hall wrote in 1973, 'there are always several possible readings of a given cultural text; some reinforce the existing power structures and status quo while other, more oppositional ones, challenge it.'[62] Though much has changed since Marx set out his critique of this system, and also since Hall developed it along post-Gramscian lines, this basic principle still holds. Hall identified three positions in relation to a text that are still available under a redefined or 'mature' era of capitalism: the 'dominant hegemonic position', the 'negotiated position' and the 'oppositional position'.[63] In another study of the rhetoric of online September 11th memorials, Aaron Hess concludes that 'the voices heard in the websites are ... speaking from the position of the "ordinary" ... which provides a reshaping of public memory from perspectives other than the privileged voices heard through granite and roped-off areas'.[64] His work, along with that of Foot, Warnick and Schneider, draws the unequivocal conclusion that these websites represent thoroughly independent, democratic, anti-hegemonic positions, and he also has a wholly positive view of their potential for emotional expression and healing. There is no question in either of these studies of the website producer being part of a system in which they are the objects of power as well as its subjects; nor of their material being appropriated from a source that might itself foreclose their capacity for autonomous interpretation. Hess, in fact, acknowledges the appropriation of various materials – photographs, flash video works, music – as constituting an 'intertextual' condition, but in no way does he consider the ideological implications of this.[65] Memorial gallery websites may to a certain extent play a role in renegotiating the meaning of images through their re-contextualization, but they cannot be said to occupy what Hall would call an oppositional position: one that defies or contests the image's original encoding. Of course, there are varieties of September 11th-related vernacular website that do set out to question the dominant account of the events, but those whose function is explicitly memorial, and certainly those which use photography as their means of expression, seem almost exclusively to show an acceptance of the picture of September 11th as it is presented in the mainstream American press, responding to the 'texts' of their chosen news photographs in a manner that overwhelmingly conforms to a dominant hegemonic position.[66] Hence, the totalizing power of this network of images operates both through the limited variety of images available for use, and, on a more fundamental level, by the foreclosure of oppositional positions inherent in the modern state apparatus itself.

Marita Sturken continues her argument about the commodification of mourning by saying that the consumption of 'memorial culture' in the United States has come to be understood as a kind of therapy.[67] The marketing of commemorative photographic books like *Aftermath, Here is New York* and *The September 11th Photo Project* as products which are inherently both patriotic and therapeutic certainly attests to this, as does the more fundamental assertion that the choice to look at photographs of the event in news magazine special editions or memorial websites is part of a process of cathartic recovery. Sturken does not entirely write off the compulsion to repetitively consume (or see), recognizing that it plays an obvious role in sense-making. However, parallel to the previous discussion of trauma, she does insist that the repetitive consumption of objects and images relating to catastrophic events equates to a kind of compulsive traumatic re-enactment: a child-like acting out. Consuming imagery of September 11th on terms that assert our own control, that comfort us, or allow us to operate as detached tourists of history, makes it much easier to adopt a position of unquestioning acquiescence with regard to war. 'The use of 9/11 as a means to justify the war in Iraq [is an example of] how narratives of victimization and trauma enable a perpetuation of violence.'[68] As tourists, we are not required to take any responsibility for what we consume.

On the surface, the use of photographs in independent memorial projects of whatever kind looks like an act of reclaiming and empowerment, on both psychological and sociopolitical levels. Some of these projects set themselves up as vehicles of 'collective memory', and some in opposition to it. But, the trap set by the spectacular state in its own visual presentation of the attacks has meant that each of these gestures was compromised from the beginning. Together with the restricted pool of images that seemed to make everything visible but did not, the apparent transparency, indexicality and openness of photography itself created ideal conditions for the kind of internalized control that caused individuals to experience manipulation as complete freedom of thought. The dual effects of this manipulation – the disabling of citizens' engagement in the political process as well as of their attempts at emotional recovery – are clear in each of these examples. But, this still leaves the question of the more general public response to photographs as a way of navigating the trauma of September 11th. For those who did not choose to create collections, books, websites or exhibitions, but simply to look, was there any hope to be found in photographs at all?

5 THE COMPULSION TO REPEAT: PHOTOGRAPHY AS A DEAD END

Sometimes it seems like nobody speaks and sometimes like everybody's talking at once.

DAVID FOSTER WALLACE[1]

For both first- and second-hand witnesses of the September 11th attacks, the uneasy relationship between words and images marked the experience from the very beginning. It was so deeply confounding, so far outside most Western viewers' conscious frames of reference, that words seemingly could not accommodate it. Some, like the journalists and TV news anchors whose job required them to find words, made recourse to superlatives and negatives – it was 'beyond words', 'unbelievable', 'indescribable' – and others to the language of cinema and dreams – 'like a movie', 'like a video game', 'surreal'. But, most people could only look on in silence. Silence is the default mode for watching television, of course, and television is the medium through which the breaking news was witnessed by the vast majority of people. But, this particular wordlessness, expressed clearly in the halting reactions of TV commentators, became a hallmark of the American response. Many sought understanding of the event not primarily through reading or listening, but looking, and subsequently responded to it not by speaking or writing, but still more looking, or by making visual tributes for others to see. Most often, words were relegated to the supplementary role of photo captions or film commentary. There are several reasons for this. One of the most obvious is that, because of the attacks' timing and location, so many photographs were taken and so much film footage gathered that this abundance of visual information was bound to characterize the event. But, Judith Lewis Herman provides a starker explanation for this kind of wordless response to the traumatic, and one that ties in with a Lacanian reading of its un-symbolizable, unassimilable effect: 'certain violations of the social contract are too terrible to utter aloud', she says. 'This is the meaning of the word unspeakable.'[2] The unspeakable nature of this event, combined with the ready overcompensation or overvisibility of particular types of image at the crucial earliest stages, largely foreclosed the kinds of meaningful verbal response that would have made the experience intelligible. And, this enduring substitution of words with pictures, enacted both by the authorities (government and media) and individual citizens (in memorial projects of various kinds, for example), while understandable in such extraordinary circumstances, ultimately contributed to a widespread failure to recover from the trauma.

When the dust had settled and the time came to move from shock to retelling and understanding, words still seemed inadequate, and the pictures that had first come to us as fragments of breaking news evolved to become signifiers that bore the weight of whole systems of meaning. Still photography in particular became hugely important. For the various individuals and groups who created photo-based memorials, from big exhibitions to personal web pages, the motivation was clear: the act of looking at these pictures was in one way or another understood to be a challenging but ultimately redemptive and healing process. Returning to photographs was the way forward. On the wall of the *September 11 Photo Project* exhibition, among a group of nine black and white photographs, a handwritten note read:

> On September 11th and in the days that followed, I didn't know what to do with myself. I was filled with so much sorrow, so many mixed emotions. I started taking pictures because I felt the need to document what was going on. But a part of me also wanted to experience the events more, to feel things more deeply in order to reach a level of acceptance and understanding. I am hoping that the images will help me sort through it all in time. – *Deborah Suchman Zeolla, New York City, November 2001.*[3]

But to what extent can looking at photographs really help anyone come to terms with tragedy? This person's testimony supports the argument that photography was both a vehicle for moving beyond trauma towards recovery through 'bearing witness' and also, in a more complicated way, of holding on to pain. In the aftermath of September 11th, Barbie Zelizer says, photography 'rose to fill the space of chaos and confusion that journalism was expected to render orderly'.[4] While journalists and commentators attempted to commit the scene to words, packaging, prioritizing and summarizing information, verifying sources, explaining and rationalizing the scene, the ubiquitous photographs that accompanied their reports were a constant reminder that no such order was really possible. Unlike the verbal reports, photographs allowed viewers to observe and contemplate the formless devastation at their own pace, taking in the represented events for themselves without prescribed conclusions. Here again, then, is the repeated association between images and disorder, words and order. And, further complicating matters, there is a pervading sense that this disorder was in fact desirable; that it had value of some kind, and that without it no account could be authentic.

Zelizer's view of what happens when pictures of a traumatic scene are looked at repeatedly is very different from the Freudian perspective explored earlier. Rather than seeing it as a destructive process of acting out, her view fits in with that of Saltzman and Rosenberg, for whom representation is the key to facing a traumatic experience and integrating its memory. For Zelizer, the constant repetition of photographs of the event helped witnesses to see and continue to see, until the recovery process was worked through. 'Just as a child reaches mastery over difficult tasks by repetition', she says, 'so too does the repeated display of images work its way into acceptance or acquiescence.'[5] As the same, or very similar, images of September 11th were repeated again and again in memorial websites and collections, just as they had been in photographic supplements in the national press at the time of the attacks and later, in commemorative publications, this repetition enabled a 'public iconography' to develop, and as these concepts and horrible facts gradually became representable, they could, as Zelizer puts it, 'work their way into acceptance'.

Implicated in this argument is the view that still photographs offer a more stable means of assimilation than moving film footage. Unlike television's slippery 'stream of underselected images', still photographs can be held.[6] The space that still photography offers for slow comprehension, possession and repeated looking is apparently key to its usefulness in recovery from trauma. Digital photography complicates this somewhat because the technology involved increasingly erodes the boundary between motion and stillness. Some of the most well-known 'photographs' of the World Trade Center attacks are actually grabbed frames from digital video footage. Others, like Lyle Oweko's picture featured on the cover of *TIME* magazine and Richard Drew's 'Falling Man', were chosen from series of very rapidly captured digital stills – so rapid, in fact, that the resulting contact sheets look as if they could quite easily be reanimated as movies.[7] In both cases, it is the careful isolation of a moment that is not only 'privileged' but strategically or even ideologically selected, which gives them their power in relation to moving images. This dual investment of the still photograph – the power to determine the exact slice of time that corresponds to a given or desired construction of events, and the stability of an object to be possessed and contemplated – secured its place in so many attempts to establish both coherent ideological meaning and psychological recovery.

In the case of Oweko's *TIME* cover, we can presume that the final image was chosen for its superior composition and drama: its perfect, movie poster-like capturing of the event's spectacular focal point. The camera's position is close-up, from below, right in the midst of the on-the-ground action, the dramatic foreshortening of the towers seeming to underscore the magnitude of this event as an episode in America's history, and signalling the opening of an uncertain but brave (even exciting?) new era. In the case of Drew's 'Falling Man', the subject of an *Esquire* article and subsequent film written by Tom Junod, the criteria for selection are different. Junod suggests that this image has become so famous primarily because it presents the subject as falling not in desperate panic, but with a kind of stoic grace.[8] But, the contact sheet of twelve successive shots from which this one was selected for release by the Associated Press shows a different story. In the other images in the sequence, this same man falls, arms and legs flailing wildly, just as desperate as any of the other 'jumpers' on that day. The apparent peace captured in Drew's final selection is illusory and fleeting. We can surmise that, though it was met by many with outrage and called inappropriate, this picture was printed in more newspapers than other 'jumper' pictures because in relative terms it was so much easier to look at. From the vantage point of this particular slice of time, the man's death is a decisive act of courage, not of frightened desperation. It is the one that best suited, to recall Jürgen Habermas's words, a land that needed heroes.

In the case of September 11th, the question of the emergence of either a 'public iconography' or any kind of 'public icon' is complex, both because of the sheer number of photographs in existence and because of the dislocation of time and processes of cognition involved in its media dissemination. But, the notion of such an icon or group of icons is central to Zelizer's theory of collective witness-bearing and recovery. She claims that frozen images mobilize the public, dislodging them from initial shock and starting the recovery process:

> The movement from trauma to a post-traumatic space may be facilitated at least in part by photography, not only in its strategic relay – the making of photographs – but also in the usage of photographs over time. In display, prominence, centrality, and sheer number, photographs create a space of contemplation in the documentary record, through which people move at varied paces on their way to recovery.[9]

Judith Lewis Herman confirms that from a clinical point of view, bearing witness is an important stage in recovery from psychological trauma, and that bearing witness *together* is particularly important in cases where that trauma is collective. Furthermore, when the trauma has been public and deliberately violent, recovery involves a shared movement towards a reconfiguration of reality and reviewing of beliefs about society.[10] In a sense, the national press performed this function in the aftermath of September 11th 2001, but the necessary sense of personal and shared subjective ownership came from other sources: impromptu displays of ephemera around Ground Zero, collective photographic exhibitions and, further afield, digital memorials. In these spaces, individuals spoke with their own voices, publicly declaring, 'we will remember'. Given the centrality images though, perhaps what they really meant was, 'we will keep looking'. While Herman seems to agree on one level with the view that bearing witness together can lead to recovery, her understanding of witnessing is not the same as Zelizer's. Most fundamentally, it is not a visual process. As suggested previously, photography as a mechanism is more closely analogous with the process by which trauma itself takes root in the psyche than with the process of recovery. In fact, Herman likens traumatic memory to 'a series of still snapshots or a silent movie; the role of therapy is to provide the music and words'.[11] In a clinical application of Freudian (and also Lacanian) theory, language is key to her prescription for recovery from trauma.[12] Specifically, the form of language that she calls for is narrative retelling. Traumatic memories are chaotic and without order. They are 'pre-narrative'. Arriving at a point of being able to tell the story of a traumatic experience out loud or in writing, and subsequently as part of the internal storytelling by which one's subjectivity is constructed, represents a conquering of the unspeakable. Beginning with the fragmented raw material of sensation and images – which, depending on the context, may be concrete objects or reside solely in the mind – the goal is to create a verbal account:

> As the narrative closes in on the most unbearable moments, the patient finds it more and more difficult to use words. At times the patient may spontaneously switch to nonverbal methods of communication, such as drawing or painting. Given the 'iconic' visual nature of traumatic memories, creating pictures may represent the most effective initial approach to these 'indelible images' … The ultimate goal, however, is to put the story, including its imagery, into words.[13]

Paul Virilio writes that in the age of 'real-time', rolling news, we have passed 'from the order of succession', to 'the disorder of simultaneity'.[14] Time that does not pass but rather 'surfaces' or 'erupts' in this way is not conducive to the formation of narrative. Though it is not quite what Virilio has in mind, this kind of chronoscopic simultaneity applies to the accumulation of still photography at least as much as it does to the video 'tele-presence' that is his main concern. In a situation like the *Here is New York* photography exhibit, where huge numbers of still photographs are collected and displayed with no regard for chronological succession, thematic coherence or even contextualizing captions, the prenarrative simultaneity of experience is potentially overwhelming. While this strategy of display was presumably a response to the perceived need to hold on to a sense of chaos, it in fact ended up 'eradicating all duration, any extension of time in the transmission of messages'.[15] There was only exposure. In Chapter 2, we discussed the implications of this kind of chaotic simultaneity in the first instance of September 11th's broadcasting. This pollution of distances had a psychological impact that was carried forward into the event's subsequent assimilation by the population at large. But, when, as a mode of visual address, it was then transferred from the initial breaking of the story to ongoing attempts at commemoration and retelling, there were even further psychic implications.

Narrative does not carry the same implications in the psychological or psychoanalytical realm as in the socio-political. The kind of integrated story or verbal account that Herman insists upon, as traumatic memory is sorted from a pile of disordered snapshots into a progressive sequence, is definitely not the same as the ideologically loaded 'metanarratives' and 'redemptive narratives' discussed in previous chapters. Indeed, looking at a range of views from different disciplinary positions, it becomes clear that narrative is a difficult notion. Within documentary photography, critics and practitioners such as Allan Sekula and Martha Rosler have long argued the political importance of integrating single photographs, which on their own represent 'fragmentary and incomplete utterances' into fuller textual forms.[16] The incorporation of text has been a crucial part of Sekula's photographic practice for a very long time, because, as he puts it, 'a moment is after all, only a moment, and only a *visible* moment at that. Speech allows for critical reflection, for complaints, for the unfolding of personal histories, for the voicing of fears and hopes'.[17] Rosler, on the other hand, is particularly wary of the ideological usefulness of the breed of narrative known as 'personal history':

> Narrative can be a homey, manageable form of address, but its very virtue, the suggestion of subjectivity and lived experience, is also its danger. The rootedness in an I, the most seductive encoding of *convincingness*, suggests an absolute inability to transcend the individual consciousness. And consciousness is the domain of ideology, so that the logic of at least the first-person narrative is that there is no appeal from ideology, no *metacritical* level.[18]

For Rosler, the individualistic relativism of contemporary society dictates that only the personal is truly knowable, and declarations based in subjective experience – typified, perhaps, by blogs – are always by definition beyond critique. This means that first-person narrative is a mode perfectly suited to reinforcing dominant ideology. However, she also insists that this is a failure 'not so much of narrative as of the naturalism that is taken as narrative's central feature. Break the bonds of that naturalism and the problem vanishes.'[19] As her own artistic practice demonstrates, the danger is not in subjective first-person narratives themselves, but in taking their political authority for granted. The kind of narrative-construction that is necessarily involved in psychological recovery from trauma is distinctive because it does not claim this kind of authority. Its meaning is primarily turned inward towards personal growth, not outwards as a framework for the interpretation of external events. And, while this applies to collective recovery from shared trauma too, the emphasis is still on a rebuilding of shared identity that does not require everyone else's narrative to be aligned with it.

Reconstruction in the aftermath of trauma inevitably leads to a review of meaning, and the question 'why?' (and subsequently, 'why me?' or 'why us?'). Where trauma seems senseless and arbitrary, recovery involves constructing some kind of logic around it, both through thought and active response. Where a previously held system of beliefs has been shattered by events, a new one must be created: a narrative that fits the subject's altered world view and their sense of place within it. This is integration – the goal of mourning. After it has been constructed and repeatedly told, this new story becomes just another part of the victim's past experience, and the memories and the grief can begin to fade. In Freudian terms, the telling of the neurotic or hysterical patient's story results in the lifting of their symptoms.[20] Then, once the story has been told and committed to the past, the next stages can begin, of rebuilding the present and facing the future. This also accords with a Lacanian view, in that if the neurotic symptom can be understood as a kind of embodied linguistic metaphor, the way to relieve the pain is not simply to use words, but, more specifically, to form part of a narrative history that can be owned: the repressed ideas or traumatic memories must be linked in to the rest of the signifying chain and finally assimilated into the ego:

> The communication of the signification to the patient cures to the extent that it produces *Überzeugung*, that is to say, conviction. The subject integrates the explication which you give him into the set of significations he has already admitted … But it is far from being generally the case. That is why we move on to the second stage, in which … the patient has to reintegrate the sequence of significations which had not been recognised (*méconnaître*) into this imaginary continuum which we call the ego, to recognise it as being his, to integrate it into his biography.[21]

As the images of the ego are integrated into the symbolic text, the subject can fully assume his or her history ('biography', or what Lacan elsewhere refers to as 'stories').[22] If we map this process onto the earlier idea that the trauma is an eruption of, or missed encounter with, the order of the real, the goal of analysis and recovery can then be seen as a passage from the effects of an encounter with the un-representable, un-symbolizable trauma, through recognition on the level of the 'imaginary continuum which we call the ego', and finally into the symbolic order of language, as the newly integrated biography is made available for retelling. The trauma, associated with the order of the real, is not representable in an image. But, in some cases – including the witnessing of September 11th – the originating traumatic event *is* a visual object. This is why any hope for collective recovery from the trauma of September 11th does not consist in trying to recapture it in pictures in order to 'face it' as Barbie Zelizer,

Michael Shulan and others have suggested – an impossible proposition – but rather in recognizing that the originating traumatic scene must be recovered, assimilated and owned, eventually assuming verbal form. Freud, in fact, writes of the patient 'getting rid' of a 'memory picture' associated with a traumatizing event 'by turning it into words'.[23] For him, it seems that the essential ingredient of the trauma itself is always fundamentally visual or pictorial, and while such pictures may present the means to uncover the causes of traumatic neurosis and signpost the way to recovery, the goal is ultimately not to assimilate them, but to destroy them altogether.[24] This, of course, is not possible in the case of the September 11th trauma, as the pictures involved are not just 'memory pictures' that can be called up from within the psyche and destroyed: they are photographic objects that remain a ubiquitous and unavoidable feature of modern visual culture. They will never be 'got rid of', so there is no other way forward but to assimilate them and make them part of some kind of signifying chain.

Sontag argues that while photographs of harrowing events have an enduring affective power, what they cannot do is offer understanding. 'Narratives can make us understand', she says. 'Photographs do something else: they haunt us.'[25] A photograph is not a route to recovery, it only represents an endless return to the trauma. It is a dead end. In looking at Jose Jiminiz's photograph of people fleeing the North Towers' collapse (Figure 5.1), it is possible to see and even feel again something of the shock and confusion of that moment. A group of people are trying to outrun the rolling dust-cloud that has already engulfed the surrounding streets. But, they do not move in unison or with the same sense of urgency. Some run, some seem to walk rather idly (including a photographer in the middle distance who appears oblivious, absorbed in reviewing pictures of his own) and some turn to look back or towards one another, as if asking whether this could really be happening. It is a scene of confusion. The central subject of the picture, though, is a young man – maybe just a schoolboy – who runs with such desperation and panic that he will narrowly miss colliding with the photographer as he rushes by. His face is frozen in a grimace that expresses more than fear, as if he is in pain, or maybe he is already exhausted. What does this picture give us? It is a document to be added to the collected record, contemplated and mused upon as a way of moving both back to the event and forward from it. It freezes but also vicariously reanimates this particular moment, seeming to offer both cathartic encounter and, simultaneously, the privilege of filing it away as a fragment of the past, flat and dead. All of this and more has been asked of photographs like this one, which in reality has nothing to offer except eternal shock and eternal panic. The young man in the foreground is not killed, nor does he reach safety. He will only ever be running in terror, as long as we are without access to his story or to the moments just before and after this moment which the photographer, probably also acting in fear for his life, has selected.

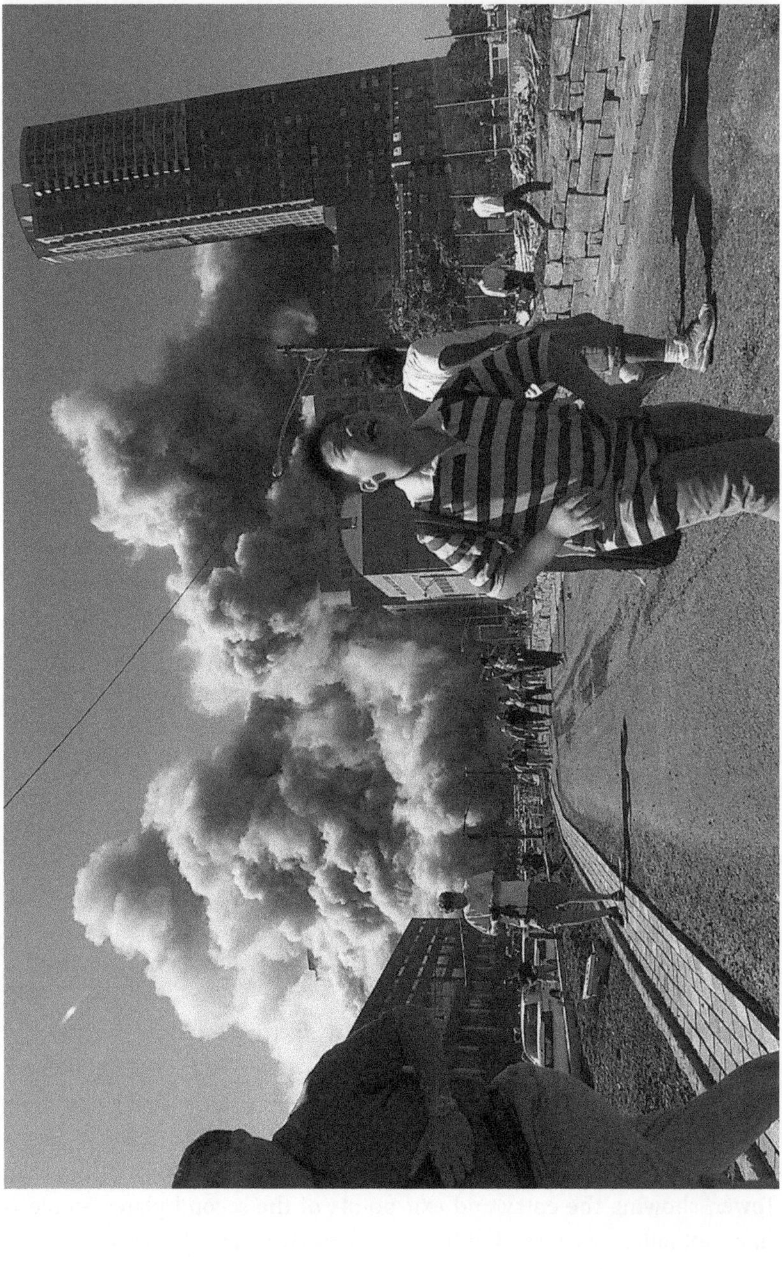

Figure 5.1 People run away as the North Tower of World Trade Center collapses, September 11th 2001. Photo by Jose Jimenez, Primera Hora/Getty Images.

One of the most telling and personal illustrations of his apparent wariness towards images is in the story of a curious encounter between Freud and Michelangelo's famous statue of Moses in Rome.[26] In response to the statue, by which he is deeply affected, Freud draws a series of four sketches showing what he imagines Moses' movements to be in the moments leading up to the final pose captured by the sculptor. In this process, Peter Benson has suggested, Freud 'seeks to quell the dangerous power of visual images by multiplying them', and that 'narrating becomes a means to pacify confusion in the visual register, supplementing what is seen by its imagined completion'.[27] He constructs a kind of story of explanation for the visual object that haunts him, contextualizing or anchoring in much the same way as a verbal narrative can have a mastering effect on visual material in memory or in the photographic record. In this instance, Freud uses pictures, not words, to do this, but the point is still the creation of a series: a progressive narrative with a beginning, middle and end. It is also especially noteworthy that this exercise is for Freud a personal journey of response to a deeply affecting encounter with a visual object, rather than a detached prescription for a patient. From her position as a New York resident impacted by the September 11th attacks, and as someone who used her own camera in an attempt to deal with this experience, Marianne Hirsch has written that 'if still photography is the visual genre that best captures the trauma and loss associated with September 2001 … it is due to the photograph's temporality'.[28] It is no wonder that photography played so key a role on this of all days, as a mechanism that offered the power to stop time. The temporal intervention of photography involves the blocking of narrative by seizing an isolated moment from the stream of experience, but the converse of this disturbance is that it also creates the opportunity for narrative to be reconstructed around this same moment on the viewer's own terms. In the days when Hirsch and other stunned New Yorkers walked the streets taking in the devastation, the longing to turn back time was surely everywhere, expressed in hundreds of different ways including the taking of photographs. But, this was a wish so simple and audacious that it could only really be spoken out loud by children. In Figure 5.2, a picture handed in to the British Embassy in New York three days after the attacks, Stanley writes, 'Dear Americans, I wish you were still here.' But, he acknowledges the impossibility of his wish by drawing what he has seen. In the bottom right hand corner of his short letter, by way of illustration, the tops of the two towers billow their clouds of smoke, and in a detail that shows how closely the child has observed (or absorbed) photographs like Spencer Platt's (Figure 1.1), additional clouds of smoky debris burst out from both sides of the South Tower, showing the entry and exit points of the second plane. Stanley's towers have not fallen down yet, but he knows exactly what will happen next. In one of the thousands of photographs in the *Here is New York* collection, another

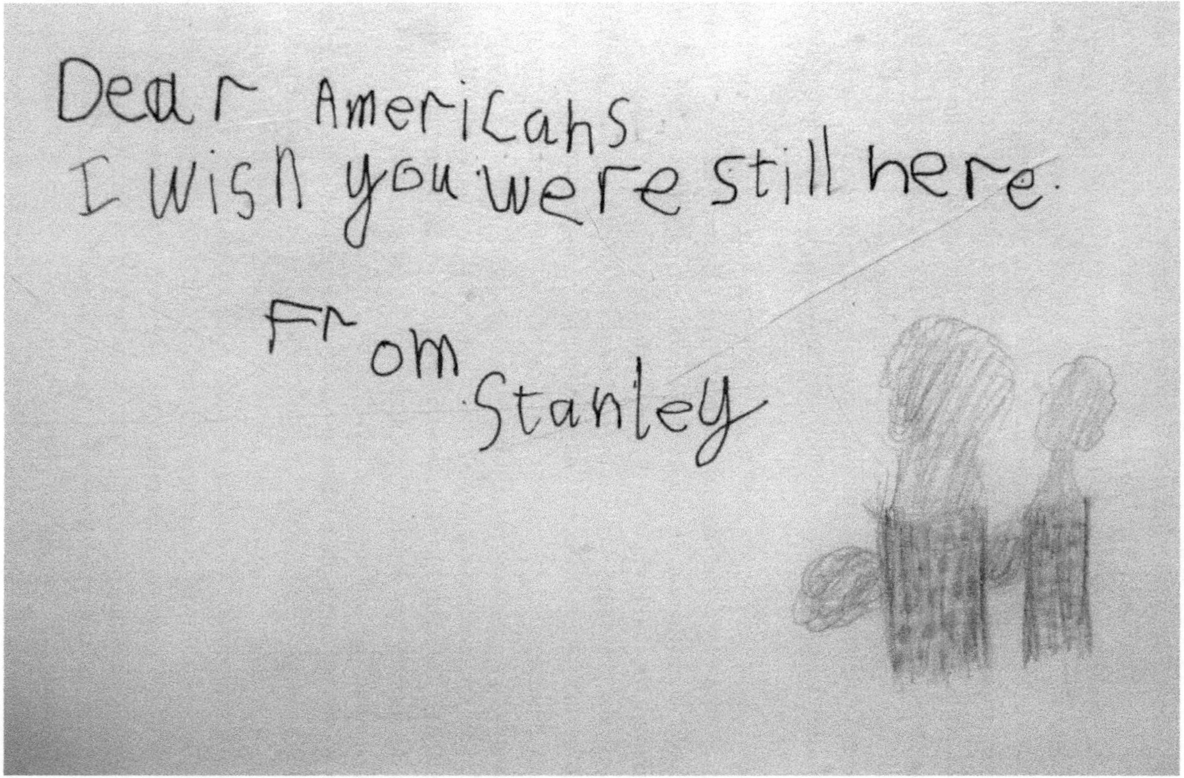

Figure 5.2 A child's drawing displayed at an exhibition of September 11th–related children's art at the International Gallery of Children's Art in London, 5 September 2002. Photo by Sion Touhig, Getty Images.

child's drawing is seen taped to a Manhattan fence. It is part of the outpouring of ephemeral memorial street art that covered walls and fences everywhere in the weeks following the attacks. The drawing shows a bright yellow sun in the sky, but it has a frowning face, watching as an aeroplane heads towards the twin towers. Underneath, in what might be the handwriting of an eight- or nine-year-old is the plea, 'turn around and go back to the airport and let those people out!! A nice lady is waiting for you at the airport and she will give you a kiss'. Unlike Stanley, whose towers are already burning, this child's attempt at mastery over her trauma involves taking the frozen moment before the first plane's impact and intervening, imposing an imagined completion on what she has seen. In the stillness of this suspended moment, she has time to reason with the pilot and impose a different narrative, taking this frozen beginning and creating a different middle and a happy ending. Narrating the preceding moments on her own terms is for her, as it is for Freud, a means to disarm and take control of a phenomenon whose visual (and hence emotional) impact is otherwise totally overwhelming.

Discussion of temporality and death in photography brings us, inevitably perhaps, to the writings of Roland Barthes, and particularly his most famous, final book. A meditation on personal loss and the enigmatic power of the photograph, *Camera Lucida* is his own work of mourning and articulates in the most stark and poignant terms that the meaning of every photograph is death. A photograph of a lost loved one says, simultaneously, 'he is dead and he is going to die'. And, in the photograph of someone still living, that same inevitability is there like a haunting experience. The 'Falling Man' is suspended. Like the screaming boy who runs from the collapsing North Tower, he will always be frozen in this moment. But, the compelling attraction of this photograph lies in the fact that, just as the running boy will always be screaming in terror, the falling man will always be alive.[29] He will always be falling, half way to the ground: always dead but always not yet dead either. Hand in hand with the perpetual *momento mori*, this is the power over death that photography offers. For Barbie Zelizer, this same power is what made it possible to look at photographs of the stricken towers, which in a similar way, all capture the suspended moment between death and life. 'By freezing the story at its most porous and suggestive moment and asking people to do no more than presume death,' she writes, 'the images prolonged public engagement long enough for them to come to grips with what was being depicted.'[30] By the time the many variations of this picture – of the twin towers billowing smoke and fire but not yet collapsed – were seen and understood around the world, we knew that the thousands of people inside were now inevitably dead. And yet, at the moment when the picture was taken, most were not. So, these photographs, as well as protecting us by keeping the graphic reality of death invisible and relying on (among other things) the anthropomorphic replacement of bodies with buildings, function as the rallying symbol of this event, even though in this moment the thousands of deaths that characterize it have not yet taken place. For Zelizer, this is a kind of suspended space that is something to be thankful for, 'even if that did not reflect an understanding of the event's causality and offered no real answers'.[31]

As we have seen though, this vacuum of answers was filled soon enough. To the president, the image of the burning towers represented not an open space between death and life, but a totally clear and unambiguous message:

> Freedom and democracy are under attack ... This enemy attacked not just our people, but all freedom-loving people everywhere in the world ... [we will] conquer this enemy ... we will not allow this enemy to win the war by changing our way of life or restricting our freedoms ... The freedom-loving nations of the world stand by our side. This will be a monumental struggle of good versus evil. But good will prevail.[32]

Into the silence that photography opened up, rushed a whole new national vocabulary: 'Ground Zero', 'freedom towers', 'war on terror', 'sacrifice', 'axis of evil', 'heroes', 'hallowed ground', 'un-American' and 'patriot act' came to proliferate American public discourse virtually overnight and without question.[33] There are helpful and unhelpful kinds of narrative. In the same way, just as the lack of words was a problem on one level, this was a case of too many of the wrong kind of words, with no space for listening. An 'Other' that is referred to wholesale as the 'axis of evil' cannot hope to have a place in a constructive dialogue.[34]

This kind of naming, loaded with value judgement, is a deliberate rhetorical device. But, there is a more subtle sense in which the automatic and seemingly innocuous designation of the event itself – '9/11' – is as problematic. One of the most basic but contentious steps in the narrativizing of a public trauma is naming. Like the photographs that depict them, it seems that events in the public sphere are no longer available for contemplation without quickly becoming subject to labels that nail down their meanings and foreclose any scope for nuances of interpretation. Jacques Derrida was quick to recognize the naming of this event as being not so much a political or ideological problem (in the way that the 'axis of evil' might be), as much as a psychic one: a symptom of the difficulty of transferring the unnameable event from the real, outside of subjects' understanding, into the order of the symbolic:

> We do not in fact know what we are saying or naming in this way ... The brevity of the appellation (September 11, 9/11) stems not only from an economic or rhetorical necessity. The telegram of this metonymy – a name, a number – points out the unqualifiable by recognising that we do not recognise or even cognise, that we do not yet know how to qualify, that we do not yet know what we are talking about.[35]

'9/11' is a numeric label, a code: not a word and thus not a proper name. The event to which it refers is singular, unprecedented and unique, and as such, perhaps, cannot have a name. It cannot be adequately represented by a signifier and cannot be part of the symbolic order. If we have so much trouble even naming this phenomenon, or if it is impossible to fit it within our symbolic system of understanding by demarcating it using language, what business do we have presuming, then, to ascribe to it a story serving nationalistic or any other ideological interests? Having arrived at this 'name', with all that that implies, Derrida says, there was no recourse but to repeat it and keep repeating it until the name seemed to have a meaning. In the absence of understanding or even logic, repetition became the desperate last resort: 'for repetition always protects by neutralizing, deadening, distancing a traumatism, and this is true for the repetition of the televised images'.[36] And here, we come back to the division of words and pictures. For Derrida, the strange 'naming' of '9/11' is a symptom of its unspeakableness:

> [to call the event '9/11' was] to deny, as close as possible to this act of language and this enunciation, our powerlessness to name in an appropriate fashion, to characterise, to think the thing in question, to get beyond the mere deictic of the date: something terrible took place on September 11, and in the end we don't know what.[37]

As long as we cannot use words to describe or, specifically, to name this thing, we cannot recover from it. We have moved too fast past the silence, past the task of reflection and basic understanding, into the neutralizing and distancing repetition of a premature ideological narrative; and with every repetition, we endlessly subject ourselves to the trauma again. Barthes notes that 'the incapacity to name is a good symptom of disturbance', and that 'what I can name cannot really prick me'.[38] According to Derrida, the traumatic event has not adequately been named because it is too painful, and because its terror and trauma are felt to be beyond words. But, the name we have given it protects us from the 'prick' of this truth. Just as the neurotic destructively repeats fragments of a trauma without really remembering in order to control and dominate it, in the same way, we repeat '9/11' (a fragment of a date) and its redemptive narratives without really knowing what this means. Again, the painful, wordless space opened up by photographs has been closed down too fast in the attempt to regain both political and psychological control. '9/11' becomes a kind of soothing ritual incantation which simply signals that a historic event has taken place. All that is offered by this label is the number of the day and month on which the unthinkable happened: no place name, no description, no details necessary. Like a photograph, it is forever expected to speak for itself, and it is further taken for granted that by default nothing that happened anywhere else in the world on that date matters. Nor is it necessary to extend the label to '9/11/2001'. By the same logic that transformed the World Trade Center site into the nominal centre of the universe – 'Ground Zero' – this is Day Zero, on which America's new relationship to the world began and after which 'nothing would be the same'. Stating the year is redundant.

What, then, is the better response? How might it have been it possible, within the context of a democratic politics and an 'over-psychologized society', to work through in a way that was not simplistic transcendence and that did not involve the endless acting out of trauma by the ritual repetition of abstracted names or the revisiting of photographs? In working through the trauma of September 11th, America has had a difficult line to tread between bearing witness and bearing false witness; between reflective narratives that process pain and acknowledge accountability, and redemptive narratives that simplify and turn away from this; between critique and rhetoric, comfort and courage, words and actions. What is perhaps needed above all is a kind of narrative that in some way acknowledges, in Derrida's words, that, even now, we do not yet know what we are talking about. The mistakes of the war on Iraq and its occupation must surely convince us, too late, that we (the 'we' who must accept ourselves as such within the democracies of Britain and the United States, the legality of the war notwithstanding) certainly did not know what we were talking about in early 2003.

September 11th was not just a private or an individual trauma, experienced solely by the people directly involved. It was at the same time precisely the opposite: collective, public, visible and political. This makes the attempt to construct any kind of narrative for it highly contentious. But, new relationships to the past must be negotiated and new group identities consolidated, taking into account notions of American national interest and serving a sense of stability and origin. This is an important part of any kind of memorial project: redrawing the lines of both personal and national identity in the aftermath of an event which has created a sense of existential crisis and brought the subject's sense of self and of the world into question. As a group, people in the United States have needed collective narratives, just like any individual victim of trauma. But, what happens, asks Peter Wollen, when history simply cannot be made sense of in a satisfactory way?

> What if it has no meaningful narrative? If the scene of the crime cannot be narrativized, if it can never be restored to the world of meaning and comprehension, then what else can it do but decay, crumble away, and become a ruin? And as we contemplate this ruin, with its eerie relics and its sinister holes and cracks, what else can we do except resort to melancholy? … We mourn for a meaningless future.[39]

This terrorist attack, horrific as it was, represented a terrible opportunity for the people of the United States to reflect on their vulnerability and their position in the world. Instead, perhaps unsurprisingly, what could have been a period for mournful self-reflection was hijacked by the simplistic rhetoric of war and turned towards an uncritical, melancholic climate of fear. This fear has been used to justify a US foreign policy of paternalistic dominance and imperialism. In short, the American people have been emotionally blackmailed: intimidated into retaliating for, rather than coming to terms with, what has happened to them. Trauma and mourning have themselves been folded easily into this rhetoric, becoming part of the short-hand vocabulary that has characterized the public discourse of the 'War on Terror'. But, in his work on mourning, Freud warns that 'we rely on its being overcome after a certain lapse of time, and we look upon any interference with it as useless or even harmful'.[40] Mourning must take its own unimpeded course in order to come to any kind of resolution. In post–September 11th America, mourning has – both as an abstract notion and in its many concrete outworkings – been at the very least 'interfered with'. And, this interference can only result in the condition identified by Freud as mourning's misdirected and sick alternative: melancholia.

> Mourning is regularly the reaction to the loss of a loved person, or to the loss of some abstraction which has taken the place of one, such as one's country, liberty, an ideal, and so on. In some people the same influences produce melancholia instead of mourning and we consequently suspect them of a pathological disposition.[41]

Mourning is, according to Freud, the normal (if not simple) reaction of a subject to loss. But, depending on the disposition of the subject, or the conditions of their loss, mourning does not always work. Melancholia is the result of its disruption or, we could say, corruption. The normal work of mourning begins with reality-testing, by which the subject confirms that the lost object is gone, demanding that all attachments to it are broken.[42] This meets with obvious opposition of will, as the libido wants to cling to the object. 'Normally', Freud tells us, 'respect for reality gains the day', but this takes time. The process is 'carried out bit by bit, at great expense of time and cathectic energy, and in the meantime the existence of the lost object is psychically prolonged'.[43] One by one, each connecting memory and expectation is brought up, 'hypercathected', and finally detached. Ultimately, given the right conditions, 'when the work of mourning is completed the ego becomes free and uninhibited again'.[44]

The suggestion that, in the aftermath of September 11th, the mourning of American society was somehow undermined, becoming instead a hopeless, self-centred, anxious melancholia, is a difficult one to substantiate when the subject is an entire nation. By way of a few brief examples though, we can see quite alarming indications of Freudian melancholia at large, based on his clearly defined system of diagnosis. This, as with the uses of Freudian and Lacanian theory in in other chapters, is attempted in the spirit of Dominick LaCapra's (and others') project of widening the territory of psychoanalysis from individual clinical practice to a kind of psychoanalysis of history. Freud himself devoted a considerable period of his career to the analysis of group behaviours and collective values such as nationhood and guilt.[45] But, for him, this does not seem to have stretched beyond general analysis of 'group psychology' to the diagnosis of particular psychological problems or conditions (such as melancholia) at a group level. LaCapra explains that rather than necessarily adhering to ideas of therapeutic psychoanalytic practice, or even to the idea of working through as a 'cure', it is possible to take psychoanalysis 'in more ethical and political directions':[46]

> I am intent on showing why psychoanalysis is misunderstood as merely a psychology of the individual, and its basic concepts are overly reduced when they are confined to a clinical context, however important the latter may be. In addition, certain key psychoanalytic concepts (such as transference, denial, resistance, repression, acting-out, and working-through) are crucial in the attempt to elucidate the relation between cultures that come into contact as well as between the present (including the analyst) and the past.[47]

This characterization of the historian as psychoanalyst has been met in recent years with accusations of reductionism (the labelling of socio-political phenomena by reference to a presumed common substream or essence of the psyche) and hastiness. It has also been identified as part of a wave of scholarship concerned with memory in historical discourse which makes uncritical assumptions about so-called collective or cultural memory, and which is guilty of 'carelessly applying psychoneurotic jargon to groups'.[48] On the other hand, however, the application of the principles of psychoanalysis to an essentialist psychology of the individual seems in some ways to be just as reductive. Psychoanalysis is founded on a social relation – that between analyst and analysand – and as Freud shows in his explorations of literature and even sculpture is surely flexible enough to be implemented not just in the observation of a society, but in the diagnosis of its prevailing pathologies too.

The first of Freud's melancholic indicators is ambivalence about the nature of loss. Unlike normal mourning in which the lost object is clearly identified (for example the death of a loved one), in the analysis of a melancholic subject, 'one cannot clearly see what it is that has been lost'.[49]

> This, indeed, might be so even if the patient is aware of the loss which has given rise to his melancholia, but only in the sense that he knows whom he has lost but not what he has lost in him. This would suggest that melancholia is in

some way related to an object-loss which is withdrawn from consciousness, in contradisctinction to mourning, in which there is nothing about the loss that is unconscious.[50]

A degree of uncertainty was quickly identified in the American press as to what exactly was lost or destabilized as a result of the September 11th attacks, and it has already been suggested that for most communities across the country, trauma resulted more from the vague sense of a new instability and insecurity than actual loss of life:

> When the smoke cleared from the collapsed world trade center towers, everything had changed. It was as if someone had yanked a cord and the walls of America fell away. Suddenly, we understood the unimaginable truth: we are as naked and vulnerable as any country. Our security, with its military might and vast network of intelligence agents, is as illusory as a Hollywood set.[51]

This highly typical press excerpt is consistent with Freud's remarks that in cases of melancholia, rather than a loss that is necessarily a death, 'one can recognize that there is a loss of a more ideal kind', like, for example, security, or faith in military might and intelligence systems.[52] These are significant but somewhat vague losses, much more difficult to define and mourn than the loss of a particular person or other tangible entity. An effect of this vagueness of loss is a correspondingly vague anxiety, a common response to which is to withdraw in a self-protective and paranoid way from the rest of the world. This is the second of Freud's indicative symptoms. In his terms, the ego cuts itself off from the world and turns to the object, rather than cutting itself off from the lost object and turning back towards a functional relation to the world, as in the work of mourning. This is also referred to as the 'regression of libido into the ego'.[53] The result of this is a kind of melancholic, anxious and paranoid self-obsession, which is arguably not difficult to discern in post–September 11th American society. Kai Erikson identifies this condition as a symptom not just of misdirected mourning, but of trauma more generally. 'People stripped of the ability to screen out signs of peril,' he says, tend to be 'unusually vigilant and unusually anxious':

> They evaluate the data of everyday life differently, read signs differently, see omens that the rest of us are for the most part spared … After all, how do you estimate the odds of being damaged by a given hazard when it has already happened to you? To consult a chart and then declare that it is a one-in-a-million shot is too abstract by far. The times call for something else.[54]

Ironically though, the state reaction to this vague anxiety in the United States was indeed a chart (Erikson's remark was made back in 1995). The Department of Homeland Security and its colour-coded Advisory System, established in November 2002, is the most obvious and commonly cited indicator of the post–September 11th climate of fear. For the vast majority of its nine-year period of implementation, the threat level advised by the five-tiered system remained at 'yellow', or 'elevated', signifying 'significant risk of terrorist attacks', and that while 'there continues to be no credible, specific intelligence to suggest an imminent threat to the homeland at this time ... all Americans should continue to be vigilant, take notice of their surroundings, and report suspicious items or activities to local authorities immediately'.[55] The effect of this non-specific call to vigilance and fear has been much commented upon and widely criticized. In the *New York Times* in 2006, Bob Herbert recalled that while in the dark days of the Depression Franklin Roosevelt counselled Americans to resist fear, George W. Bush had chosen instead to use the public's fear as his most powerful political asset.[56] Jürgen Habermas has also reflected on this aspect of the attacks' aftermath, perhaps little knowing that the conditions he describes would continue to be carefully sustained for years afterwards:

> I do not know whether the US government itself was slightly paranoid or merely shunning responsibility. At any rate, the repeated and utterly nonspecific announcements of possible new terror attacks and the senseless calls to 'be alert' further stirred a vague feeling of angst along with an uncertain readiness – precisely the intention of the terrorists.[57]

Habermas's language points directly to melancholia. As well as the melancholic symptoms of vague paranoid anxiety and angst, he also names a third sign of the condition: the shunning of responsibility. Here, the straightforward application of Freud's principles to post–September 11th American society breaks down somewhat, because a key characteristic of melancholia appears to be missing: that of self-reproach. In what seems at first like a paradox, Freud identifies a kind of misdirected or inauthentic self-reproach within melancholia that is linked directly with the avoidance of responsibility. While there were those within American society who urged critical reflection and consideration of responsibility on a state level, particularly with regard to foreign policy decisions, the majority-voice of patriotism, hero-worship and national triumph that followed left little room for reflexive examination or awareness, let alone reproach.[58] But, the faux self-reproach that tends, for Freud, to come with melancholia gives way something that *is* identifiable in the American post–September 11th flag-waving frenzy: blame.[59] While it is normal to direct blame at those responsible for such a horrific act, no community can recover from trauma and loss, Judith Lewis Herman reminds us, without adequately addressing its own responsibilities and moving forward with some measure of humility. 'Like traumatized individuals', she writes, 'traumatized countries need to remember, grieve, and atone for their wrongs in order to avoid reliving them.'[60] They must not, she says, rush to a premature peace that is really only appeasement, amnesia or denial and that corresponds to acting out. In fact, we might say that in Freud's terms, mourning is to melancholia as working through is to acting out. While the mourner can work through their loss and recover, the melancholic is condemned to perpetual repetition and anxiety. The repetition compulsion is based on a need for the subject endlessly to replay the traumatic experience in order to reassure themselves that they have withstood it. This acting out is a destructive and hopeless process that became even more destructive when performed by the American media and the political administration for their own ends, as it both exacerbated and manipulated the already destructive repetition of the traumatic scene through photography. Without the endless and ideologically over-determined re-presentation of photographic images, the process of constructive public mourning would more easily have been allowed to run its course.[61]

But, photography was also the medium most commonly used in individual attempts to confront reality, often in concerted efforts to break out of the interpretive frames put forward by the culture industry. This brings us back again to the ubiquitous, misguided idea of pictures telling stories, standing in for words, and providing the fullness of meaning that so many needed so badly, and still do. Barthes argues that no photograph contains anything but 'flat death', but for many people, there was the ongoing compulsion to collect masses of photographs in search of life, or truth, or presence, or essence, which would 'stand for' or make sense of what happened. Barthes testifies in *Camera Lucida* to this same frustration as he searches through piles of photographs for the essence of his mother. No single image or even stack of images can sum her up. They offer no being, only fragments. In a hopeless riposte to Allan Sekula's 'archival ambition', by which more photographs must equal more knowledge, Barthes admits that 'straining towards the essence of her identity, I was struggling among images partially true, and therefore totally false'.[62] Then, on finding the one image that brings his mother closer than any other, the 'winter garden photograph', what confronts him is only the further hopelessness of finding any healing in it:

> I cannot transform my grief, I cannot let my gaze drift ... the photograph ... is without culture: when it is painful, nothing in it can transform grief into mourning. And if dialectic is that thought which masters the corruptible and converts the negation of death into the power to work, then the photograph is undialectical: it is a denatured theatre where death cannot 'be contemplated', reflected and interiorised; or again: the dead theatre of Death, the foreclosure of the Tragic, excludes all purification, all catharsis.[63]

'Painful' photographs, or those associated with loss, disrupt the dialectical process by which the pain of this loss might be transformed into the progress of mourning. They are a short circuit. Even though we can hold them in our hands and look at them for as long as we like, they offer too small a slice of time to be grasped. They do not allow for real contemplation and cannot offer any helpful transition towards order or recovery. This is confirmed and made more complex still when the loss under consideration is violent and traumatic:

> The trauma is a suspension of language, a blocking of meaning. Certainly situations which are normally traumatic can be seized in a process of photographic signification but then precisely they are indicated via a rhetorical code which distances, sublimates and pacifies them. Truly traumatic photographs are rare … the traumatic photograph (fires, shipwrecks, catastrophes, violent deaths, all captured 'from life as lived') is the photograph about which there is nothing to say; the shock-photo is by structure insignificant: no value, no knowledge, at the limit; no verbal categorization can have a hold on the process instituting the signification. One could imagine a kind of law: the more direct the trauma, the more difficult is connotation; or again, the 'mythological' effect of a photograph is inversely proportional to its traumatic effect.[64]

That traumatic experience blocks or suspends language is now accepted. What Barthes offers us here, however, is an explanation for what photographic representation, in such cases of violence or trauma, does to this element of the traumatic. For him, most photographs of such events do not repeat the trauma or confront the viewer with it, but rather 'denature' and 'sublimate' it by subjecting it to photography's own limited rhetorical frame. This would apply to most, if not, all of the September 11th photographs circulating in the public sphere, about whose 'mythological rhetoric' there is so much to say. The genuinely traumatic or shocking photograph – which, Barthes stresses, is rare, and which would here refer to photographs of the attacks deemed by the press to be too graphic or upsetting to be released to a general public audience – is insignificant because it is beyond linguistic categorization. Photographs of this kind, about which there is nothing to say, which are beyond connotation, are, in the vast public archive of September 11th images, all but non-existent. Instead, this archive consists only of images that, according to Barthes's logic, can neither heal the psychic wounds of trauma nor exacerbate them. They are ultimately irrelevant and without any meaning other than the signification of mythology and rhetoric. Rather than exhibiting death, they present analogies for it, the most basic of which is the substitution of fallen and broken bodies with fallen and broken buildings. Just as the most horrific events are the ones that cannot adequately be named, the most moving or arresting photographs are the ones whose effect cannot be put into words. Photography can be called the perfect realization of the human aspiration to defeat death – to stop it in its tracks by freezing and preserving life for all time. (As André Bazin writes, 'death is but the victory of time. To preserve the bodily appearance artificially is to snatch it from the flow of time, to stow it neatly away, so to speak, in the hold of life.'[65]) While projects like *Here is New York* seem to hold this as their foundational assumption not exactly the preservation of life but preservation of the moments of death in the hope of finding meaning, Barthes warns that the opposite is true: photography does not represent the transcendence of death, but the dive right into it. In fact, photography's intimate connection with death, for Barthes, corresponds with a profound shift in Western thinking and custom surrounding death:

> Contemporary with the withdrawal of rites, Photography may correspond to the intrusion, in our modern society, of an asymbolic Death, outside of religion, outside of ritual, a kind of abrupt dive into literal Death. Life/Death: the paradigm is reduced to a simple click, the one separating the initial pose from the final click ... Earlier societies managed so that memory, the substitute for life, was eternal and that at least the thing which spoke of Death should itself be immortal: this was the monument. But by making the (mortal) photograph into the general and somehow natural witness of 'what has been', modern society has renounced the monument.[66]

If photographs cannot help us in the process of coming to terms with death, neither can they effectively serve as the monuments to death that many seek to use them for. Barthes's comments are particularly interesting when viewed alongside what would seem to be the most ephemeral kind of monument imaginable: digital photographs circulating immaterially in cyberspace, or on newsprint that is made to last just a day before being discarded. Even large-scale memorial exhibitions like *Here is New York* or the US State Department's *After September 11*, which point to photographs as the most fitting tributes to September 11th, in Barthes's terms fall far short of what a monument should be. In her personal account of using photography to come to terms with the September 11th experience, Marianne Hirsch acknowledges how little sensory and emotional substance is accessible through photographs – specifically her own: 'it is this ordinariness, this platitude that I find frustrating in the pictures. I look at them and I seek out the monumentality I feel. I wonder how, through these photographs, others who are not here might be able to share in the dimensions of these deaths, their grandeur. But perhaps the flatness of the images is precisely what we need.'[67] One of her conclusions is that of the many things we ask photography to do, all it really can do is prove that something happened and that the photographer was there. Beyond that, her experience seems very much like Barthes's, recognizing that in the flatness of photographs, there is a kind of comforting, empty numbness that no-one wants to admit they are looking for.

Of the rites of death that Barthes says have been 'withdrawn' in modern Western society, perhaps the most significant are the rites of looking and watching. There was a time not long ago when it was a normal part of life to be brought face to face with death; when through wakes, vigils and even the custom of post-mortem photography, we were as European and (until less recently) American societies very familiar with seeing the bodies of our communities' dead. The vigil (from the Latin *vigilia*, or 'wakefulness') is a period of sleepless devotional watching or observance. This practice, in which a group of mourners sit together through the night watching over a loved one's coffin, and indeed the convention of open coffins for visitation at funeral homes have all but disappeared. While traditionally a means of making sure the lost person was really dead and that the spirit would not leave their body before the funeral rites had been performed, these practices have also been shown to be psychically beneficial in the grieving process of mourners themselves because they make way for acceptance. Watching – particularly *prolonged* watching – and being brought 'face to face' with death, while painful, helps to integrate the truth of death in a much more complete way than if this truth is quickly hidden from view in the name of discretion or minimizing distress. As Barthes acknowledges, however, death in our medicalized industrial culture is now just a momentary 'click', which might be less painful in the short term but puts us at a disadvantage in fully coming to terms with it.

James O'Brien, a contributor to the *September 11 Photo Project*, recalls, 'I then returned to Ground Zero on Thursday, September 13, to turn in my photos to the FBI. I also felt the need to see the towers buried in the ground firsthand so that I could begin to grieve.'[68] Most people could not go and visit the spot where the towers were 'buried in the ground', so they looked at photographs instead. But, either way, does this impulse indicate that something in us remembers the significance of looking to mourn, as a necessary part of dealing with death, especially when that death is shocking and unexpected? Barthes would then say that this is a vain exercise, because photography itself is 'flat death' and offers only the shallowest kind of looking. While our looking may be prolonged, it is only at a thin, instantaneous slice of time that is inherently violent, and so cannot ease the pain of violence. Besides, if we see no bodies in these photographs, we are not really bearing witness to death on any level at all.

'Images anaesthetize', Susan Sontag has famously said. Repeated exposure to photographs of an event makes the event less real, rather than more. Initial shock wears off with familiarity and saturation, and 'photographs, which turn the past into a consumable object, are a short cut.'[69] Though she herself has been accused of paying too little attention to the specificity of what it means to look at actual photographs, her words indicate that a collection of photographs, whether in an exhibition space, in a book, or on a memorial website, while powerful in one sense, cannot ever be a tool in coming to terms with the reality of what is pictured, being instead a reductive abbreviation. Neither the collection nor the repetition of photographs really brings any psychological healing, because though anaesthesia might feel like healing, it is not. Ulrich Baer identifies this phenomenon in another context: the gradual transformation of photographs of the 1945 liberation of

Nazi death camps from unspeakably shocking documents to ubiquitous clichés. Their overuse, he argues, has led to the 'disappearance of memory in the act of commemoration':

> They represent the past as fully retrievable (as simply a matter of searching the archive), instead of situating vis-à-vis the intangible presence of an absence, which Jacques Derrida has called the 'hell in our memory'. When they have not become mute clichés, on the other hand, the graphic images of death are likely to disable the viewer's capacity to remember or to respond, either critically or with empathy. In their irreversible finality, such pictures represent history as locked in the past.[70]

Baer points to a whole range of dangers here. Photographs make remembering too easy. They seem to commodify even that which is invisible. They are 'mute clichés'. Most seriously, perhaps, they are paralysing barriers to history: recalling Marita Sturken's accusation that we are all detached tourists of the past, photographs are a means of putting the past firmly beyond our reach and absolving us of any responsibility to act (or even think) in the present. Photographs verify our impotence, and the cycle of melancholy continues.

While pictures have an important role to play, recovery from a trauma like September 11th cannot progress as long as a community continues trying to make images do things that cannot be asked of them. Recovery involves the construction of coherent meaning, so that decisions can be made about the future and the community's new relationship to the world based on what has happened. The effective use of words is not only crucial in this process, in the movement from acting out to remembering and working through, or from melancholia to mourning, but also for the democratic process of truth-telling, accountability and genuine public debate. Dissenting public voices were marginalized, stigmatized and silenced in regard to many of the Bush administration's most significant post–September 11th policies. Instead of reason and reflection, the government promoted fear; instead of memory, patriotic commemoration; and instead of open verbal debate, a mesmerising and endless vista of photographs that were said to speak for themselves and tell the whole story.

What hope is there, then, for photographs like the ones discussed here, which surely have value beyond their ideological mobilization, their deflection of psychological recovery and their capacity to offer false comfort? They are still traces, albeit incomplete, of an event that was not just a spectacle but a brutal reality. My aim is not to propose how they might, in practice, be reclaimed, but it seems clear that two things would need to happen. First, these images would need to be removed from the redemptive narratives constructed around them (because redemptive narrative, when combined with spectacular images, has been shown to equal spectacular power), and separated from their ideological investments.

This is the only way that, second, words can be given their proper place. Addressing a conference on globalization and photography in 2007, Iain Boal, member of Retort and co-author of *Afflicted Powers*, spoke against the common misconception that in this 'globalized image culture', images have somehow trumped or superseded words. On the contrary, he claimed, they have never been more *subject* to words – framing systems of power, politics and ideology.[71] Images are everywhere used by and in the service of words, to the point where words have become truncated in comparison. A prime example of this is the centrality of photography in the manipulative arsenal of Islamist terrorists, who use images of destruction to spread fear and to enforce fundamentalist views. Boal went on in his lecture to question how the art world might 'image back' in response to the use of images not only by terrorists but by the American (and British) governments. He toyed with phrases such as 'anti-imaging' and 'counter-hegemonic image-making', as if experimenting with language and searching for a term to describe a practice that is unnameable because it has never existed before, presumably because it has never before been so necessary. Whether what is implied by these terms is a reclaiming of the image ('imaging back') or a triumph of the verbal over the visual ('anti-imaging'), the danger is that they each posit the replacement of one received narrative of September 11th with a different one – perhaps less redemptive, but still inevitably reductive and, presumably, equally loaded with moral value judgements. The answer is not more words, or more pictures, but a new and radically reflective use of both, the highest goal of which should be a renewed understanding of, and empathy with, the other. At the time of writing, even as the image-frenzy seems to have abated giving way to a verbally coherent tackling of the question 'why?' or 'why us?', the legacy of the post–September 11th image-overload is still very present. Images, not words, are still how the world remembers September 11th 2001, because that is how it was first communicated, and how viewers worldwide were encouraged to remember it, bear witness to it and reflect upon it. If this endless, emotive image spectacle was used to obscure more critical questions and verbal dialogue, America is still paying the price in an inability to truly mourn and recover, remaining still in a stage of incoherent, unspeakable anger and fear, struggling through piles of photographs for a picture that is only partially true, and therefore totally false.

CONCLUSION: BEYOND WORDS

Everyone knows that we need two eyes in order to see anything in relief and make a choice. Anyone who aims a gun knows this.

PAUL VIRILIO[1]

If the World Trade Center attacks occupy not only Ground Zero, but Day Zero: a turning point after which nothing can ever be the same, this day becomes fixed as a historical moment around which there can be no ambiguity. With this belief comes such a strong determination to respond and push forward into the future that everything before that September day ceases to exist and looking back is seemingly not required. This is another compelling truism that is just as likely to block the way for critical engagement as the temptation to wait for an 'ideal time'. The figure who has perhaps most powerfully denounced this kind of thinking is Walter Benjamin. In his last major work, written in the midst of the Second World War shortly before he committed suicide, he recognized the importance of looking backwards, but in doing so, he did not see a narrative that could help him make any sense of the present. Instead, he gives an account of the 'angel of history': a metaphorical figure (inspired by a painting by Paul Klee) who stands with his back to the future, arrested by a vision of the past which is laid out before him. But, rather than a sequential chain of events, what he sees instead is that history is a perpetual accumulation: 'one single catastrophe which keeps piling wreckage upon wreckage and hurls it in front of his feet'.[2] For Benjamin, this kind of historical consciousness is our best hope for understanding the present, even if it leaves us helpless to intervene:

> The angel would like to stay, awaken the dead, and make whole what has been smashed. But a storm is blowing from Paradise; it has got caught in his wings with such violence that the angel can no longer close them. The storm irresistibly propels him into the future to which his back is turned, while the pile of debris before him grows skyward.[3]

Like the eyewitness in the street who is caught by the camera and held forever in a tension between looking on and turning away (Figure I.1), the angel is condemned to remain a perpetual bearer of witness. The context of Benjamin's vision is a critique of Marxist historical materialism, which understands the past as a continuum of progress; a sequence of intelligible events that can be read as culminating in a revolutionary future. Instead, Benjamin argues for a looking back that understands history as, above all else, an encounter. For him, 'to articulate the past historically does not mean to recognise it "the way it really was". It means to seize hold of a memory as it flashes up at a moment of danger.'[4] To suggest that history can be perceived or interpreted as a stable narrative is ideological fallacy.

A few years earlier, Benjamin had written about a different kind of witnessing, of a different kind of aftermath. Considering the photography of Eugène Atget, whose pictures of deserted Parisian streets looked to Benjamin like 'the scene of a crime', he argued that a space for the political use or abuse of photography is opened up above all by aesthetic emptiness: no human figures, no faces and no emotive details. All is open to interpretation because these photographs 'pump the aura out of reality like water from a sinking ship'.[5] Benjamin very much approved of this kind of 'forensic' anti-aesthetic, in which there was no room for psychological melodrama or emotional identification, and this made Atget's work in his opinion the first model for a fully realized photographic practice. Maybe it is paradoxical, though, that Benjamin should have associated this ultimate ideal of empty neutrality with the photography of crime scenes: the very locations of human drama. Or, maybe that was the whole point. His angel of history surveys a crime scene too, in an image loaded with pathos. It is the job of the forensic photographer to arrive at the scene of suffering, violence, pain, death and fear, and to 'pump the aura out'. Why? So that even though we cannot bring the victim back to life, we can still learn something useful. Like the angel, the forensic photographer's job is not to change what took place amidst the wreckage but to bear witness to it.

Crime scenes, of course, are sacred places. As Peter Wollen writes, 'anybody who watches Court TV knows that crime scenes should never be disturbed. They should never be contaminated. They should never be entered by unauthorized people. Nothing should ever be moved until it has been photographed … In fact, it should be treated exactly as if it were sacred. In this context the photographer's camera is not simply a recording device, but an officiant's ceremonial object, and the photograph itself can be regarded as a kind of icon or relic.'[6] Perhaps this indicates why the cultural response to September 11th has allowed for an abundance of photography, which seems to record without touching but has largely banished critique, which might tamper, interfere or disturb. Sacred spaces are exempt from theory, especially theory borne out of a tradition as disruptive as 'deconstruction'.

Nowhere in history has the sacredness of a crime scene been more vigorously upheld than Ground Zero – one tenet of the mission statement of the National September 11 Memorial Museum is to 'respect this place made sacred through tragic loss' – and as we have seen, no photographer has been more firmly identified with the role of ceremonial officiant than Joel Meyerowitz. (David Campany goes further, calling him an 'undertaker'.[7]) His work shows, though, how great an interpretive leap there can be from the forensic to the ceremonial. Four masked men in hard hats stoop in the rubble of the Pit, one holding a lamp to better see into the gaps between the twisted pieces of metal and concrete. One of them (possibly two) has 'Police' marked across his back. The caption of the photograph reads 'Searchers in Rubble', and the date only '2001'. No month is specified, so we can't tell much about what stage of the process the image records. We don't know how much time has passed since the crime, what these searchers have already uncovered, or how wearied they have become from the tension of looking and the horror of finding. They are in the extreme foreground, so close to us that two of their bodies are bisected by the frame. But they are not its focus. So small are they in comparison to the rising majesty of the ruins that surround them, in scale so much more like the bits of building on the ground, that they are just part of the texture of the periphery, and the eye finds them only after the picture has already made its impact. Wreckage piled upon wreckage and hurled at their feet, the searchers keep their gaze close to the ground and are unmoved by the spectacle that we see behind them. They are tending to the victims as best they can, leaving us free to look on in awe at the play of light on the latticework of the remaining façades and the impossible grandeur of this edifice that looks more like a cathedral than when the towers were standing tall in its place. Within the hallowed perimeter of Ground Zero, Meyerowitz made a set of photographs that could not have been further away from the work of Atget, and of which Walter Benjamin would certainly not have approved. Rather than being stripped away, aura is ramped up to an epic level, suggesting not a single, emptied instant of frozen reality or a momentary flash of experience but the whole arc of history, stable and continuous.[8] The attack on the twin towers is fixed within a great unfolding story of which we already know the ending because good triumphs over evil, inevitably and always.

By contrast with this presentation of the aftermath, the succession of moments that unfolded on September 11th was compressed and disordered, as the combination of 'real-time' broadcasting, an overload of imagery and the uncoupling of that imagery from words created what seemed to many like one single catastrophe. It is tempting to connect this phenomenon – this simultaneous piling of wreckage – with Paul Virilio's conception of mediated time: instead of an unfolding story, a disorder of synchronicity; an exposure of compressed, chronoscopic time that left us transfixed and helpless.[9] Judith Lewis Herman writes of the 'pile of snapshots' that constitutes traumatic memory – another potent metaphor in the light of Benjamin's vision – which can play a role in recovery, but only if the subject is able to sort through them, overcoming the entropy of time and space and committing them to some kind of sequence.[10]

The role of Benjamin's allegorical angel is to learn: he is history reflexively re-examining itself. But, the angel is powerless and so the lessons he learns are ultimately painful. He has given up searching in the rubble for any trace of meaning and is resigned to standing still. For Benjamin, writing in despair and exile near the end of his own life, this is still a worthwhile pursuit. But, in twenty-first-century American public discourse, there is still, over a decade on, little room for existential nihilism, just as there is little room for the ambiguity of the uncanny, or even for the painful course of true mourning. It cannot be tolerated, and for many, looking to the past with a critical eye is not an option. Faced with Meyerowitz's photographs, we may look on in grief, but we are not positioned as helpless onlookers. There is wreckage and catastrophe, but there is no paralysis here. We are invited instead to identify with the heroic protagonists, woven into their redemptive narrative, reassured that the story will move forward from this moment towards a better one. From Day Zero, the point at which the lines of history are redrawn, the only value to be gained from looking back is in finding patterns that confirm what we want to see in the present.[11] As the years have gone by, these photographs, along with all the others discussed here, have moved back and forth through the signifying chains of discourse and memory-work, dynamic carriers of meaning that continues to shift and change. But, their collective status as the definitive record of public memory only intensifies. The further this terrible event recedes into history, the greater the weight of memory becomes. Each image is required to transport us over a greater distance, show more, reveal more and explain more. The passage of time allows for more critical detachment in how we talk about them, but it also makes them more sacred, as pieces of the past that gradually become more vivid than our own memories.

The pain of September 11th, that isolated, exceptional, unprecedented point in history, seemed to make way for a glorious new mission: a war with a whole new set of rules, justification not only for a new ruthlessness in rooting out and punishing anyone who might pose a threat, but in the suspension of rights in the American Homeland: rights to privacy, free speech and, most significantly, the right to freedom from fear. The climate of fear that was cultivated by the American administration, keeping the public in a manipulable state of anxious support for the 'War on Terror', has been commented on widely. It is another part of the same network of cultural phenomena implicated in the representations of September 11th. But, while it was extraordinary and in many ways unique, September 11th 2001 was not, of course, Year Zero, or Day Zero. The discontinuous irruption that Paul Virilio describes – the chronoscopic funnelling of all time into an instant that can only lead to obsessive fixation – is thus the description of an ideological apparatus. As well as being a senseless and indefensible act to which no logic can be applied, it was also a convergence of histories: complex international political and diplomatic issues, globalization and antiglobalization movements, the diversification and misconceptions of Islam and others. America was part of a fragile world order long before there was a colour-coded warning system by which to measure its fragility on a given day. September 11th provoked a sense of unprecedentedness on the one hand, but also, for some, of culmination, and this confusion prevails.

Since that day, commentators from both inside and outside the United States have expressed grave concerns about breaches of human rights and civil liberties that have taken place under the auspices of its new war. In writing this book, my motivation has been a concern not primarily with this issue, important as it is, but with other aspects of that war that are more difficult both to implement and to quantify: the engineering of emotions, corrosive campaigns of distraction and social phenomena that ostensibly fall within the critical remit of the humanities but have implications that do not. I have explored some of the disjunctures between looking and not looking, the visible and the invisible, the invisible and the overvisible, looking and witnessing, seeing and thinking, seeing and speaking, seeing and being traumatized, seeing to recover and seeing to redeem an unspeakable sight. For most people in the United States, the kind of trauma involved in experiencing September 11th was characterized by technological mediation and distance. In this sense, the event signalled a new paradigm of perception, even introduced new kinds of traumatic encounter that have not existed before. In such a context, images are so potent that they can be blinding. They are also wide open to manipulation, precisely because of their capacity to evade language: most of us do not have the vocabulary to define just what goes on in, through, around and because of images like these. In showing how photographs formed part of an attempted collective recovery process as well as part of a political state apparatus, I have tried to help build this vocabulary.

For the ideology of chronoscopic time, in which there can be no process, only the paralysing and eternal instant of exposure, photographs are the perfect vehicles. Whether in the frozen snapshot that holds forever the falling tower and the running schoolboy, or in the extended stillness of Joel Meyerowitz's hallowed crime scene, time erupts, breaks the surface and becomes space: the eternal, overexposed Zero. Because of how it came to us, September 11th was not just an event, it was a photographic event. And the photographs of it are not just photographs, they are violent exposures of the real-time instant. It is not an exaggeration to say that by this process of compression, in which the protocols of understanding were so spectacularly broken, millions of people have remained collectively locked in a repetitive cycle of fearful melancholia, prevented from engaging in the psychological work of moving on. Photographs have played a part in laying the foundations for this and other, much more obvious forms of violence, and of abuses of human rights and civil liberties. Does this mean that governments are responsible for managing the seeing of catastrophe? Does it mean that specific photographs can dictate public policy? No, but it means that a multitude of photographs made in good faith: immediate, urgent, plural, necessary, personal, up close, far away, hopeful, hopeless, as chaotic as they should be; have been hijacked, slotted into politically expedient narratives and adopted by a population that was already hurting, vulnerable and hungry for sense. People need photographs in times of such confusion. The collection and display of photographs in the aftermath of this violence was an entirely necessary exercise. Photographs were necessary because they had the power to show a thousand different subject positions and reflect a thousand different experiences. As part of the work of grief, individual people could hold on to them not as stable documents but as symbols that could mean what they needed them to mean. As well as being vehicles for ideology, photographs were, and continue to be, visual objects that helped reconstruct meaningful social realities and participated in the act of bearing witness to the events. But at the same time that this quiet work was going on, we were being told much more loudly and in no uncertain terms what they meant.

We were also told to look and not speak. In a message that resonated conveniently with what many people instinctively felt – that the pictures were beyond words – we were urged to remain in stunned, broken silence. Despite the critical attention that has been paid to these photographs over the years, they have ultimately, again and again, been held up as self-evident signals of the redundancy of words. Photographs do indeed exceed words, but words are also necessary in order not only to ask questions about them as some have done, but to find a way of moving forward through the chaotic spaces that they open up. Pictures do many things within us, between us, and around us, in the places where meaning does not easily take shape because it is not there, and where reason fails. But what they never do is speak. When these pictures emerged, there were no words for them, not because they spoke for themselves, but because in that moment *there was nothing to say*. There was only fragmented horror: shattered and shattering glimpses of senselessness. The pictures did not come together to form a whole or to tell a story, though many grasped frantically for them in the hope that they would, because there was no whole; there was no grand, tidy, overarching narrative. There were only millions of individual experiences and small personal narratives of recovery to be navigated and pieced together bit by bit. Photographs can help with this process, because this is a power that they do have – it is a legitimate request that we can make of photography – but this power was curtailed as their meanings were bent and turned towards further violence and further terror waged far away in the name of everyone who had ever looked at a photograph of downtown Manhattan and wordlessly wept.

These are the stakes involved in talking about pictures well: carefully, slowly, humbly, openly, in dialogue, together. It is not reactionary iconoclasm to say that photographs are dangerous. They are exactly as dangerous, ambiguous and contradictory as they should be. If I look at a photograph of a human being suffering injustice and feel emotion rise in me, and you tell me, before my emotion has even taken shape, what I am feeling, what it means and what I should do about it, you have wronged me. You have robbed me of my voice, taken the power of the photograph for yourself and taken advantage of that suffering person for your own ends. In the turmoil of late 2001, this happened on a vast scale. And, this would have been more than enough wrongdoing, had it not also formed the background to a series of public policy decisions that have ultimately led to thousands more deaths in two unwinnable wars of which there is still no true end. I make no argument for a solution. Projects that aim to reclaim the photograph in some way, to create alternative interpretations or to supplant the visual with the verbal, only amount to replacing one reductive account of September 11th with another. The only conclusion is a call for space, plurality, freedom to speak and to choose. Let the images come as they will, but give me the space to see.

NOTES

Preface: *I was there*

1 Susan Sontag, *Regarding the Pain of Others* (London: Penguin, 2004), pp. 76–77.

Introduction

1 Barbie Zelizer in Barbie Zelizer and Stuart Allan (eds), *Journalism After September 11* (London: Routledge, 2002), p. 63.

2 Slavoj Žižek, *Welcome to the Desert of the Real* (London: Verso, 2002), pp. 11–15.

3 The term 'image event' comes from Nicholas Mirzoeff, *The Visual Culture Reader* (second edition) (London: Routledge, 2002), but he may not have been the first to use it.

4 Marianne Hirsch, 'I Took Pictures: September 2001 and Beyond', in Judith Greenberg (ed.), *Trauma at Home: After 9/11* (Lincoln: University of Nebraska Press, 2003).

5 E. Ann Kaplan, 'A Camera and a Catastrophe', in Greenberg (ed.), *Trauma at Home: After 9/11*.

6 Andrea D. Fitzpatrick, 'The Movement of Vulnerability: Images of Falling and September 11', *Art Journal*, vol. 66, no. 4 (2007), pp. 85–102; Rob Kroes, 'The Ascent of the Falling Man: Establishing a Picture's Iconicity', *Journal of American Studies*, vol. 45, no. 4 (2011), pp. 47–67.

7 Robert Hariman and John Louis Lucaites, *No Caption Needed: Iconic Photographs, Public Culture, and Liberal Democracy* (London: University of Chicago Press, 2007), p. 46.

8 David Simpson, *9/11: The Culture of Commemoration* (London: The University of Chicago Press, 2006), p. 7.

9 As well as those that I will go on to cite here, other examples of serious, critical/theoretical critique include Žižek, *Welcome to the Desert of the Real*; Noam Chomsky, *Pirates and Emperors, Old and New: International Terrorism in the Real World* (London: Pluto, 2002); and Denzin and Lincoln (eds), *9/11 in American Culture*. None of these, however, make a sustained attempt to address September 11th's visual representation in particular.

10 Dominick LaCapra, *Representing the Holocaust: History, Theory, Trauma* (London and Ithaca: Cornell University Press, 1994), p. 1.

11 Giovanna Borradori, *Philosophy in a Time of Terror: Dialogues with Jürgen Habermas and Jacques Derrida* (London: University of Chicago Press, 2003). These views are expounded by Habermas in *The Structural Transformation of the Public Sphere: An Inquiry into a Category of Bourgeois Society* (trans. Thomas Burger and Frederick Lawrence) (London: Polity Press, 1989).

12 Borradori, *Philosophy in a Time of Terror*, p. 17.

13 Borradori, *Philosophy in a Time of Terror*, p. 86.

14 Powell cited in *After September 11: Images from Ground Zero: An Exhibition by the US Department of State, Bureau of Educational and Cultural Affairs, with Photographs by Joel Meyerowitz* (exhibition catalogue, 2004), pp. 1 and 5.

15 Victor Burgin, 'Looking at Photographs', in Victor Burgin (ed.), *Thinking Photography* (London: Macmillan, 1982), p. 148.

16 Borradori, *Philosophy in a Time of Terror*, pp. 26–27.

17 Simpson, *9/11*, p. 11.

18 Paul Virilio, *Open Sky* (London: Verso, 1997), p. 3. This book builds on arguments established in his previous book, *Polar Inertia*.

19 Virilio, *Open Sky*, p. 27.

20 Virilio, *Open Sky*, p. 39.

21 Virilio, *Open Sky*, p. 40.

22 David Foster Wallace, 'The View from Mrs. Thompson's', *Rolling Stone* (25 October 2001), p. 132.

23 W.J.T. Mitchell, 'Criticism and Crisis', *Critical Inquiry*, vol. 28, no. 2 (2002), p. 571.

24 Frank Rich, 'Whatever Happened to the America of 9/12?', *The New York Times* (10 September 2006).

25 Thomas Hoepker, 'I Took That 9/11 Photo', *Slate.com* (14 September 2006).

26 Jonathan Jones, 'The Meaning of 9/11's Most Controversial Photo', *The Guardian* (2 September 2011).

Chapter 1

1 The (unnamed) director of the Stockholm Cultural Centre, Sweden, referring to the *After September 11: Images From Ground Zero* photographic exhibition, quoted in the exhibition catalogue: *After September 11: Images from Ground Zero. An Exhibition by the US Department of State, Bureau of Educational and Cultural Affairs, with Photographs by Joel Meyerowitz* (2004), p. 20.

2 This article continues: 'this job somebody did on us yesterday was a message, a symbol job, the Mount Rushmore of terrorist attacks ... but so many people didn't seem to get it. Some of them didn't even get that there was a message at all ... Imperial nations don't get messages fast. They don't think they have to. Some of us tried.' Henry Allen, 'The Message in the Smoke', *Washington Post* (12 September 2001), p. C1.

3 Barbie Zelizer in Zelizer and Allan (eds), *Journalism After September 11*.

4 The CNN network issued the first reports, beginning transmission of live footage of the smoking first tower at exactly 8:49:36 a.m. David Friend, *Watching the World Change: The Stories Behind the Images of 9/11* (New York: Picador, 2006), p. 26.

5 According to David Campany, this is typical of a broader tendency within the media: photography is rarely the medium by which events are first experienced. Because photography rarely 'breaks the news' any more, this changes the role of newspapers to one of commentary rather than coverage. Campany, 'Safety in Numbness: Some Remarks on the Problems of "Late Photography"', in David Green, (ed.), *Where Is the Photograph?* (London: Photoworks, 1999), p. 127.

6 Dana Calvo and David Shaw, 'Overwhelming Coverage: As News Organizations Struggle to Meet the Public's Demand for Information, They Often Find Themselves Part of the Story', *Los Angeles Times* (13 September 2001), p. A33.

7 Calvo and Shaw, 'Overwhelming Coverage', p. A33.

8 *Chicago Tribune* (13 September 2001), p. A13.

9 Zelizer in Zelizer and Allan (eds), *Journalism After September 11*, pp. 58–64.

10 Friend, *Watching the World Change*, p. 13.

11 'Photojournalism' is defined here as the communication of news by photographs, referring specifically to the making, editing and displaying of photographs themselves, to be supplemented by text.

12 *The New York Times* (15 September 2001), p. A6.

13 Zelizer in Zelizer and Allan (eds), *Journalism After September 11*, pp. 60–62.

14 Friend, *Watching the World Change*, p. 62.

15 Friend, *Watching the World Change*, p. 62.

16 *Los Angeles Times* (14 September 2001), p. A3.

17 Jim Rutenberg and Felicity Barringer, 'News Media Try to Sort Out Policy on Graphic Images', *The New York Times* (13 September 2001), p. A24.

18 Rutenberg and Barringer, 'News Media Try to Sort Out Policy on Graphic Images', p. A24.

19 Rutenberg and Barringer, 'News Media Try to Sort Out Policy on Graphic Images', p. A24.

20 Rutenberg and Barringer, 'News Media Try to Sort Out Policy on Graphic Images', p. A24. Similar articles, voicing similar concerns and debate, were common across the American press, and the British too. See for example Raymond Snoddy, 'When Pictures Tell Too Much of the Story', *The Times T2* supplement (14 September 2001), p. 22.

21 James Kelly, 'Brokering the Power of the Image', *Time.com* (24 May 2004), www.time.com/time.

22 Zelizer in Zelizer and Allan (eds), *Journalism After September 11*, p. 66.

23 John Taylor, *Body Horror: Photojournalism, Catastrophe and War* (New York: New York University Press, 1998), p. 7.

24 Taylor, *Body Horror*, p. 194.

25 Sontag, *Regarding the Pain of Others*, p. 77.

26 Theodor Adorno, 'The Culture Industry: Enlightenment as Mass Deception', in Theodor Adorno and Max Horkheimer (eds), *The Dialectic of Enlightenment* (New York: Continuum, 1995), p. 121.

27 J.M. Bernstein notes that, 'while Adorno nowhere identifies the culture industry with the political triumph of fascism, he does imply, both directly and indirectly, that the culture industry's effective integration of society marks an equivalent triumph of repressive unification in liberal democratic states to that which was achieved politically under fascism.' J.M. Bernstein in Theodor Adorno, *The Culture Industry: Selected Essays on Mass Culture* (London: Routledge, 1991), p. 4.

28 This is comparable to Walter Benjamin's theory of distraction, a mode of visual attention characteristic of modern urban life. However, Benjamin is not so negative about the state of distraction, seeing it as a necessary adaptation to modern life, and even as a potentially counter-hegemonic mode of apperception that reveals the truly fragmentary nature of society and production. Walter Benjamin, *Illuminations* (trans. Harry Zohn) (London: Fontana, 1992), pp. 211–235.

29 See Richard W. Allen, 'The Aesthetic Experience of Modernity: Benjamin, Adorno, and Contemporary Film Theory', *New German Critique*, no. 40 (Winter 1987), pp. 236–237.

30 Adorno, *The Culture Industry*, p. 121.

31 Adorno, *The Culture Industry*, p. 167. In a later essay, 'The Culture Industry Reconsidered', this is put even more forcefully: 'People are not only, as the saying goes, falling for the swindle; if it guarantees them even the most fleeting gratification they desire a deception which is nonetheless transparent to them. They force their eyes shut and voice approval, in a kind of self-loathing, for what is meted out to them, knowing fully the purpose for which it is manufactured. Without admitting it they sense that their lives would be completely intolerable as soon as they no longer clung to satisfactions which are none at all.' Theodor Adorno and Anson G. Rabinbach, 'The Culture Industry Reconsidered', *New German Critique*, no. 6 (Autumn 1975), pp. 12–19.

32 Bob Kempur, *Chicago Tribune* (12 September 2001), p. A1; *Los Angeles Times* (12 September 2001), p. A24.

33 *Los Angeles Times* (13 September 2001), p. A1.

34 Friend, *Watching the World Change*, p. 58.

35 Friend, *Watching the World Change*, p. 59.

36 The *Los Angeles Times* (13 September 2001), p. A1 front page headline reads: '"Acts of War": Bush vows full assault, says "Good will prevail"'. Quotation here is from Dean E. Murray, *The New York Times* (15 September 2001), p. A7.

37 *The New York Times* (12 September 2001), p. A4.

38 Friend, *Watching the World Change*, p. 61.

39 *The Times* (14 September 2001), p. A1.

40 Howard Rosenberg, 'Bush's Image Fails to Fill the Screen', *Los Angeles Times* (14 September 2001), p. A19.

41 *Chicago Tribune* (12 September 2001), p. E6.

42 *The New York Times, A Nation Challenged* (New York: Jonathan Cape, 2002), p. 98. (Commemorative book produced by *The New York Times*.)

43 The small image of an injured woman being tended to while seated on a kerb, featured bottom right on the *New York Times* front page, is another example. This image appeared in several newspapers, as did others of this same scene taken from different angles, for example in the *Chicago Tribune* (12 September 2001), p. A9.

44 Most notably Jürgen Habermas: see p. 30.

45 *LIFE: One Nation: America Remembers September 11, 2001* (New York: Little, Brown & Co., 2001), p. 6. In the same passage, he goes on to say that 'we have an obligation to honour their memory by doing everything we can to eradicate terrorism, so that no other child is orphaned by its evil'.

46 Borradori, *Philosophy in a Time of Terror*, p. 43.

47 Friend, *Watching the World Change*, p. 197.

48 Friend, *Watching the World Change*, p. 198.

49 See William Rees-Mogg, 'Attacks Are Worst on US Since Pearl Harbour', *The Times* (12 September 2001), p. A19.

50 Taylor, *Body Horror*, p. 90.

51 *The New York Times* (12 September 2001), p. A3.

52 Daniel J. Sherman, and Terry Nardin, *Terror, Culture, Politics: Rethinking 9/11* (Bloomington: Indiana University Press, 2006), p. 51.

53 Sherman and Nardin, *Terror, Culture, Politics*, p. 106.

54 Adorno, 'The Fetish Character in Music and the Regression of Listening', in Andrew Arato and Eike Gebhardt (eds), *The Essential Frankfurt School Reader* (New York: Continuum, 1982), p. 286.

55 See for example Susie Orbach, 'Staying Vulnerable', OpenDemocracy.com: www.opendemocracy.net/conflict-911/article_186.jsp (11 September 2002).

56 Iain Boal, T.J. Clark, Joseph Matthews and Michael Watts (Retort), *Afflicted Powers: Capital and Spectacle in a New Age of War* (London: Verso, 2005), p. 19.

57 Retort, *Afflicted Powers*, p. 15.

58 Guy Debord, 'The Society of the Spectacle', reprinted in Nicholas Mirzoeff (ed.), *The Visual Culture Reader* (second edition) (London: Routledge, 2002), p. 142.

59 Debord, 'The Society of the Spectacle', p. 144: 'The spectacle is *capital* accumulated to the point where it becomes image.'

60 Retort, *Afflicted Powers*, p. 14.

61 Retort, *Afflicted Powers*, p. 14.

62 In his popular book, *The Culture of Fear: Why American Are Afraid of the Wrong Things* (New York: Basic Books 1999), Barry Glassner proposes that there is a tendency in American public life towards scare-mongering and smoke-screening for political ends. He gives examples of cases in which public attention is deflected from the important onto the trivial in a manner consistent with Zelizer's suggestion, and also with that of Elaine Scarry, below.

63 Elaine Scarry, 'Watching and Authorising the Gulf War', in Marjorie Garber, Jann Matlock and Rebecca L. Walkowitz (eds), *Media Spectacles* (New York: Routledge, 1993), pp. 57–64.

64 Scarry, 'Watching and Authorising the Gulf War', pp. 57–64.

65 Scarry, 'Watching and Authorising the Gulf War', pp. 57–64.

66 Debord in Mirzoeff (ed.), *The Visual Culture Reader*, p. 142.

67 Scarry, 'Watching and Authorising the Gulf War', p. 64.

68 Sontag, *Regarding the Pain of Others*, p. 79.

69 *The New York Times, A Nation Challenged*, p. 98.

70 Retort, *Afflicted Powers*, p. 22.

71 Debord, 'Comments on the Society of the Spectacle', cited in Retort, *Afflicted Powers*, p. 22.

72 Taylor, *Body Horror*, p. 162.

73 Taylor, *Body Horror*, p. 162.

74 Michelle Fine in Norman K. Denzin and Yvonna S. Lincoln (eds), *9/11 in American Culture* (London: Altamira Press, 2003), p. 58.

75 Borradori, *Philosophy in a Time of Terror*, p. 153.

76 *After September 11* (exhibition catalogue, 2004).

77 Joel Meyerowitz, *Aftermath: World Trade Center Archive* (New York: Phaidon, 2006). *Aftermath* is distinct from the State Department exhibition (and catalogue) *After September 11: Images from Ground Zero*, which featured many of the same photographs.

78 http://uk.phaidon.com/store/photography/aftermath-9780714862125/

79 In his own words, 'I will be the Mathew Brady.' In Vince Aletti, 'Site Specific: with Joel Meyerowitz in the forbidden city', *Village Voice* (2 November 2001), p. 13. At the time of the attacks, several journalists drew comparisons between the devastation at Ground Zero and that experienced during the American Civil War. See John Carman, 'Mesmerizing Scenes of Hell', *San Francisco Chronicle* (12 September 2001), p. A14, in which the attacks' death toll is compared to that of the battle of Antietam.

80 Alan Trachtenberg, 'Albums of War: On Reading Civil War Photographs', in Philip Fisher (ed.), *The New American Studies: Essays from Representation*s (Berkeley: University of California Press, 1991), p. 287.

81 *LIFE: One Nation*, p. 80.

82 *LIFE: One Nation*, p. 89.

83 Michael Feldschuh (ed.), *The September 11 Photo Project* (New York: HarperCollins, 2002), p. 141. Archive of the exhibition's original photographic and written materials accessed at New York Public Library, 16 January 2008.

84 Feldschuh, *The September 11 Photo Project*, p. 60.

85 *After September 11*, exhibition catalogue, p. 52.

86 Oliver Wendell Holmes, 1863, in Trachtenberg, 'Albums of War', p. 294.

87 Roland Barthes, *Camera Lucida: Reflections on Photography* (London: Vintage, 1993), p. 92.

88 Steven Diamond, www.aspp.com

89 Diamond, www.aspp.com

90 Liam Kennedy, 'Remembering September 11: Photography as Cultural Diplomacy', *International Affairs*, vol. 2, no. 79 (2003), p. 320.

91 The particular work that comes to mind is J.M.W. Turner's 'The Shipwreck', first exhibited 1805, Tate.

92 http://uk.phaidon.com/store/photography/aftermath-9780714862125/

93 Terry Smith, *The Architecture of Aftermath* (Chicago: University of Chicago Press, 2006), p. 146.

94 Powell cited in *After September 11* (catalogue), pp. 1 and 5.

95 Bush cited in *After September 11* (catalogue), p. 3.

96 Campany, 'Safety in Numbness', p. 132.

97 Retort, *Afflicted Powers*, p. 25.

98 Retort, *Afflicted Powers*, p. 35.

Chapter 2

1 Editorial, 'Time Out to Deal with Trauma', *San Francisco Chronicle* (13 September 2001), p. A24.

2 Barbara Rose, 'Technology Provides Lifeline During Disaster', *Chicago Tribune Business* supplement (13 September 2001), p. 1.

3 Joan Ryan, 'Terrorists Have Riddled Us All with Fear', *San Francisco Chronicle* (12 September 2001), p. 2.

4 PTSD was mentioned in several major American newspaper articles in the days following the attacks, citing psychiatric and psychology professionals and other 'experts'. Unlike many of the journalists themselves, most of these experts were slow to use the terms 'PSTD' or 'trauma'. One, Dr Rachel Yehuda, encouraged a 'wait and see' attitude to the attacks' psychological effects, saying 'circle your calendar for October. We're really not post-traumatic yet'. In Erica Goode, 'Trauma, Felt Directly or Not, Takes a Psychic Toll', *The New York Times* (13 September 2001), p. A2.

5 Mark Jarzombek in Liza Saltzman and Eric Rosenberg (eds), *Trauma & Visuality in Modernity* (Lebanon: Dartmouth College Press, 2006), p. 250.

6 Saltzman and Rosenberg, *Trauma & Visuality in Modernity*, p. 251. Since the Vietnam War, the fields of psychiatry, psychoanalysis and sociology have taken renewed interest in trauma. In 1985, the International Society for Traumatic Stress Studies (ITSS) was formed. In 1989, the US Congress created an umbrella organization, the National Center for PTSD, to coordinate research. State and government agencies set up outreach counselling programs, and self-help groups proliferated. An important factor in this trend, it seems, was the raised profile of the Holocaust during the 1970s. Later, in 1995, the Oklahoma bombing happened at such a time that trauma studies research could come into play in an unprecedented way, analysing and treating a whole community of traumatized civilians. Consequently, understanding of the issues of trauma and PTSD expanded in cultural discourse and in the media around this time. Saltzman and Rosenberg, *Trauma & Visuality in Modernity*.

7 Saltzman and Rosenberg, *Trauma & Visuality in Modernity*, p. 266.

8 See Josef Breuer and Sigmund Freud (trans. James and Alix Strachey), *Studies on Hysteria* (London: Penguin, 1974), and also Sigmund Freud (trans. James Strachey, ed. James Strachey and Angela Richards), *Introductory Lectures on Psychoanalysis* (London: Penguin, 1991).

9 The term 'subject' is used in the psychoanalytical sense, as employed in LaPlanche and Pontalis's definition of trauma, below.

10 Habermas in Borradori, *Philosophy in a Time of Terror*, p. 28.

11 Friend, *Watching the World Change*, p. 34.

12 Friend, *Watching the World Change*, p. 34.

13 Sigmund Freud (trans. James Strachey), 'Remembering, Repeating and Working Through', *The Standard Edition of the Complete Psychological Works of Sigmund Freud, vol. XII* (London: The Hogarth Press, 1958), p. 149. See also Breuer and Freud, *Studies on Hysteria*, p. 37.

14 Jean LaPlanche and Jean-Bertrand Pontalis (trans. Donald Nicholson), *The Language of Psychoanalysis* (London: The Hogarth Press, 1973), p. 465.

15 Judith Lewis Herman, *Trauma and Recovery: The Aftermath of Violence from Domestic Abuse to Political Terror* (New York: Basic Books, 1997) p. 33.

16 Saltzman and Rosenberg, *Trauma & Visuality in Modernity*, p. 51.

17 Kai Erikson in Cathy Caruth (ed.), *Trauma: Explorations in Memory* (London: The Johns Hopkins University Press, 1995), pp. 183 and 168. See also Kai Erikson, *A New Species of Trouble: Explorations in Disaster, Trauma and Community* (New York: W.W. Norton & Company, 1994).

18 Erikson in Caruth, *Trauma*, p. 191.

19 Adair Lara, 'The Day the World Changed', *San Francisco Chronicle* (12 September 2001), p. E8.

20 Dominick LaCapra, *Writing History, Writing Trauma* (London: The Johns Hopkins University Press, 2001), pp. 47 and 79.

21 Dominick LaCapra, *History & Memory After Auschwitz* (London and Ithaca: Cornell University Press, 1998), p. 195.

22 LaCapra, *History & Memory After Auschwitz*, p. 181.

23 Patrick T. Reardon, 'Fear: "What Makes Anybody Safe Anywhere?"', *Chicago Tribune* (12 September 2001), p. 18.

24 Joan Ryan, 'Terrorists Have Riddled Us All with Fear', *San Francisco Chronicle* (12 September 2001), p. A2.

25 E. Ann Kaplan, 'Imaging Catastrophe', in Amy Coplan and Peter Goldie (eds), *Empathy: Philosophical and Psychological Perspectives* (New York: Oxford University Press, 2011), p. 259.

26 Coplan and Goldie, *Empathy*, p. 256.

27 Coplan and Goldie, *Empathy*, p. 276.

28 Saltzman and Rosenberg, *Trauma & Visuality in Modernity*, p. 51.

29 Saltzman and Rosenberg, *Trauma & Visuality in Modernity*, pp. xi–xii.

30 www.crowleyonline.com/911.

31 Margaret Olin, *Touching Photographs* (University of Chicago Press, 2012), p. 178.

32 Sigmund Freud, 'Screen Memories', *Standard Edition, vol. III*, p. 307 (the reference to omission is from Sigmund Freud, 'Screen Memories', *Standard Edition, vol. III*, p. 306). The term 'mnemic symbols' is used slightly earlier, in Breuer and Freud, *Studies on Hysteria*, p. 37. Both of these works appear quite early in Freud's career, and his understanding of trauma continued to develop, particularly in the context of the First World War and his clinical work with victims of so-called war neurosis. The most significant work in this regard is perhaps *Beyond the Pleasure Principle*, 1920, in which he introduces the concept of the 'compulsion to repeat': Sigmund Freud (trans. James Strachey), *Beyond the Pleasure Principle* (New York: W. W. Norton & Company, 1990).

33 Sigmund Freud, 'Remembering, Repeating and Working Through', p. 155.

34 Sigmund Freud, 'From the History of an Infantile Neurosis', *Standard Edition, vol. XVII* (London: The Hogarth Press, 1957), pp. 1–122.

35 The very specific meaning that Lacan ascribes to the 'real' will be discussed in Chapter 3. In his words, 'the function of the *tuché*, of the real as encounter – the encounter in so far as it may be missed, in so far as it is essentially the missed encounter – first presented itself in the history of psychoanalysis in a form that was in itself already enough to arouse our attention, that of the trauma'. Jacques Lacan, *The Four Fundamental Concepts of Psycho-Analysis* (London: Penguin, 1994), p. 55.

36 Freud, *Introductory Lectures on Psychoanalysis*.

37 Sigmund Freud, 'The Claims of Psycho-Analysis to Scientific Interest', *Standard Edition, vol. XIII* (London: The Hogarth Press, 1913), p. 177.

38 To this same paragraph, Jacques Lacan responds, 'this passage is clear enough. The apparent flagrant contradiction that you can draw from it on the basis of Freud's remark that dreams are expressed in images rather than otherwise is restored and resituated as soon as he shows the sort of images in question – namely, images that occur in writing.' Jacques Lacan, *Seminar Book III: The Psychoses* (New York: W. W. Norton & Company, 1997) p. 247.

39 Freud, from *Moses and Monotheism*, cited in Ulrich Baer, *Spectral Evidence: The Photography of Trauma* (London: MIT Press, 2002), p. 25.

40 Baer, *Spectral Evidence*, pp. 9–10.

41 Cited in Anne Wilkes Tucker et al., *War/Photography: Images of Armed Conflict and its Aftermath* (New Haven and London: Yale University Press, 2012), p. 167.

42 Sharon Sliwinski elaborates both on Lee Miller's experience and on this phenomenon, which she calls, '*testimony visualis*, or, communication without understanding', in *Human Rights in Camera* (Chicago: University of Chicago Press, 2011), p. vi.

43 Hirsch, 'I Took Pictures'.

44 Jones, 'The Meaning of 9/11's Most Controversial Photo'.

45 Geoffrey Batchen discusses this early use of the camera metaphor by Freud in Geoffrey Batchen *Burning with Desire: The Conception of Photography* (Cambridge: MIT Press, 1997), p. 187.

46 Baer, *Spectral Evidence*, p. 9. This is also discussed by Batchen above.

47 Baer, *Spectral Evidence*, pp. 25–60. For an evaluation of the importance of these photographs within Charcot's work, see Stephen Heath, 'Difference', in Screen, *The Sexual Subject: A Screen Reader in Sexuality* (London: Routledge, 1992), pp. 52 and 53 ('so dear to Charcot in his endeavour to bring hysteria into the order of medicine, to define a clinical *picture* ... '), and David Lomas, *The Haunted Self: Surrealism, Psychoanalysis, Subjectivity* (New Haven and London: Yale University Press, 2000), pp. 87–88 ('The primacy of vision in Charcot's diagnostic method, its ocularcentrism, meant the hysterical woman was effectively denied a voice ... ').

48 Cited in Lomas, *The Haunted Self*, p. 83. See Breuer and Freud, *Studies on Hysteria*, p. 14.

49 Baer, *Spectral Evidence*, p. 9.

50 Baer, *Spectral Evidence*, p. 9.

51 Baer, *Spectral Evidence*, p. 11.

52 Baer, *Spectral Evidence*, p. 12.

53 Freud, 'Remembering, Repeating & Working Through', p. 150.

54 Freud, 'Remembering, Repeating & Working Through', p. 151.

55 Baer, *Spectral Evidence*, p. 6.

56 John Carman, 'Mesmerizing Scenes of Hell', p. E1.

57 Jacques Lacan (trans. Alan Sheridan), *Écrits* (New York: W.W. Norton & Company, 1977), p. 148.

58 Lacan, *Écrits*, pp. 148–155.

59 Lacan, *Écrits*, p. 166.

60 Lacan, *Écrits*, p. 59.

61 Herman, *Trauma & Recovery*, p. 2.

62 R.W. Apple, 'A Creeping Horror', *The New York Times* (12 September 2001), p. A1.

63 Michiko Katukani, 'Struggling to Find Words for a Horror Beyond Words', *The New York Times* (13 September 2001), p. E1.

64 Caryn James, 'Live Images Make Viewers Witnesses to Horror', *The New York Times* (12 September 2001), p. A25.

65 James, 'Live Images Make Viewers Witnesses to Horror'.

66 James, 'Live Images Make Viewers Witnesses to Horror'.

67 James, 'Live Images Make Viewers Witnesses to Horror'.

68 James, 'Live Images Make Viewers Witnesses to Horror'.

69 Christopher Knight, 'Elusive and Illusionary: A single, iconic image has not emerged from coverage of last week's attack. The reason has to do with the flood of pictures and our proximity to the event', *Los Angeles Times* (16 September 2001), pp. A6 and A7.

70 Knight, 'Elusive and Illusionary', pp. A6 and A7.

71 Knight, 'Elusive and Illusionary', pp. A6 and A7.

72 Hariman and Lucaites, *No Caption Needed*, pp. 27, 1.

73 Hariman and Lucaites, *No Caption Needed*, p. 301.

74 Baer, *Spectral Evidence*, p. 6.

75 Kroes, 'The Ascent of the Falling Man', p. 47.

76 Susan Sontag, *On Photography* (London: Penguin, 1979), p. 19.

77 Sontag, *On Photography*, p. 19. See also Walter Benjamin's discussion of the significance of captions accompanying news photographs, in Walter Benjamin, 'A Short History of Photography', reprinted in Alan Trachtenberg (ed.), *Classic Essays on Photography* (Stoney Creek: Leete's Island Books, 1980), p. 215; and also in Walter Benjamin (trans. Harry Zohn), 'The Work of Art in the Age of Mechanical Reproduction', in *Illuminations* (London: Fontana, 1992).

78 Lacan, *Écrits*, p. 175.

79 Saltzman and Rosenberg, *Trauma & Visuality in Modernity*, p. 272.

80 Paul Virilio in Sylvère Lotringer and Paul Virilio, *The Accident of Art* (New York: Semiotext(e), 2005), p. 26.

81 Saltzman and Rosenberg, *Trauma & Visuality in Modernity*, p. 257.

82 Steve Johnston, 'Attack on TV Was Surreal', *Chicago Tribune 'Evening Extra'* (11 September 2001), p. 21.

Chapter 3

1 See for example Michiko Kakutani, *The New York Times* (13 September 2001), p. E1.

2 Sigmund Freud, 'The Uncanny', *Standard Edition, vol. VXII* (London: The Hogarth Press, 1957), p. 244.

3 Following Freud's statement in 'The Uncanny' that 'I have not made a very thorough examination of the literature, especially the foreign literature, relating to this present modest contribution of mine, for reasons which, as may easily be guessed, lie in the times in which we live', his translator James Strachey claims in a footnote that this is 'an allusion to the first World War only just concluded'. Freud, 'The Uncanny', p. 220.

4 Freud, 'The Uncanny', p. 219. Aesthetics here is understood to refer to the branch of philosophy concerned with the study of sensory or sensory-emotional values, and also this field's close association with the philosophy of art. For an example of the very large literature on the subject of the uncanny and aesthetics, see David Ellison, *Ethics and Aesthetics in European Modernist Literature, From the Sublime to the Uncanny* (Cambridge: Cambridge University Press, 2001).

5 It is important to note the distinct difference between how Freud deals with the eyes as organs and the phenomenon of sight. Peter Benson has claimed that Freud downplays his visual references in 'The Uncanny' in spite of their obvious prevalence, dismissing them as mere substitutes for the genital organs. This is given as another example of his wary ambivalence towards images and the visual. Peter Benson, 'Freud and the Visual', *Representations*, vol. 45 (Winter 1994), p. 111.

6 Freud, 'The Uncanny', pp. 227 and 230. The prevalence of references to vision and the eyes in the essay as a whole has been remarked upon by Nicholas Royle, who says that it is 'pervasively concerned with the visual. Its ocularcentrism is perhaps nowhere more marked than in its *focus* on castration and the fear of blindness … No doubt uncanny feelings are very often generated by strange sights, unveilings, revelations, by what should have remained out of sight; and "The Sandman" is a magnificent, relentless exploration of the uncanniness of seeing and not seeing, of the optical imagination.' Nicholas Royle, *The Uncanny* (London: Routledge, 2003), p. 45.

7 Freud, 'The Uncanny', p. 231.

8 Christopher Knight, 'Elusive and Illusionary: A single, iconic image has not emerged from coverage of last week's attack. The reason has to do with the flood of pictures and our proximity to the event', *Los Angeles Times* (16 September 2001), p. A7.

9 Anthony Vidler, *The Architectural Uncanny: Essays in the Modern Unhomely* (London and Cambridge: MIT Press, 1992), p. 11.

10 Lewis Mumford, *The Pentagon of Power: The Myth of the Machine Volume Two* (San Diego: Harcourt, Brace Jovanovich, 1974), p. 342.

11 Sontag, *Regarding the Pain of Others*, p. 7.

12 Jonathan Hyman, *Landscapes of 9/11: A Photographer's Journey* (Austin: University of Texas Press, 2013).

13 The 'last beam' was also preceded in the procession by an empty stretcher symbolizing the missing in a more overt reference to the tradition of the unknown soldier.

14 See Hyman, *Landscapes of 9/11*, 2013.

15 However, Vidler does also trace the subsequent rejection and recent negative re-invention of this concept by architects in the twentieth century. Vidler, *The Architectural Uncanny*, pp. 69–71.

16 The story of this photograph is told in the documentary film, *9/11: The Falling Man* (dir: Singer, Henry, 2006, Channel 4, first aired 15 March 2006).

17 Freud, 'The Uncanny', p. 235.

18 Smith, *The Architecture of Aftermath*, p. 117.

19 Smith, *The Architecture of Aftermath*, p. 119.

20 Freud, 'The Uncanny', p. 235.

21 Smith, *The Architecture of Aftermath*, p. 122.

22 Smith, *The Architecture of Aftermath*, p. 122.

23 See for example http://urbanlegends.about.com/library/bltabloid-arch10.htm. A photograph by AP photographer Mark D. Phillips is one commonly cited as revealing a 'devilish' face in the clouds of dust. This is an example of what psychologists call 'pareidolia': the human tendency to perceive meaningful symbols where there are none.

24 Freud, 'The Uncanny', p. 234.

25 Simpson, *9/11*, p. 58.

26 Freud, 'The Uncanny', p. 219.

27 Freud, 'The Uncanny', p. 220.

28 This phenomenon has been widely commented on. For one prominent example, see Žižek, *Welcome to the Desert of the Real*, p. 17.

29 Steve Johnson, 'Attack on TV Was Surreal', *Chicago Tribune 'Evening Extra'* (11 September 2001), p. 21.

30 Kakutani, *The New York Times*, p. E1.

31 Freud, 'The Uncanny', p. 241.

32 Freud, 'The Uncanny', p. 249.

33 Freud, 'The Uncanny', p. 244.

34 In a further interesting link with the film industry, Žižek recounts that in October 2001, a group of Hollywood scenarists and directors specializing in catastrophe movies were gathered by the Pentagon to imagine possible scenarios for terrorist attacks and how to respond to them. Then, in November 2001, a series of meetings took place between White House advisors and senior Hollywood executives to establish Hollywood's role in the 'War on Terror' by 'getting the right ideological message across' in America and to the rest of the world. Žižek, *Welcome to the Desert of the Real*, p. 16.

35 Oscar Villalon, *The San Francisco Chronicle* (13 September 2001), p. B1.

36 Specifically in Freud 'Remembering, Repeating and Working Through', pp. 147–156.

37 Freud, 'The Uncanny', p. 238.

38 Jacques Lacan (trans. Dennis Porter), *The Seminar of Jacques Lacan, Book VII, 1959–1960: The Ethics of Psychoanalysis* (London: Routledge, 1992): here, *jouissance* is 'perverse' and must be 'tamed' (p. 4); it is 'evil'; it is 'harmful' and 'malignant' (p. 187); and '*jouissance* appears not purely and simply as the satisfaction of a need but as the satisfaction of a drive' (p. 209).

39 Lacan, *The Four Fundamental Concepts of Psycho-Analysis*, pp. 185–186.

40 Žižek, *Welcome to the Desert of the Real*, pp. 11–12.

41 Freud, 'The Uncanny', p. 241.

42 Radstone in Greenberg (ed.), *Trauma at Home*, p. 117.

43 In Jacques Lacan (trans. Bruce Fink), *The Seminar of Jacques Lacan, Book XX, 1972–1973: Encore: On Feminine Sexuality, the Limits of Love and Knowledge* (New York: W. W. Norton & Company, 1999), *jouissance* is conceived primarily in terms of ambiguous sexual satisfaction or enjoyment (p. 8).

44 Radstone in Greenberg (ed.), *Trauma at Home*, p. 120.

45 Radstone in Greenberg (ed.), *Trauma at Home*, p. 120.

46 Freud, 'The Uncanny', p. 220 (terms used throughout).

47 LaCapra, *History & Memory After Auschwitz*, p. 181.

48 LaCapra, *History & Memory After Auschwitz*, p. 181.

49 Jacques Lacan (trans. Sylvana Tomaselli), *The Seminar of Jacques Lacan, Book II, 1954–1955: The Ego in Freud's Theory and in the Technique of Psychoanalysis*

(Cambridge: Cambridge University Press, 1988), p. 97: 'the real is without fissure. What I teach you ... is that we have no means of apprehending this real – on any level and not only on that of knowledge – except via the go-between of the symbolic.' Also Jacques Lacan (trans. Russel Grigg), *The Seminar of Jacques Lacan, Book III, 1955–1965: The Psychoses* (London: Routledge, 1993), pp. 12–13: in the case of psychosis, for example, 'what is refused in the symbolic order re-emerges in the real'.

50 Lacan, *Seminar Book III*, pp. 12–13.

51 Mladen Dolar, '"I Shall Be with You on Your Wedding-Night": Lacan and the Uncanny', *October*, vol. 58 (Autumn 1991), p. 14.

52 Lacan, *The Four Fundamental Concepts of Psycho-Analysis*, p. 55.

53 LaCapra, *Writing History, Writing Trauma*, p. 67.

54 LaCapra, *Writing History, Writing Trauma*, p. 53.

55 Baer, *Spectral Evidence*, p. 105.

56 Sontag, *Regarding the Pain of Others*, p. 71.

57 Hariman and Lucaites, *No Caption Needed*, p. 290.

58 Jonathan Hyman, 'The Public Face of 9/11: Memory and Portraiture in the Landscape', *Journal of American History*, vol. 94 (June 2007), pp. 183–192.

59 Hyman, 'The Public Face of 9/11'.

60 Lacan, *Seminar Book III: The Psychoses*, pp. 86 and 88. The term 'woof' is a reference to weaving: the warp – the threads that run lengthwise – and the woof – the threads that run across – make up the structure of fabrics such as the tapestry in Lacan's metaphor. Thus when the horizontal threads of the 'woof' are removed from a tapestry leaving only the vertical 'warp', the fabric disintegrates in a way comparable, Lacan suggests, to the disintegration of the psyche following a sudden encounter with the real.

61 Hariman and Lucaites, *No Caption Needed*, p. 291.

62 Dolar, 'I Shall Be with You on Your Wedding-Night', p. 19.

Chapter 4

1 Shulan in George et al. (eds), *Here is New York: A Democracy of Photographs* (Zurich: Scalo, 2002), p. 9.

2 Barbie Zelizer, 'Finding Aids to the Past: Bearing Personal Witness to Traumatic Public Events', *Departmental Papers (ASC), Annenberg School for Communication, University of Pennsylvania* ScholarlyCommons: http://repository.upenn.edu/ascpapers/87 (2002), p. 1.

3 Sontag, *On Photography*, pp. 8–9.

4 Allan Sekula, 'Reading an Archive: Photography between Labour and Capital', in Patricia Holland, Jo Spence and Simon Watney (eds), *Photography/Politics: Two* (London: Photography Workshop, 1986), p. 154.

5 Sekula, 'Reading an Archive', p. 156.

6 Shulan in George et al. (eds), *Here is New York*, p. 9.

7 Olin, *Touching Photographs*, p. 185. Olin goes on to note that the exhibition did offer the opportunity for visitors to recount their own personal memories in video booths, but 'these narratives, however, were separated from the photographs themselves'. Olin, *Touching Photographs*, p. 185.

8 Michel Foucault (ed. James D. Faubion), *Power* (New York: The New Press, 1994), p. 332.

9 Michel Foucault (ed. Colin Gordon), *Power/Knowledge* (London: Harvester Wheatsheaf, 1980), p. 334.

10 Adorno, 'The Culture Industry', p. 121.

11 http://hereisnewyork.org

12 Sekula, 'Reading an Archive', p. 157.

13 Net proceeds from the sale of the book (which retailed at $49.95) went to the Children's Aid Society (as did proceeds from original exhibition print sales) and other charities. George et al. (eds), *Here is New York*, p. 9.

14 George et al. (eds), *Here is New York*, pp. 7–8.

15 Feldschuh (ed.), *The September 11 Photo Project*, pp. viii–ix.

16 Feldschuh (ed.), *The September 11 Photo Project*, pp. viii–ix.

17 Feldschuh writes, 'The decision to make this book presented a dilemma for the project; from the start we avoided anything commercial. Listening to the participants and visitors to the project settled it for us. They said that if a book could help fund a tour of the exhibition and bring even some of the experience to those who could not see it, we had to do it. We agree.' Feldschuh (ed.), *The September 11 Photo Project*, p. x.

18 Feldschuh (ed.), *The September 11 Photo Project*, p. 22.

19 Feldschuh, *The September 11 Photo Project*, p. viii.

20 Pages 58–59, 68–69 and pages 36–39 feature photographs taken in Afghanistan in October 2001, including one of a 'Baba Jan' carrying his injured grandson to a hospital. The photographer's handwritten comment reads, 'on the first day of the humanitarian convoy in Dasht-e-Qaleh, I looked at my country through the truck window and noticed the symbolism before my eyes. I saw through this window a magnificent country but every inch of it was broken.' Feldschuh, *The September 11 Photo Project*, p. viii.

21 The terms 'net or internet' are understood to refer to the global system of networked computers; the infrastructure via which the World Wide Web operates, and with which it is not to be confused. Fittingly for a discussion of Foucault's thought, it is the apparatus, not its content or application. See Tim Berners Lee, *Weaving The Web: The Original Design and Ultimate Destiny of the World Wide Web* (London: Harper Business, 2000).

22 Karl Marx and Friedrich Engels (ed. C.J. Arthur), *The German Ideology* (New York: International Publishers, 1970); Foucault, *Power*, p. 98.

23 Allan in Zelizer and Allan (eds), *Journalism After September 11*, p. 127.

24 Allan in Zelizer and Allan (eds), *Journalism After September 11*, p. 136.

25 *The Times* (9 July 2005), pp. A20–A21. Other major events in which vernacular online newsgathering played a pivotal role included the violent riots in Paris (October–November 2005) and London (August 2011), the Tunisian uprising of 2011 and other episodes of the 'Arab Spring'.

26 Zelizer and Allan, *Journalism After September 11*, p. 130.

27 Amy Harmon, 'Web Offers Both News and Comfort', *The New York Times* (12 September 2001), p. A25.

28 See P.J. Huffstutter, Dave Wilson and Christine Frey, 'News Web sites clogged in Aftermath: Breakdown highlights weakness of medium not ready to compete with radio, TV', *Los Angeles Times* (12 September 2001), p. A31.

29 The September 11th Web Archive: http://september11.archive.org.

30 Kirsten Foot, Barbara Warnick and Steven M. Schneider, 'Web-Based Memorializing After September 11: Toward a Conceptual Framework', *Journal of Computer-Mediated Communication*, vol. 11 (2006), pp. 93–94.

31 See for example Aaron Hess, 'In Digital Remembrance: Vernacular Memory and the Rhetorical Construction of Web Memorials', *Media, Culture and Society*, vol. 29 (2007), pp. 812–830 (and other material cited therein).

32 Foot et al., 'Web-Based Memorializing', p. 93.

33 See http://crowleyonline.com/911/default.htm and http://www.stangbangers.com/September_11,_2001.htm

34 Foucault, *Power/Knowledge*, p. 98.

35 Kevin Robins, *Into the Image: Culture and Politics in the Field of Vision* (London: Routledge, 1996).

36 Robins, *Into the Image*. A connection might be observed between this regression of consciousness and Adorno's concept of 'regressive listening', imposed by the domination of the music industry, which I have suggested could equate to a kind of 'regressive seeing' imposed by the dominance and control of the Western visual media. Adorno, 'The Fetish Character in Music and the Regression of Listening', pp. 270–299.

37 Michael Shulan, www.hereisnewyork.org.

38 Anonymous, 'Awaiting the Aftershocks', *The New York Times* (12 September 2001), p. A1.

39 Foot et al., 'Web-Based Memorializing', p. 92.

40 Herman, *Trauma and Recovery*, p. 70.

41 Retort, *Afflicted Powers*.

42 Retort, *Afflicted Powers*, p. 4.

43 Retort, *Afflicted Powers*.

44 Retort, *Afflicted Powers*, pp. 188–189.

45 Žižek, *Welcome to the Desert of the Real*, p. 3. This 'choice', for him, is specifically the one presented by the American government in the wake of September 11th, between fundamentalism and democracy. Žižek argues that though we live in an era of ultimate freedom of choice, the framing of this question negates choice.

46 See the *Times* (12 September 2001), pp. A13–A14, which features varied reactions to the attacks from the Arab world, including photographs of celebrations in Palestine.

47 Birgit Richard in Norman K. Denzin and Yvonna S. Lincoln (eds), *9/11 in American Culture* (London: Altamira Press, 2003), p. 131.

48 The Panopticon is a model prison system designed by Jeremy Bentham in the late eighteenth century, which Foucault uses as a detailed schema for illustrating some of his key ideas about power. He writes, 'the Panopticon functions as a kind of laboratory of power. Thanks to its mechanisms of observation, it gains in efficiency and in the ability to penetrate into men's behaviour; knowledge follows the advance of power, discovering new objects of knowledge over all the surfaces on which power is exercised.' Michel Foucault (trans. Alan Sheridan), *Discipline and Punish: The Birth of the Prison* (London: Penguin, 1991), p. 204.

49 Sekula 'Reading an Archive', p. 154.

50 Sekula 'Reading an Archive', p. 156.

51 John Tagg, 1984, in Liz Wells (ed.), *The Photography Reader* (London: Routledge, 2003), p. 257.

52 Foucault, *Power/Knowledge*, p. 98.

53 Adorno, 'The Culture Industry', p. 167.

54 Ziauddin Sardar, 'Alt.Civilizations.Faq: Cyberspace as the Darker Side of the West', *Futures*, vol. 27, no. 7 (September 1995), p. 735.

55 Foucault, *Power*, p. 333.

56 Foucault, *Power*, p. 336.

57 Karl Marx, *Capital Volume 1* (London: Penguin, 1976).

58 John Roberts, 'Realism, Modernism and Photography: "At last, at last the mask has been torn away"', in Matthew Beaumont (ed.), *Adventures in Realism* (London: Blackwell, 2007), p. 159.

59 Marita Sturken, *Tourists of History: Memory, Kitsch, and Consumerism from Oklahoma City to Ground Zero* (Durham: Duke University Press, 2007), p. 5.

60 Sturken, *Tourists of History*, p. 10.

61 See Daniel Miller cited in Alison Landsberg, *Prosthetic Memory: The Transformation of American Remembrance in the Age of Mass Culture* (New York: Columbia University Press, 2004), pp. 144–145.

62 Stuart Hall, 'Encoding, Decoding', in Simon During (ed.), *The Cultural Studies Reader* (London: Routledge, 1993), p. 100.

63 Hall, 'Encoding, Decoding', p. 100.

64 Hess, 'In Digital Remembrance', p. 820.

65 Hess, 'In Digital Remembrance', p. 824. Hess writes that the production of websites is subject to controlling factors and authorities such as fees for domain space and the constraints of advertisers: 'Rhetorically, the individual, while provided with a forum for free speech, is required to interact with the corporate owners of websites and the official discourse of the digital gate-keeping elite.' Hess, 'In Digital Remembrance', p. 821.

66 Examples of vernacular websites that occupy counter-hegemonic positions include the many 'conspiracy theory' sites springing up in response to September 11th. Some of these make their arguments by scrutinizing press photographs, particularly of the rubble at the Pentagon site, see www.conspiracyplanet.com and www.9/11truth.org.

67 Sturken, *Tourists of History*, p. 14.

68 Sturken, *Tourists of History*, pp. 28–29.

Chapter 5

1 David Foster Wallace, 'The View from Mrs. Thompson's', *Rolling Stone* (25 October 2001), p. 132.

2 Herman, *Trauma and Recovery*, p. 1.

3 In Feldschuh (ed.), *The September 11 Photo Project*.

4 Zelizer in Zelizer and Allan (eds), *Journalism After September 11*, p. 48.

5 Zelizer in Zelizer and Allan (eds), *Journalism After September 11*, p. 66.

6 Sontag, *On Photography*, pp. 17–18.

7 For the stories of how both of these images were captured, see Friend, *Watching the World Change*.

8 *9/11: The Falling Man*, produced and directed by Henry Singer. Presented by Junod, Henry Singer's film details how, after appearing in Pennsylvania's *Morning Call* newspaper (on the front page and larger than in any other paper) and causing many complaints, the image disappeared from view. 'No one wanted to confront the existence of the jumpers', he says. Americans had 'recoiled' from the distasteful deaths of the 'jumpers', choosing instead to rally around images of heroic rescue workers that illustrated American spirit.

9 Zelizer, in Zelizer and Allan (eds), *Journalism After September 11*, p. 49.

10 Herman, *Trauma and Recovery*, pp. 237–243.

11 Herman, *Trauma and Recovery*, p. 174.

12 Breuer and Freud write, 'each individual hysterical symptom immediately and permanently disappeared when . . . the patient had described that event in the greatest possible detail and had put the affect into words.' Breuer and Freud, *Studies on Hysteria*, p. 57. I base this assertion regarding Lacanian theory primarily on two statements in his *Écrits*; first: 'what the psychoanalytic experience discovers in the unconscious is the whole structure of language . . .', p. 147, and second: 'if this [traumatic] event was recognised as being the cause of the symptom, it was because the putting into words of the event (in the patient's "stories") determined the lifting of the symptom', p. 46.

13 Herman, *Trauma and Recovery*. Of course, images themselves have been shown to play an effective part in recovery from trauma, as demonstrated in the field of art therapy. David Friend recounts several examples of the productive use of such therapy for bereaved families of September 11th victims, with particular emphasis on the use of photography. An important distinction, though, is that the photographs used are not ones depicting the scene of the attacks (these are repeatedly referred to by victims in Friend's account as being highly upsetting and destructive to their recovery process), but positive images of the deceased family members in happy times, for example; or the project of photographing nature as a way of re-engaging with life. See Friend, *Watching the World Change*, pp. 267–269.

14 Virilio, *Open Sky*, p. 63.

15 Virilio, *Open Sky*, p. 9.

16 Allan Sekula, 'Dismantling Modernism, Reinventing Photography', in *Photography Against the Grain: Essays and Photoworks 1973–1983* (Halifax: Nova Scotia, 1994), p. 73.

17 Sekula, 'Dismantling Modernism', p. 73.

18 Martha Rosler, *Decoys and Disruptions: Selected Writings, 1975–2001* (MIT Press, 2004), p. 7.

19 Rosler, *Decoys and Disruptions*, p. 7.

20 For an example of this process in the case of one of Freud's patients, see Breuer and Freud, *Studies on Hysteria*, p. 289.

21 Lacan, *Seminar Book II: The Ego in Freud's Theory and in the Technique of Psychoanalysis* (New York: W. W. Norton & Company, 1991), p. 320.

22 'If this [traumatic] event was recognised as being the cause of the symptom, it was because the putting into words of the event (in the patient's "stories") determined the lifting of the symptom.' Lacan, *Écrits*, p. 46.

23 Breuer and Freud, *Studies on Hysteria*, p. 365.

24 Freud continues: 'we go on to examine the memory picture itself in order to discover the direction in which our work is to proceed. "Look at the picture once more. Has it disappeared?" "Most of it, yes, but I still see this detail". "Then this residue must still mean something new in addition to it, or something will occur to you in connection with it". When this work has been accomplished, the patient's field of vision is once more free and we can conjure up another picture.' Breuer and Freud, *Studies on Hysteria*, pp. 365–366.

25 Sontag, *Regarding the Pain of Others*, p. 80.

26 Sigmund Freud (trans. James Strachey), 'The Moses of Michelangelo', *The Standard Edition of the Complete Psychological Works of Sigmund Freud, vol. XIII* (London: The Hogarth Press, 1964), pp. 211–238.

27 Benson, 'Freud and the Visual', p. 110.

28 Marianne Hirsch in Greenberg (ed.), *Trauma at Home*, p. 72.

29 Fitzpatrick provides a fuller Barthesian reading of this image in her essay, 'The Movement of Vulnerability', pp. 85–102.

30 Barbie Zelizer, *About to Die: How News Images Move the Public* (New York: Oxford University Press, 2010), p. 120.

31 Zelizer, *About to Die*, p. 120.

32 From the transcript of an address by George W. Bush, *The New York Times* (13 September 2001), p.A16. In an example of binary rhetoric from the other side, in the aftermath of the first US aerial attacks on Afghanistan, Osama bin Laden declared on the Al-Jazeera network that 'these events have divided the world into two sides. The side of believers and the side of infidels'. See Friend, *Watching the World Change*, p. 176.

33 Bush's public use of language in this period has been analysed using various rhetorical frames, predominantly religious in association, including those of political demonology and Puritanical covenant renewal. See for example Joshua Gunn, 'The Rhetoric of Exorcism: George W. Bush and the Return of Political Demonology', *Western Journal of Communication*, vol. 68 (2004); and Denise M. Borstoff, 'George W. Bush's Post-September 11 Rhetoric of Covenant

Renewal: Upholding the Faith of the Greatest Generation', *Quarterly Journal of Speech*, vol. 89, no. 4 (November 2003), pp. 293–319.

34 It also is noteworthy that this 'other' appears entirely annexed from Western discourse though the distancing effect of the Arabic language: a distance that recalls the Biblical curse of the Tower of Babel (Genesis 11: 1–9), whereby the people of the Earth were condemned to be scattered and divided by barriers of language as a punishment for arrogance.

35 Derrida in Borradori, *Philosophy in a Time of Terror*, p. 86.

36 Derrida in Borradori, *Philosophy in a Time of Terror*, p. 87.

37 Derrida in Borradori, *Philosophy in a Time of Terror*, p. 87.

38 Barthes, *Camera Lucida*, p. 51.

39 Peter Wollen, 'Vectors of Melancholy', in Ralph Rugoff (ed.), *Scene of the Crime* (Cambridge: MIT Press, 1997), p. 34.

40 Freud 'Mourning and Melancholia', p. 244.

41 Freud 'Mourning and Melancholia', p. 243.

42 Freud arguably departs from what he says in 'Mourning and Melancholia', stating later, in 'The Ego and the Id', that rather than severing the attachment in order to mourn successfully, the lost one must actually be internalized in a way that sounds, in fact, rather like melancholia.

43 Freud 'Mourning and Melancholia', p. 244.

44 Freud 'Mourning and Melancholia', p. 245.

45 See Freud, *Civilization, Society and Religion: Group Psychology, Civilization and Its Discontents and Other Works* (London: Penguin, 1991). See also Robert A. Nye, *The Origins of Crowd Psychology: Gustave LeBon and the Crisis of Mass Democracy in the Third Republic* (London and Beverly Hills: Sage, 1975). Both Freud and, later, Nye, base their studies of group psychology on the foundational work of LeBon.

46 LaCapra, *Writing History, Writing Trauma*, p. 143. This is of course also consistent with the work of psychologists such as Judith Lewis Herman, who seems to see no conceptual or practical problem in applying her clinical analysis to social, historical or even national subjects.

47 LaCapra, *Representing the Holocaust*, p. 9.

48 Kerwin Lee Klein, 'On the Emergence of Memory in Historical Discourse', *Representations*, vol. 69 (Winter 2000), pp. 127–150.

49 Freud, 'Mourning and Melancholia', p. 245.

50 Freud, 'Mourning and Melancholia', p. 245.

51 Ryan, 'Terrorists Have Riddled Us All with Fear', p. 2.

52 Freud, 'Mourning and Melancholia', p. 245.

53 Freud, 'Mourning and Melancholia', p. 258.

54 Kai Erikson in Caruth (ed.), *Trauma: Explorations in Memory*, p. 195.

55 United States Department of Homeland Security web page: www.dhs.gov. When this much-derided system was replaced in 2011 with a new 'National Terrorism Advisory System', Homeland Security Secretary Janet Napolitano announced that 'the alerts will be specific to the threat. They may recommend certain actions or suggest looking for specific suspicious behaviour. And they will have a specified end date.' 'U.S. replaces color-coded terror alerts' (27 January 2011), CNN web page: http://edition.cnn.com/2011/TRAVEL/01/27/terror.threats/

56 Bob Herbert, 'America the Fearful', *The New York Times* (15 May 2006).

57 Habermas in Borradori, *Philosophy in a Time of Terror*, p. 26.

58 In the *Here is New York* archive, there are numerous photographs showing the public display of messages in New York City urging reflection and acceptance of responsibility in the attacks' aftermath. See also Michael E. Ross, 'Poll: US Patriotism Continues to Soar' (4 July 2005), MSNBC web page: www.msnbc.msn.com. The suggestion here is that September 11th initiated a surge of triumphal but misguided patriotism which has continued to grow in the years following.

59 Freud, 'Mourning and Melancholia', p. 248.

60 Herman, *Trauma and Recovery*, p. 242.

61 It is worth mentioning, however, as suggested by LaCapra, that a certain amount of repetition of and return to the traumatic memory is a necessary part of the forming and completion of an integrated narrative. Common sense dictates that repetition, within reason, cannot be excluded from the process. See LaCapra *Representing the Holocaust*, pp. 208–209.

62 Barthes, *Camera Lucida*, p. 66.

63 Barthes, *Camera Lucida*, pp. 90–91.

64 Roland Barthes (trans. Stephen Heath), *Image Music Text* (London: Fontana Press, 1977), p. 30.

65 André Bazin, 'The Ontology of the Photographic Image', in *What Is Cinema?* (Berkeley: University of California Press, 1976), p. 10.

66 Barthes, *Image Music Text*, pp. 92–93.

67 Marianne Hirsch Greenberg (ed.), *Trauma at Home*, p. 79.

68 Feldschuh, *The September 11 Photo Project*, p. 185.

69 Sontag, *On Photography*, p. 68.

70 Baer, *Spectral Evidence*, p. 70.

71 Iain Boal, plenary lecture at *Global Photographies: Histories: Theories: Practices* conference, Institute of Art, Design & Technology, Dun Laoghaire, Ireland (29 June 2007).

Conclusion

1 Virilio in Lotringer and Virilio, *The Accident of Art*, p. 26.

2 Walter Benjamin, *Illuminations* (New York: Schocken, 1985), p. 257.

3 Benjamin, *Illuminations*, p. 257.

4 Benjamin, *Illuminations*, p. 247.

5 Walter Benjamin (trans. Edmund Jephcott and Kingsley Shorter), 'A Small History of Photography', *One Way Street* (London: NLB, 1979), p. 250.

6 Wollen 'Vectors of Melancholy', p. 25.

7 Campany, 'Safety in Numbness', p. 124.

8 As already discussed in Chapter 1, Liam Kennedy has called Meyerowitz's images 'extended moments rather than decisive moments': 'Remembering September 11', p. 320.

9 Virilio, *Open Sky*.

10 Here, I connect Benjamin's piling of wreckage, Virlio's compression of instants and Herman's pile of snapshots only inasmuch as they are metaphors that are suggestive of one another. They in fact each refer to very different concepts that are not to be confused with each other, but which do point towards a confusion, and this is essentially my argument.

11 This is best illustrated using a photographic example: the ready comparison between Thomas Franklin's photograph of firefighters raising the flag at Ground Zero with Joe Rosenthal's World War Two icon 'Flag Raising at Iwo Jima'. The apparent (but unintentional) formal reference made by Franklin made it easy to slot his image into the historical framework of military victory, national glory and righteous struggle.

REFERENCES

Adorno, T. (ed. Bernstein, J. M.) (1991), *The Culture Industry: Selected Essays on Mass Culture*, London: Routledge.

Adorno, T. and Rabinbach, A. G. (1975), 'The Culture Industry Reconsidered', *New German Critique*, 6: 12–19.

Allen, R. W. (1987), 'The Aesthetic Experience of Modernity: Benjamin, Adorno, and Contemporary Film Theory', *New German Critique*, 40: 225–240.

Arato, A. and Gebhardt, E. (1982), *The Essential Frankfurt School Reader*, New York: Continuum, 1982.

Baer, U. (2002), *Spectral Evidence: The Photography of Trauma*, Cambridge, MA: MIT Press.

Barthes, R. (trans. Heath, S.) (1977), *Image Music Text*, London: Fontana Press.

——. (1993), *Camera Lucida: Reflections on Photography*, London: Vintage.

Batchen, G. (1999), *Burning with Desire: The Conception of Photography*, Cambridge, MA: MIT Press.

Baudrillard, J. (trans. Schutze, B.; ed. Lotringer, S.) (1988), *The Ecstasy of Communication*, New York: Semiotext(e).

——. (trans. Benedict, J.) (1993), *The Transparency of Evil: Essays on Extreme Phenomena*, London: Verso.

Bazin, A. (1976), *What Is Cinema?*, Berkeley, CA: University of California Press.

Beaumont, M. (ed.) (2007), *Adventures in Realism*, London: Blackwell.

Benjamin, W. (trans. Jephcott E. and Shorter, K.) (1979), *One Way Street*, London: NLB.

——. (trans. Zohn, H.) (1992), *Illuminations*, London: Fontana.

Benson, P. (1994), 'Freud and the Visual', *Representations*, 45: 101–116.

Berners Lee, T. (2000), *Weaving the Web: The Original Design and Ultimate Destiny of the World Wide Web*, London: Harper Business.

Boal, I., Clark, T. J., Matthews, J. and Watts, M. (Retort) (2005), *Afflicted Powers: Capital and Spectacle in a New Age of War*, London: Verso.

Borradori, G. (2003), *Philosophy in a Time of Terror: Dialogues with Jürgen Habermas and Jacques Derrida*, London: University of Chicago Press.

Borstoff, D. M. (2003), 'George W. Bush's Post-September 11 Rhetoric of Covenant Renewal: Upholding the Faith of the Greatest Generation', *Quarterly Journal of Speech*, 89(4): 293–319.

Breuer, J. and Freud, S. (trans. Strachey, J. & A.) (1974), *Studies on Hysteria*, London: Penguin.

Bryson, N., Holly, M. A. and Moxey, K. (1994), *Visual Culture: Images and Interpretations*, Lebanon: University Press of New England.

Burgin, V. (ed.) (1982), *Thinking Photography*, London: Macmillan.
Cadava, E. (1997), *Words of Light: Theses on the Photography of History*, Princeton, NJ; Chichester, West Sussex: Princeton University Press.
Cadava, E. and Cortes-Rocca, P. (2006), 'Notes on Love and Photography', *October*, 116: 3–34.
Caruth, C. (ed.) (1995), *Trauma: Explorations in Memory*, London: The Johns Hopkins University Press.
Chomsky, N. (2002), *Pirates and Emperors, Old and New: International Terrorism in the Real World*, London: Pluto.
Coplan, A. and Goldie, P. (eds) (2011), *Empathy: Philosophical and Psychological Perspectives*, New York: Oxford University Press.
Davis, R. (1999), *The Web of Politics: The Internet's Impact on the American Political System*, New York: Oxford University Press.
Denzin, N. K. and Lincoln, Y. S. (eds) (2003), *9/11 in American Culture*, London: Altamira Press.
Dikovitskaya, M. (2006), *Visual Culture: The Study of the Visual after the Cultural Turn*, Cambridge, MA: MIT Press.
Dolar, M. (1991), '"I Shall Be with You on Your Wedding-Night": Lacan and the Uncanny', *October*, 58: 5–23.
During, S. (1993), *The Cultural Studies Reader*, London: Routledge.
Eagleton, T. (1996), *Literary Theory: An Introduction (*second edition*)*, Oxford: Blackwell.
Elkins, J. (2003), *Visual Studies: A Skeptical Introduction*, London: Routledge.
Ellison, D. (2001), *Ethics and Aesthetics in European Modernist Literature, From the Sublime to the Uncanny*, Cambridge, MA: Cambridge University Press.
Erikson, K. (1994), *A New Species of Trouble: Explorations in Disaster, Trauma and Community*, New York: W.W. Norton & Company.
Feldschuh, M. (ed.) (2002), *The September 11 Photo Project*, New York: HarperCollins.
Fisher, P. (ed.) (1991), *The New American Studies: Essays from Representations*, Berkeley, CA: University of California Press.
Fitzpatrick, A. D. (2007), 'The Movement of Vulnerability: Images of Falling and September 11', *Art Journal*, 66(4): 85–102.
Foot, K., Warnick, B. and Schneider, S. M. (2006), 'Web-Based Memorializing After September 11: Toward a Conceptual Framework', *Journal of Computer-Mediated Communication*, 11: 93–94.
Foucault, M. (ed. Gordon, C.) (1980), *Power/Knowledge*, London: Harvester Wheatsheaf.
———. (trans. Sheridan, A.) (1991), *Discipline and Punish: The Birth of the Prison*, London: Penguin.
———. (ed. Faubion, J. D.) (1994), *Power*, New York: The New Press.
Freud, S. (trans. Strachey, J.) (1957a), 'From the History of an Infantile Neurosis', *The Standard Edition of the Complete Psychological Works of Sigmund Freud, vol. XVII*, London: The Hogarth Press.
———. (trans. Strachey, J.) (1957b), 'Mourning and Melancholia', *The Standard Edition of the Complete Psychological Works of Sigmund Freud*, vol. XIV, London: The Hogarth Press.
———. (trans. Strachey, J.) (1957c), 'The Uncanny', *The Standard Edition of the Complete Psychological Works of Sigmund Freud, vol. XVII*, London: The Hogarth Press.
———. (trans. Strachey, J.), (1958), 'Remembering, Repeating and Working Through', *The Standard Edition of the Complete Psychological Works of Sigmund Freud, vol. XII*, London: The Hogarth Press.

———. (trans. Strachey, J.) (1962a), 'Screen Memories', *The Standard Edition of the Complete Psychological Works of Sigmund Freud, vol. III*, London: The Hogarth Press.
———. (trans. Strachey, J.) (1962b), 'The Aetiology of Hysteria', *The Standard Edition of the Complete Psychological Works of Sigmund Freud, vol. III*, London: The Hogarth Press.
———. (trans. Strachey, J.) (1964), 'The Moses of Michelangelo', *The Standard Edition of the Complete Psychological Works of Sigmund Freud, vol. XIII*, London: The Hogarth Press.
———. (trans. Strachey, J.) (1990), *Beyond the Pleasure Principle*, New York: W.W. Norton & Company.
———. (trans. Strachey, J.) (1991a), *Civilization, Society and Religion: Group Psychology, Civilization and Its Discontents and Other Works*, London: Penguin.
———. (trans. Strachey, J.) (1991b), *Introductory Lectures on Psychoanalysis*, London: Penguin.
———. (trans. Bell, A.) (2002), *The Psychopathology of Everyday Life*, London: Penguin.
Friend, D. (2006), *Watching the World Change: The Stories Behind the Images of 9/11*, New York: Picador.
Garber, M., Matlock, J. and Walkowitz, R. L. (eds) (1993), *Media Spectacles*, New York: Routledge.
George, A. R., Peress, G., Shulan, M. and Traub, C. (2002), *Here is New York: A Democracy of Photographs*, Zurich: Scalo.
Glassner, B. (1999), *The Culture of Fear: Why Americans Are Afraid of the Wrong Things*, New York: Basic Books.
Green, D. (2003), *Where Is the Photograph?* London: Photoworks/Photoforum.
Greenberg, J. (ed.) (2003), *Trauma at Home: After 9/11*, Lincoln, NE: University of Nebraska Press.
Gunn, J. (2004), 'The Rhetoric of Exorcism: George W. Bush and the Return of Political Demonology', *Western Journal of Communication*, 68: 166–192.
Habermas, J. (trans. Burger, T. and Lawrence, F.) (1989), *The Structural Transformation of the Public Sphere: An Enquiry into a Category of Bourgeois Society*, London: Polity Press.
Hariman, R. and Lucaites, J. L. (2007), *No Caption Needed: Iconic Photographs, Public Culture, and Liberal Democracy*, Chicago: University of Chicago Press.
Herman, J. L. (1997), *Trauma and Recovery: The Aftermath of Violence from Domestic Abuse to Political Terror*, New York: Basic Books.
Hess, A. (2007), 'In Digital Remembrance: Vernacular Memory and the Rhetorical Construction of Web Memorials', *Media, Culture and Society*, 29: 812–830.
Holland, P., Spence, J. and Watney, S. (eds) (1986), *Photography/Politics: Two*, London: Photography Workshop.
Holt, Y. and Barlow, P. (2000), 'Visual Culture in Britain: An Introduction and a Debate', *Visual Culture in Britain*, 1(1): 1–13.
Homer, S. (2005), *Jacques Lacan*, London and New York: Routledge.
Horkheimer, M. (trans. O'Connel, M. J.) (1995), *Critical Theory: Selected Essays*, New York: Continuum.
Horkheimer, M. and Adorno, T. (1995), *The Dialectic of Enlightenment*, New York: Continuum.
Hyman, J. (2007), 'The Public Face of 9/11: Memory and Portraiture in the Landscape', *Journal of American History*, 94: 183–192.

——. (2013), *Landscapes of 9/11: A Photographer's Journey*, Austin: University of Texas Press.
Kennedy, L. (2003), 'Remembering September 11: Photography as Cultural Diplomacy', *International Affairs*, 2(79): 315–326.
Klein, K. L. (2000), 'On the Emergence of Memory in Historical Discourse', *Representations*, 69: 127–150.
Kroes, R. (2011), 'The Ascent of the Falling Man: Establishing a Picture's Iconicity', *Journal of American Studies*, 45(4): 47–67.
Lacan, J. (trans. Sheridan, A.) (1977), *Écrits: A Selection*, New York: W.W. Norton & Company.
——. (trans. Porter, D.) (1992), *The Seminar of Jacques Lacan, Book VII, 1959–1960: The Ethics of Psychoanalysis*, London: Routledge.
——. (trans. Grigg, R.) (1993), *The Seminar of Jacques Lacan, Book III, 1955–1965: The Psychoses*, London: Routledge.
——. (trans. Sheridan, A.) (1994), *The Four Fundamental Concepts of Psycho-Analysis*, London: Penguin.
——. (ed. Miller, J-A.) (1998), *The Seminar of Jacques Lacan, Book II: The Ego in Freud's Theory and the Technique of Psychoanalysis*, Cambridge, MA: Cambridge University Press.
——. (trans. Fink, B.) (1999), *The Seminar of Jacques Lacan, Book XX, 1972–1973: Encore: On Feminine Sexuality, the Limits of Love and Knowledge*, New York: W.W. Norton & Company.
LaCapra, D. (1994), *Representing the Holocaust: History, Theory, Trauma*, London and Ithaca, NY: Cornell University Press.
——. (1998), *History & Memory After Auschwitz*, London andIthaca, NY: Cornell University Press.
——. (2001), *Writing History, Writing Trauma*, London: The Johns Hopkins University Press.
Landsberg, A. (2004), *Prosthetic Memory: The Transformation of American Remembrance in the Age of Mass Culture*, New York: Columbia University Press.
LaPlanche, J. and Pontalis, J-B. (trans. Nicholson, D.) (1973), *The Language of Psychoanalysis*, London: The Hogarth Press.
LIFE (2001), *LIFE: One Nation: America Remembers September 11, 2001*, New York: Little, Brown & Co.
Lomas, D. (2000), *The Haunted Self: Surrealism, Psychoanalysis, Subjectivity*, New Haven, CT and London: Yale University Press.
Lotringer, S. and Virilio, P. (2005), *The Accident of Art*, New York: Semiotext(e).
Marx, K. (1976), *Capital Volume 1*, London: Penguin.
Marx, K. and Engels, F. (ed. Arthur, C. J.) (1970), *The German Ideology*, New York: International Publishers.
McQuire, S. (1998), *Visions of Modernity: Representation, Memory, Time and Space in the Age of the Camera*, London: Sage.
Melville, S (1987), 'Psychoanalysis and the Place of "Jouissance"', *Critical Inquiry*, 13(2): 349–370.
Meyerowitz, J. (2006), *Aftermath: World Trade Center Archive*, New York: Phaidon.
Mirzoeff, N. (1999), *Introduction to Visual Culture*, London: Routledge.
——. (ed.) (2002), *The Visual Culture Reader (second edition)*, London: Routledge.
Mitchell, W. J. T. (2002), 'Criticism and Crisis', *Critical Inquiry*, 28(2): 567–572.
Olin, M. (2012), *Touching Photographs*, Chicago: University of Chicago Press.

Roberts, J. (1998), *The Art of Interruption: Realism, Photography and the Everyday*, Manchester: Manchester University Press.
Robins, K. (1996), *Into the Image: Culture and Politics in the Field of Vision*, London: Routledge.
Rosler, M. (2004), *Decoys and Disruptions: Selected Writings, 1975–2001*, Cambridge, MA: MIT Press.
Royle, N. (2003), *The Uncanny*, London: Routledge.
Rugoff, R. (ed.) (1997), *Scene of the Crime*, Cambridge, MA: MIT Press.
Sadoff, D. F. (1998), *Sciences of the Flesh: Representing Body and Subject in Psychoanalysis*, Stanford: Stanford University Press.
Saltzman, L. and Rosenberg, E. (2006), *Trauma and Visuality in Modernity*, Lebanon, NH: Dartmouth College Press.
Sardar, Z. (1995), 'Alt.Civilizations.Faq: Cyberspace as the Darker Side of the West', *Futures*, 27(7): 777–794.
Scott, C. (1999), *The Spoken Image: Photography and Language*, London: Reaktion Books.
Sherman, D. J. and Nardin, T. (2006), *Terror, Culture, Politics: Rethinking 9/11*, Bloomington, IN: Indiana University Press.
Simpson, D. (2006), *9/11: The Culture of Commemoration*, London: The University of Chicago Press.
Sliwinski, S. (2011), *Human Rights in Camera*, Chicago: University of Chicago Press.
Smith, T. (2006), *The Architecture of Aftermath*, London: University of Chicago Press.
Sontag, S. (1979), *On Photography*, London: Penguin.
———. (2004), *Regarding the Pain of Others*, London: Penguin.
Sturken, M. (2007), *Tourists of History: Memory, Kitsch, and Consumerism from Oklahoma City to Ground Zero*, Durham: Duke University Press.
Sturken, M. and Cartwright, L. (2001), *Practices of Looking: An Introduction to Visual Culture*, New York: Oxford University Press.
Tagg, J. (1988), *The Burden of Representation: Essays on Photographies and Histories*, London: Macmillan.
Taylor, J. (1998), *Body Horror: Photojournalism, Catastrophe and War*, New York: New York University Press.
The New York Times (2002), *A Nation Challenged*, New York: Jonathan Cape.
———. (2002), *A Nation Challenged: Young Reader's Edition*, New York: Scholastic Reference.
Trachtenberg, A. (ed.) (1980), *Classic Essays on Photography*, Stoney Creek, CT: Leete's Island Books.
———. (1985), 'Albums of War: On Reading Civil War Photographs', *Representations*, 9: 1–32.
US Department of State, Bureau of Educational and Cultural Affairs (2004), *After September 11: Images from Ground Zero: An exhibition by the US Department of State, Bureau of Educational and Cultural Affairs, with Photographs by Joel Meyerowitz* (exhibition catalogue).
Vidler, A. (1992), *The Architectural Uncanny: Essays in the Modern Unhomely*, Cambridge, MA: MIT Press.
Virilio, P. (1997), *Open Sky*, London: Verso.
———. (1999), *Polar Inertia*, London: Sage.
———. (2002), *Ground Zero*, London: Verso.
Wells, L. (ed.) (2003), *The Photography Reader*, London: Routledge.

Wilkes Tucker, A. et al. (2012), *War/Photography: Images of Armed Conflict and Its Aftermath*, New Haven, CT and London: Yale University Press.
Zelizer, B. (2010), *About to Die: How News Images Move the Public*, New York: Oxford University Press.
Zelizer, B. and Allan, S. (eds) (2002), *Journalism After September 11*, London: Routledge.
Žižek, S. (1997), 'The Big Other Doesn't Exist', *Journal of European Psychoanalysis: Humanities, Philosophy, Psychotherapies*, 5. Available at http://www.lacan.com/zizekother.htm. Accessed 27 June 2013.
——. (2002), *Welcome to the Desert of the Real*, London: Verso.

INDEX

Note: Locators followed by the letter 'n' refer to notes.